最新中国俚语(修订版)
New Slang of China(Revised Edition)

汉 英 对 照
Chinese–English

李淑娟　颜力钢　编著

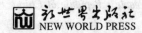

新世界出版社
NEW WORLD PRESS

First Edition 2000
Third Edition 2006
Compiled and Translated by Li Shujuan and Yan Ligang
Cover and Book Design by He Yuting

ISBN 7 – 80005 – 564 – 7

Published by
NEW WORLD PRESS
24 Baiwanzhuang Road, Beijing 100037, China

Distributed by
NEW WORLD PRESS
24 Baiwanzhuang Road, Beijing 100037, China
Tel:0086 – 10 – 68994118
Fax:0086 – 10 – 68326679
E-mail:frank@nwp.com.cn

Printed in the People's Republic of China

前　　言

　　这是一本汉英对照的俚语工具书,共收集了近年来中国最流行的俚语 1300 余条。此书大部分俚语以北方话为主,兼收入一些其他方言和外来语。

　　俚语作为一种通俗的口语和俗语,常带有浓郁的生活气息和强烈的地方色彩。虽然它比书面语显得粗俗不雅,但就其表情达意而言却有一针见血、要言不烦、入木三分的特点。它往往以其直率、生动、诙谐、幽默的风格深受大众的喜爱,可以说它是中国语言中极富生命力的一部分。

　　俚语同其他语言一样在不断地产生、发展和变化。它在一定程度上反映了社会经济文化生活的千变万化。我们编辑此书正是为了满足不同层次的国内外读者的需要,为他们学习、研究、掌握俚语提供参考,为翻译工作者带来方便。

　　我们在编辑、翻译此书过程中得到了许多热爱语言文字的中外朋友的关心和支持,在此谨向他们表示最衷心的感谢。愿以此书奉献给一切热爱语言和生活的朋友们。

编者

2000 年 7 月

Preface

This new dictionary of modern Chinese slang contains more than 1,300 entries of the most popular and widely used slang which has emerged in recent years. Most of the expressions in this dictionary are widely used in northern areask while a few expressions originating from foreign words or from the south of China.

Slang, as a colloquial spoken language, is vividly flavored with local color. Although it is both informal and vulgar, many of the slang expressions commonly used are direct, simple and apt. People tend to like the frankness, the satire and the humor of slang. In fact, it can be considered as a living part of the Chinese language.

Slang, like other languages, continues to emerge, develop, and change. To a certain extent, it reveals various changes in the economy, culture, and standard of living of a society. We compiled this dictionary to meet the needs of readers at home and abroad at all levels, to supply them with a reference book to study, research, and master, as well as providing a tool for translators.

We wish to acknowledge our debt to all who gave us so much love, kindness and support in compiling and translating this dictionary. May we dedicate this dictionary to all those who share our enthusiasm for Chinese slang.

Li Shujuan, Yan Ligang

July 2000

前　言

　　《最新中国俚语》面市以来在社会上引起了不小的反响，它的出版能得到社会各界人士的关注，并对此发表各自不同的观点和看法，为此，我们感到十分高兴。同时，我们也想借修订版出版的机会向所有关心和爱护我们的人表示衷心的感谢。

　　工具书，顾名思义，本身就是为大众服务的工具。它为我们查阅、了解、学习、借鉴、掌握和使用社会上出现的词汇，提供必要的帮助。我们编辑此书的目的，就是要将散落在社会上的，那些生动、鲜活、人情味十足，又被老百姓所乐意使用的语言收集起来，编辑成册，从而方便人们的使用和交流。

　　俚语是通俗的口头语，带有浓郁的地方色彩和民间韵味。它的存在范围十分广泛，其中包括土语、行话、隐语、暗语、黑话、禁语。使用者大多是各行各业的老百姓。它代表了大众文化，是一种非书面的特定群体的语言。它虽然不雅，甚至粗俗，但却具有极强的表情达意的功能。其中一些俚语词汇，经过多年的使用，也会演化为书面语言。

　　俚语是语言形式中的一种，它来源于大众，为大众服务，并为大众所喜闻乐见。其中有些词的词义和用法是多种多样的。它们随着社会环境、谈话的特定语境和谈话对象的变化而变化。

　　例如，"老不死的"一词，如果用于大街上碰到的一个陌生人，就有骂人的意思；但如果是欣欣然用于一对恩爱的老夫老妻之间的偶然调侃中，则能充分表现出人与人之间的那种坦荡、乐观、真诚、自信、诙谐、幽默、亲昵，而又略带嗔怪色彩的复杂情感。而这正是其他任何正规语言和书面语言所无法表达的。

　　中国的语言浩如烟海，丰富多彩，其中也包含着一些"荤词"

（粗词脏话）。我们在本书最初的编辑过程中，对于那些目前还不易被人接受的"荤词"未予以全部收录，只是酌情收录了一些。此次修订版除对本书收录的少量这类词汇加以注释，以提醒读者留心使用之外，还对一些特定时间出现的词予以注释说明。另外，本次修订版还增加了近一两年来涌现出来的新俚语。

语言是人们交际的工具。了解、学习、掌握各种语言，是为了更好地进行人际交往。俗话说："在什么山上唱什么歌。"学习一些俗语、俚语，除了能更好地体味语言的丰富性和佳妙之处外，更重要的还在于增进谈话双方的相互了解，缩短谈话双方之间的距离，给人以亲切感，从而使人们能够更有效地进行沟通与交流。此次修订，我们真诚希望能为广大读者在了解、学习、掌握和使用语言方面，提供更有效、更令读者满意的借鉴和帮助。同时，我们也衷心地欢迎广大读者能够继续提出自己的宝贵意见和建议，以使我们今后的编辑工作能够变得更加完善，更符合读者的需要。

在此，我们再次向一切关心、热爱语言的人们表示由衷的敬意和感谢！

编者

2005 年 11 月 6 日

Preface

(Revised Edition)

Since its publication, New Slang of China has generated buzz nationwide, catching the interest of individuals within a wide range of circles, prompting an onslaught of opinions and viewpoints on this facet of the Chinese language. We are extremely pleased, and would like to show our gratitude to those who have so actively expressed their interest and love for the book by publishing a revised edition.

A dictionary or a reference book is, as the term suggests, a tool intended to serve the public, providing a necessary aid for pinpointing, understanding, mastering and using current vocabulary. Our original purpose in compiling this book was to condense the vivid, vital, earthy, slang terms that are the lingua franca of the masses into one book, thereby enabling them to be understood and communicated to an even greater extent.

As a patois, or colloquial language, slang is permeated with rich local color and flavor. It covers a wide linguistic scope, including local dialect, jargon, cant, and blasphemy. Its use embraces the masses and subdivides further into members of specific occupations, trades, professions, sects, classes, and age groups.

It represents popular culture, as well as being an informal language used by specific groups. Although it is often vulgar and unrefined, its implied meaning can be both deep and eloquent. After an unspecified length of time, slang terms often pass into standard language usage.

Slang is a type of language in itself. Its origins are embedded in the lives of the general public, whom it serves, and who love to use it. There are certain terms that have multiple meanings and usage, and change according to their specific social and conversational context.

For example, "老不死的(lǎo bù sǐ de)" meaning old fellow or old folk, when uttered by strangers colliding on the street, can be offensive. However, when occasionally used in a ribbing, teasing sense, by, say, an elderly loving couple, it expresses complex feelings of frankness, optimism, sincerity, self-confidence, humor, jocularity, and intimacy, which would be impossible to express through any standard or formal language.

The Chinese language is as vast, rich and colorful as the ocean, and naturally contains terms that could be termed vulgar or obscene. In compiling this book, we have left out a number of unacceptable obscenities, but kept others, according to our own discretion. In this revised edition, we not only have added explanations to, and identification of, specific words in order to make potential users fully aware of their appropriate use, we have also added some notes to words mostly used in a past period of time. In addition, some new words have come forth in the past two years, and have also been included in this new edition in order to meet the needs of the people.

Language is the main tool of human communication. The purpose of learning, understanding, and mastering various levels of language is to deepen human communication. There is a Chinese saying: "Different songs are sung on different mountains." Using slang expressions not only enables the speaker to savor more fully the richness and excellence of language, but also enhances mutual understanding between speaker and listener. It narrows any social or other gap, inducing a feeling of easy familiarity that makes for more fluent verbal exchange.

We sincerely hope that readers of this revised edition find it an even more effective and satisfactory reference aid for learning, understanding, mastering and using slang. We also hope that we may continue to receive feedback, in order that our future works may be perfected and better suited to the needs of the public.

Once again, we express our heartfelt thanks to all that have shown such a keen interest, care and love for language.

Li Shujuan, Yan Ligang
Nov. 6, 2005

目　录

9

10

13

14

A

阿木林 ā mù lín

指呆头呆脑，动作言语迟缓的人（骂人话）。stupid person；flow-witted person；wooden-headed person

例：你真是个阿木林，这么简单的事也做不好。

You're such a fool. You can't even do the simplest thing well.

阿乡 ā xiāng

指土里土气的乡下人。country bumpkin；yokel

例：她带着阿乡买东西去了。

She took the country bumpkin shopping.

挨不上 āi bù shàng

指不着边，没有关系。have no relations；be irrelevant；be extraneous

例：这两件事根本挨不上。

The two matters are totally unrelated.

挨呲儿 āi cīr

指受到训斥，批评。get a talking-to；get a dressing down

例：小男孩怕挨呲儿便偷偷地把打碎的盘子扔掉。

The little boy furtively threw away the broken dish so as not to get a dressing down.

挨个儿 āi gèr

一个接一个；依次顺序。one by one；in proper order；successively；in turn

例:学生们站好队挨个儿上了汽车。

The students lined up and got on the bus in single file.

挨剋 āi kēi

受到训斥、批评或责骂。get a talking-to; told off; get a dressing-down

例:瞧,挨剋了吧。你没瞧见你爸正忙着吗,还去给他捣乱。

See, you got a good talking-to. Didn't you see your dad was busy when you went to interrupt him?

矮半截 ǎi bàn jié

比喻低人一等;不如别人或比别人差。be inferior to others; be worse than others

例:他认为清洁工的职业并不比别人矮半截。

He doesn't think his job as a street cleaner is inferior to others.

案子 àn zi

案件。case; law case

例:这是一起不小的案子。

This is a rather big case.

B

八九不离十 bā jiǔ bù lí shí

指相差不多；多数是正确的；百分之八九十是这样。

mostly correct; pretty close; eighty percent or more right

例：他每次的估计都八九不离十。

His prediction each time mostly pans out correct.

巴不得 bā bu de

迫切盼望。earnestly wish; itching to do sth.

例：她巴不得马上就走。

She is anxious to go at once.

吧嗒 bā da

抽旱烟。pull at (a pipe); smoke (a pipe)

例：他吧嗒了两口烟袋又继续讲下去。

He pulled at his pipe for a while and continued to talk.

吧娘 bā niáng

称酒吧间的女老板。female owner of a bar

例：张三是这儿的常客。每次来吧娘都给他特殊的招待。他们的关系可不一般。

Zhang San is a frequent customer of the bar here. Every time he comes the female owner of the bar gives him special treatment. Their relationship is not usual.

吧女 bā nǚ

称在酒吧间工作的女招待。bar girl

例：为了能多挣些钱，阿美白天在工厂里打工，晚上去做吧女。

To make more money A'mei goes to work in a factory during the day, and works as a bar girl in the evening.

吧台 bā tái

指酒吧的柜台。bar counter

例:如今吧台已不再是酒吧的专利。它已进入了追求时尚的百姓家庭。

Nowadays, a bar counter is no longer only found in a bar. It can be found in the homes of ordinary people.

扒带子 bā dài zi

非法盗版磁带或录像带。to make illegal copies of legally published cassettes or videotapes

例:这小子不干好事。十年前他扒带子,这几年又卖起盗版光碟了。

This guy's up to no good. He made illegal copies of cassettes and videotapes ten years ago, and in the past few years he's started selling pirated CDs.

扒分 bā fēn

指利用业余时间打工赚钱。work in spare time for money

例:为了供儿子上大学,老冯每逢周末都去扒分做小时工。

Lao Feng works as an hourly worker in his spare time every weekend so that he can support his son's attendance at university.

扒面 bā miàn

指占公家的便宜,为自己得好处。take advantage of the state or a company for one's own benefit; profit at the state's or a company's expense

例:那小子近几年可是发了,还买了汽车,一定没少扒面。

That guy made a fortune in those years and even bought a car. He must have benefited by taking advantage of his company.

拔 bá

把烫的东西放在凉水里使它变凉。cool in water

例：她把热粥放在凉水里拔。

She cooled the hot porridge in cold water.

拔撞 bá chuàng

1. 争光。win honor for sb.

例：他真给我们拔撞。

He really pulled through for us.

2. 撑腰。back sb. up

例：当我遇到麻烦时，他总为我拔撞。

He always backs me up when I get into trouble.

3. 扬威风，长志气。boast one's morale; pump up one's courage

例：她从不畏强暴，敢为弱者拔撞。

She always defies brute force, but boasts the morale of the weak.

拔份儿 bá fènr

1. 炫耀自己的威风；显示自己比别人厉害。show off one's strength or power; demonstrate one's power and courage over others

例：我看不起那些好在人群前拔份儿的人。

I look down on those who like to show off their strength in front of others.

2. 逞凶；称霸。dominate; act violently

例：他不该拔这个份儿（他不该在这儿拔份儿）。

He shouldn't dominate the situation.

把 bǎ

数量词,指次,回。time; rounds

例:老王每次看见人家玩儿牌就手痒,非得玩上几把才心里舒坦。

Lao Wang gets an itch to play cards as soon as he sees someone else playing. He won't feel comfortable unless he plays a few rounds.

把势 bǎ shi

1. 武术。martial art

例:瞧他那把势练得多地道!

Look, how good he is at martial arts!

2. 会武术的人;专精某种技术的人。person skilled in martial art or trade

例:他是个养猪的好把势。

He is skilled at raising pigs.

3. 技术。skill; technique

例:他把修理汽车的全套把势都教给了我。

He taught me all the techniques I need to repair a car.

掰 bāi

断绝友谊;分手。break up; break off a friendship

例:汤姆在一次激烈的争吵后和史蒂夫掰了。

Tom broke with his friend Steve after a wrangling.

掰哧 bāi chi

解释;分析。explain; analyze

例:这件事情已经过去了就别再掰哧了。

This matter is over, so it's useless explaining it any more.

白鼻仔 bái bí zǎi

指好吃懒做,游手好闲,贪图享受的人。Literally it means a white-nose boy/A term for a loafer, vagrant, vagabond or someone who is fond of eating and averse to work, or idle but seeking a life of pleasure.

例:你得尽快找份差使干,不能再这样闲下去了,像个白鼻仔。

You'd better find a job quickly. You can't idle about like a white-nose boy any more.

白搭 bái dā

没有用处;白费力气。have no use; futile; spend effort in vain

例:找到她也白搭。她不会把钱退给你。

It is no use to find her. She won't give the money back to you.

白骨精 bái gǔ jīng

指白领、骨干、精英的缩写。Abbreviation for white collar, cadre, and elite.

例:既然你有志要当个未来的白骨精,现在为何不努力学习呢?

Since you are determined to be a white-collar worker, a cadre and an elite in the future, why don't you study harder now?

白话 bái huo (话,此处不念 huà,念 huo)

胡扯;胡说八道;说不能实现或没有根据的话;能说会道。

make empty talk; talk big; talk nonsense; be blah-blah

例:别信他,他总爱瞎白话。

Don't believe him. He always talk nonsense.

白毛 bái máo

指白发。white (gray) hair (an impolite term)

例:您能不能少管我的事,小心操心多了会长白毛的。

Won't you please keep your nose out of my business. Be careful! Your hair will turn gray if you worry too much.

白毛风 bái máo fēng

暴风雪。snowstorm; blizzard

例:我听说东北的白毛风特别可怕,一旦刮起来两三天也不停。

I heard that the snowstorms in Northeast China are very frightening. Once one starts, it won't stop for two or three days.

白生生 bái shēng shēng

形容(女人)皮肤洁白,细嫩。(of women's skin) pure white and delicate; as white as snow

例:她的腿白生生的,真漂亮。

She's got beautiful legs with lily-white and delicate skin.

白玩儿 bái wánr

(事情)很容易干,不费力气。easy to do; not difficult; not hard

例:喝一瓶啤酒对我来说简直是白玩儿。

It's a cinch for me to drink one bottle of beer.

白眼儿狼 bái yǎnr láng

比喻忘恩负义之徒。ingrate; treacherous and ruthless person

例:我要是早知道他是个白眼儿狼才不会帮助他呢!

I wouldn't have helped him if I knew he was an ingrate earlier.

白相 bái xiàng

1.指游玩；玩耍。go on an outing

例：今天我们出去白相好不好？

Shall we go on an outing today?

2.指戏弄；开玩笑。make a fool of sb. ; make fun of sb.

例：别白相我。

Don't make fun of me!

拜拜 bái bái

再见。bye-bye (transliteration of English phrase)

例：咱们还是拜拜吧！否则你上班又要迟到了。

Let's say good-bye now, otherwise you will be late for work again.

摆龙门阵 bǎi lóng mén zhèn

闲扯；讲故事。chat; engage in chitchat; tell a story

例：他最善于和人摆龙门阵。

He is fond of chatting with people.

摆谱 bǎi pǔ

讲排场；撑门面；显示气派、阔气。keep up appearance; go in for extravagance; show off one's wealth

例：他真能摆谱，给我们叫了一桌最贵的菜。

He ordered a table of the most expensive dishes for us in order to show off his wealth.

摆摊儿 bǎi tānr

在路旁或市场中陈列货物出售。set up a stall along the street or in a market

例：退休后他去摆摊儿卖金鱼了。

He set up a stall to sell goldfish after he retired.

扳大闸 bān dà zhá

盗窃时撬锁。pry open a lock（to steal sth.）

例：他在一家仓库扳大闸时被抓获。

He was caught prying open the lock of a warehouse.

搬 bān

弄钱；搞钱。rake in money

例：今天他运气不错，搬了不少钱。

He was lucky and raked in a goodly amount of bucks today.

板凳狗 bǎn dèng gǒu

指轻便摩托车。light motorcycle；scooter

例：小谷的家离工厂很远。为了方便她上下班，她老公特地买了个板凳狗给她。

Xiao Gu's home is very far from her factory. Her husband specially bought her a scooter for her convenience when she goes to work.

板儿寸 bǎnr cùn

头顶和后脑平直的一种男子短发型。hairstyle in which the hair is cropped close to the head；closely cropped hair；bush-top

例：今年北京的男青年流行板儿寸。

The bush-top became a fad this year in Beijing.

板儿脊 bǎnr jí

男子上身不穿衣服；光着膀子；裸露上身。（of a man）bare-chested

例：酷热的夏天有的小伙子爱光着大板儿脊上街。

Some young men like to go bare-chested on hot summer days.

板儿爷 bǎnr yé

蹬平板三轮车挣钱的人。pedicab man/A term refers to one who makes a living driving a pedicab.

例：作为板儿爷的他，对每条大街小巷都了如指掌。

As a pedicab man, he knows every street and alley like the back of his hand.

办 bàn

惩处；制裁。punish；penalize

例：那伙歹徒让警察给办了。

The gangsters were punished by the police.

半半拉拉 bàn bàn lā lā

不完全；不完整；没有全部完成。incomplete；unfinished

例：把东西都吃光，别给我剩的半半拉拉的。

Eat them up. Don't give your left-overs to me.

半吊子 bàn diào zi

指人办事不太靠得住。A term refers to one who does things unreliably.

例：这么重要的事情还是你跟他一起办吧。他这人半吊子，我不放心。

You'd better do it with him since it is such an important thing. He is such an unreliable person, I don't trust him.

半残废 bàn cán fèi

戏称身高只有一米七或不到一米七但也不算太矮的男人。

half-crippled/A metaphor for a man of 170 cm or below in height who is not tall enough for the woman he's romantically interested in and therefore jokingly called "half-crippled".

例:我老婆自从决定嫁给我这半残废时,就把她所有的高跟鞋都处理了。

When my wife decided to marry me, a "half-crippled" man, she threw all her high-heels away.

半拉 bàn lǎ

半个;一半。half

例1:他把那半拉纸扔了。

He threw the other half of the paper away.

例2:那儿还剩了半拉西瓜。

There is half of a watermelon left there.

半晌 bàn shǎng

半天;形容很长。half a day/A metaphor for quite a long time.

例1:他半晌没说一句话。

He couldn't say a word for ages.

例2:前半晌 morning;后半晌 afternoon;晚半晌 evening

半仙 bàn xiān

指对算命、占卜略知一二的人。a minor sorcerer/sorceress, used to refer to one who knows a little about fortune telling or astrology

例:别信那个路边算命人的话,他绝对是个骗子,顶多是个半仙。

Don't listen to what the fortune teller on the street said. He is a swindler at worst, or a minor sorcerer at best.

扮靓 bàn liàng

指为了引人注目而打扮得很时髦漂亮。dress in the best and the most fashionable way to catch people's attention

例:如今的姑娘个个扮靓,每月都不少为此花钱。

Nowadays all the young women dress beautifully and fashionably. They spend lots of money to keep up appearances every month.

棒 bàng

（体力或能力）强；（水平）高；（成绩）好。strong; excellent; great

例 1：他身体真棒。

He is very strong.

例 2：这鞋真棒。

The shoes are excellent.

例 3：这场演出棒极了。

The show is great.

棒槌 bàng chui

比喻不懂内行规矩的外行人。wooden club (used to beat clothes when washing them in the old days)/A metaphor for a layman or an amateur.

例：他笑我是个棒槌，根本不懂出版。

He laughed at me for not knowing anything about publishing at all.

傍 bàng

1. 依靠，陪伴有钱有地位的人。rely on or accompany (a rich person)

例：她专傍洋人寻机出国。

She goes around with foreigners in hopes of getting a chance to go abroad.

2. 关系暧昧；相好。love; have an intimate relationship with sb.

例：他们俩已暗地里傍了一年了。

They have had a secret relationship for over a year.

傍大款 bàng dà kuǎn

女性陪伴有钱的男人。(for a woman)to accompany a rich man; have an intimate relationship with a rich man

例1:有些女孩发现傍大款是一个致富的捷径。

Some girls think they can have a better life by accompanying rich men.

例2:她无职业,只不过是以傍大款为生。

She has no job, but she's supported by a rich man.

傍家儿 bàng jiār

1.指情人。lover or mistress

例:他是我的老傍家儿。

He is my old lover.

2.指朋友;伙伴;帮手。friend; partner; assistant

例:我们可是傍家儿,不该相互欺骗。

As friends, we should not cheat each other.

3.指夫妻,两口子。couple; husband and wife

例:这对傍家儿总是出双入对,形影不离,就像新婚燕尔。

That couple always goes out together.

包爷 bāo yé

1.包揽诉讼案件,在当事各方之间穿梭,从中得到利益。

a person who undertakes a lawsuit

例:他多次充当包爷,从中获取了大量的钱财。

He took on several lawsuits and made a lot of money.

2.包揽生意,充当中间商或中间介绍人,从中获利。

the go-between in business who receives a cut of the profit

例:他分文没有,于是决定当包爷。

He's out of money, so he has decided to work as a go-between in business.

包圆儿 bāo yuánr

1.把货物或剩下的货物全部买下。buy the whole lot or the remainder

例：他用便宜的价钱把剩下的苹果都包圆儿了。

He bought the rest of the apples at a low price.

2.全部担当；全部包揽。take on the whole thing；finish off

例：他的胃口真大，把整个工程都给包圆儿了。

He is so ambitious. He took on the whole project.

煲电话粥 bāo diàn huà zhōu

指打电话时间长。boil (cook) porridge of telephone/A metaphor for talking on the phone for a long time.

例：她总爱煲电话粥，所以每月的电话费都很多。

She likes to chat too long on the phone so she spends much money paying her telephone bill.

保不齐 bǎo bù qí

难免；可能；没准儿；没把握。not sure；hard to avoid；may well

例1：我可保不齐说这天不会下雨。

I'm not sure it won't rain.

例2：这么热的天，食物保不齐要变坏。

It's hard to avoid food spoiling in such a hot weather.

报虫儿 bào chóngr

比喻非常爱看报纸的人。newspaper worm/A metaphor for someone who likes to read newspapers a lot.

例：我认识一个报虫儿，他每年订几十种报纸。

I know a newspaper worm who subscribes to a dozen newspapers every year.

报口 bào kǒu

旧时江湖用语，指身份或从事的行当。an old term used among vagrants and itinerants, referring to social status or profession

例：听说他前一段时间转报口卖药去了。

I heard that he switched to selling medicine a few weeks ago.

报冷门 bào lěng mén

1. 发生意想不到的事情。produce unexpected results

例：这次比赛大报冷门，杀出一批更年轻的选手。

This competition produced many unexpected results and created a group of young winners.

2. 选择不受别人重视的行业。choose a profession, trade or branch of learning which receives little attention

例：我劝她报冷门专业以躲避激烈的竞争。

I persuaded her to choose a profession little in the spotlight to avoid fierce competition.

报料 bào liào

为记者提供线索或材料。to provide news clues or information to journalists

例：游乐园出了事故，一位游客立刻给当地的晚报热线报料。

When an accident took place in an amusement park, a tourist immediately called a local evening paper's hotline and provided them with the news.

暴打 bào dǎ

狠命地打。beat sb. severely; give a good thrashing

例：他因为偷东西而被人暴打了一顿。

He was beaten severely for stealing things.

16

暴侃 bào kǎn

指一通乱说；特别能吹能聊。talk big；boast；shoot the bull

例：他善暴侃。只要他一来，我们就坐着听他神聊一通。

He likes to shoot the bull. Whenever he comes, we sit around and listen to him talk.

暴头 bào tóu

源自游戏 CS,本指在游戏中一枪毙命,后用来表示遭受突如其来的打击。Originally meaning "shot to death" in the computer game Counter Strike, it now means to "suffer a sudden attack or unexpected blow".

例：当他得知期中数学成绩时,一下子有种被暴头的感觉,心里难受极了。

As soon as he heard his math score from the mid-term test, he felt he had received a sudden blow. He was very upset.

暴笑 bào xiào

大笑。laugh

例：谁也没有想到,平日少言寡语的他说出的一句话竟然能引起大伙儿暴笑了好一阵。

He hardly ever speaks in public, and it took everyone by surprise when what he said made everyone laugh for quite a while.

曝光 bào guāng

公布于众；让世人知道。make public；expose；make known to the public

例：假冒伪劣产品该通过新闻媒介曝光。

Imitations and inferior products should be exposed through the media.

爆炒 bào chǎo

指在短时间内发起强大的宣传攻势,得到较快的宣传效果。
quick-fry/A metaphor for launching a whirlwind mass media advertising campaign for quick and optimum commercial impact in a short period.

例:电影还未上映,电影公司对此片的爆炒就已经开始,以吸引大众媒体的注意。

Before the film hit the theaters, the film company had already started to quick-fry it in order to arouse more media attention.

爆料 bào liào

指媒体刊登或播出的鲜为人知的消息。rarely known information which is exposed through the media

例:在许多娱乐节目中,明星访谈节目无疑是最开心的,因为节目中时常会有爆料场景出现,令在场嘉宾猝不及防。

There's no doubt that interviews with popular singers or movie stars are the most exciting of all the entertainment programs. That's because they often catch the interviewees off guard by suddenly revealing inside information.

爆棚 bào péng

形容某事特别受欢迎,参加者人满为患。Literally it means a tent is too crowded with people and may explode. A metaphor for something that is very popular and loved by people so that too many wish to join it, participate or go for it.

例:音乐剧《美女与野兽》去年年底在京城上演三天,场场爆棚,不得不又加演两场。

The musical play "The Beauty and the Beast" had three shows in Beijing at the end of last year. It was full every time so that they had to put on two extra performances.

北漂 běi piāo

1.指漂泊到北京。to come to Beijing and lead a wandering life there

例:对于我,一个北漂将近三年的人来说,第一次见到她,就有这样一种感觉:这就是我需要的地方。

I have led a wandering life in Beijing for nearly three years. The first time I saw Beijing, I thought to myself — this is the place I need.

2.指到北京或北方城市谋求发展的个体艺术人才。artists, actors and artisans who come to cities in northern China, particularly Beijing, to development their careers

例:如今的娱乐圈中有不少明星都是北漂,其中最有代表性的就有张国立和孙楠。

Nowadays in the entertainment circle many stars have come to Beijing for personal development. Among them, Zhang Guoli and Sun Nan are the most representative ones.

背 bèi

不顺;倒霉;运气不佳。be unlucky; have bad luck

例:这些天我特背,干什么,什么不成。

I'm very unlucky these days. Everything that I do simply goes wrong.

背过气 bèi guò qì

指停止呼吸;喘不上气。stop breathing; be out of breath; gasp for breath

例:这个不幸的消息差点儿让她背过气去。

The bad news almost took her breath away.

备不住 bèi bù zhù

说不定;或许。perhaps; maybe

例：她备不住已经去上海了。

Maybe·she has already left for Shanghai.

备份 bèi fèn

复制品；副本；留作备用的东西。copy

例：别忘了给自己留个备份。

Don't forget to keep a copy for yourself.

倍儿 bèir

指特别。extremely

例：这本小说倍儿有意思。

This novel is terribly interesting.

倍儿棒 bèir bàng

指特别好。awfully good；great

例：这人干的活儿倍儿棒，谁也比不过。

This man's work is so great that no one else's can compare with it.

本儿 běnr

指千元人民币。thousand *yuan*

例：这家饭馆每天至少挣一本儿。

This small restaurant makes at least a thousand *yuan* a day.

本子 běn zi

1. 多指汽车驾驶执照。driver's license

例1：领本子

take out a driver's license

例2：考本子

take a test for a driver's license

例3：他的本子给警察扣了。

His driver's license was taken away by the policeman.

2. 剧本。script

例：他近来搞到一个好本子，决定尽快将它搬上银幕。

He got a good script recently and decided to make it into a film as soon as possible.

奔命 bèn mìng

拼命赶路或做事。drive（push）oneself hard to hurry on with one's journey or work

例：他每天都在奔命，为的是多挣一点儿钱。

He drives himself hard to rush his work in order to make more money every day.

崩 bēng

枪毙。shoot to death; execute by shooting

例：那小子昨天让人给崩了。

That fellow was shot to death yesterday.

绷 bēng

憋住，故意不说；收住；忍住。hold back; deliberately withhold information

例：她再也绷不住了，最后还是把父亲去逝的消息告诉了她的母亲。

When she could not hold out any longer, she told her mother about her father's death.

绷儿 bèngr

用在"硬、直、亮"一类形容词的前面，表示程度深。very; so; extremely

例 1：这木头绷儿硬。

The wood is very hard.

例 2：这汤绷儿好喝。

The soup is so delicious.

例 3：这灯绷儿亮。

The light is extremely bright.

蹦迪 bèng dī

跳迪斯科舞。disco dance

例：最近他很忙，没有时间去蹦迪了。

He has been so busy recently that he has had no time to go to the disco.

蹦极 bèng jí

一种极限体育娱乐活动。参加者要将一根有强力弹性的绳索绑住双脚，然后从高处（高台，桥梁，山）纵身跳下。bungee

例：蹦极是一项勇敢者的运动。如果你有胆量，不妨玩儿它一把。

Bungee is a sport for brave people. If you are fearless, you might as well try it once.

鼻子不是鼻子,脸不是脸 bí zi bù shi bí zi, liǎn bù shi liǎn

形容人生气或愤怒时的表情;表情很难看。angry looks; unpleasant look

例：我没招她也没惹她,她凭什么对我鼻子不是鼻子,脸不是脸的?

I haven't got in the bad books with her. Why does she give me an unpleasant look?

毙 bì

1.枪毙。shoot to death; execute by shooting

例：杀人犯被毙了。

The murder was shot to death.

2.否决;不予通过;拒绝。reject; vote down; veto

例：这项议案让总统毙了。

The bill has been rejected by the president.

飙车 biāo chē

指开快车。drive violently (madly)

例：我儿子就喜欢飙车，谁劝他也不听。我真担心有一天他会出事。

My son is fond of driving violently and listens to nobody's warnings. I'm so worried that he will have an accident one day.

表叔 biǎo shū

指香港人对大陆派往香港工作的政府官员或干部的称呼（含贬义）。

uncle/An impolite term used by people in Hong Kong to refer to government official from the mainland of China to work in Hong Kong.

例：最近我们公司又来了一个表叔。

Lately another government official has joined our company.

憋镜头 biē jìng tóu

1. 摄影机器出故障。bad camera shot；a shot gone wrong

例：小心点儿，别憋了镜头。

Be careful，don't make the shot go wrong.

2. 比喻人长相不好，不上相。a metaphor for an ugly or unphotogenic person

例：别把相机对着我，我可憋镜头。

Don't take my picture. I'm very unphotogenic.

蹩脚 bié jiǎo

1. 质量差；低劣；本领不强。inferior；poor；unskilled

例：这是一篇蹩脚的文章。

This is a bad article.

2.不舒服。be uncomfortable; stinko

例：她的演唱让我听起来感到蹩脚。

Her singing rubs me the wrong way.

冰舞 bīng wǔ

在冰上所进行的舞蹈。dancing on skates (ice)

例：冰舞是她最喜欢的一项体育运动。

Dancing on skates is her favorite sport.

病秧子 bìng yāng zi

指经常生病、身体不好的人。sick vine; person in poor health; someone vulnerable to illness

例：她看起来挺结实,实际上却是个病秧子。

She looks very healthy. But actually she is often laid low by illness.

波霸 bō bà

指胸部特别丰满的女子。woman with big breasts

例：你瞧外国电影或电视片中的女演员多数是波霸,性感十足。最有代表性的要算玛莉莲·梦露了。

You see that most actresses in foreign movies or telefilms have big breasts, very sexy. The most typical is Marylin Munro.

泊车 bó chē

停车。parking

例：为了解决泊车难的问题,街道两旁都新设置了停车线。

New parking lines were drawn on both sides of the street to solve the parking problem.

脖儿切 bór qiē

用手掌侧面击打人的脖颈。neck cut；to hit the neck with the side of the palm

例：他们只不过是在闹着玩，可是一个脖儿切却送他进了医院。

They were only playing around，but that neck cut sent him to the hospital.

不颤 bù chàn

不害怕。to not be afraid；to not be scared

例：他谁也不颤，包括他的老板。

He is not afraid of anyone，even his boss.

不错 bù cùo

不坏；好 not bad；good；OK

例：这件衬衫不错。

This shirt is not bad.

不搭脉 bù dā mài

指两者间属于不同档次，不能相提并论。two things entirely different，like chalk and cheese

例：你们俩别争了。一个是名牌，一个是杂牌，根本不搭脉，争也白争。

Stop arguing you two. One is a famous brand，another is an inferior brand. They can't be mentioned in the same breath. It is useless to argue any more.

不待见 bù dài jiàn

指不受别人欢迎、喜欢；讨厌。annoy；dislike

例：我知道我赚钱不多，所以你父母最不待见我。

I know I don't make a lot of money，so your parents really dislike me.

不忿儿 bù fènr

1. 不服气。refuse to obey；to not give in to

例：他就不忿儿他的班长。

He refuses to obey the class monitor.

2. 不佩服。to not admire；to not look up to

例：她才不忿儿那些明星呢。她认为自己比她们都强。

She doesn't look up to other movie stars because she considers herself a better actress than any of them.

不赖 bù lài

不坏；好。not bad；good

例：你的测试结果还不赖。

The result of your test is not bad.

不吝 bù lìn

不在乎；无所谓。not care；not mind

例：她从不吝别人对她是怎么想的。

She doesn't care what other people think about her.

不吝秧子 bù lìn yāng zi

指人做事情不顾一切，什么都不怕。(someone) care about nothing；have no fear of anything；have no regard for sth.

例：你就是用死来吓唬他也没用，因为他这个人从不吝秧子。

It's useless even to frighten him for he is a person who cares about nothing.

不是个儿 bù shi gèr

指（人）不行，不是对手。be not good；incapable；but no match

例1：干这种活儿她可不是个儿。

She is no good for this kind of work.

例2：他又高又壮。如果论打架,这里谁也不是他的个儿。

He is very tall and strong. Nobody here is a match for him if he wants to fight.

不是玩儿的 bù shi wánr de

不是儿戏;不是小事;严肃认真的。be no joke; be serious; no kidding; not a trifling matter

例1：别坐在窗台上,这不是玩儿的。

Don't sit on the windows. This is no trifling matter.

例2：告诉你不要碰插座,这不是玩儿的。

I'm serious in telling you not to touch the socket.

不要脸 bù yào liǎn

1.这是一种女性常用的口头语,表示对某人的讨厌、愤怒,有时会在前面加上"臭",表示讨厌或愤怒的程度更深。disgusting; shameless; A colloquial expression often used by women to express their disgust or hatred for someone. Sometimes, "chòu (stinking)" is added in front of the phrase to increase the degree of disgust and hatred.

例：A:嗨,小姐,你真漂亮,能让我亲一下吗？

Hi, Miss. You're so pretty. Can I kiss you?

B:真不要脸。

How disgusting!

2.不知羞耻。shameless

例：你怎么能当众说瞎话呢！简直是不要脸到家了。

How can you tell lies in public?! You are completely shameless.

不搭界 bù dā gā (界,此处念 gā,不念 jiè)

指不着边;没有关系。(a common expression in Shanghai dialect) have no relation; have nothing to do with

例:这跟婚姻不搭界。

This has nothing to do with the marriage.

不感冒 bù gǎn mào

不感兴趣;(没有兴趣)不重视。have no interest; to not be interested in sth.; pay little attention to

例:对这种鸡毛蒜皮的事他从不感冒。

He's not interested in these kinds of petty matters.

不起眼儿 bù qǐ yǎnr

不受重视;不引人注目。not eye-catching; trivial; unremarkable

例:虽然影片中描写的都是不起眼儿的事情,但它还是一部十分感人和有教育意义的电影。

The film is very moving and instructive although what it depicts is trivial.

C

擦屁股 cā pì gu

比喻处理别人留下的、未干完的事情；收拾残局；进行扫尾工作。clean up the dirt/A metaphor for one who clears up a messy situation or finishes work others leave behind.

例：他出国了，留给我们的全都是擦屁股的活儿。

He went abroad and left us all the mess to be cleared up.

彩儿 cǎir

指精彩之处；趣味；热烈的气氛。interest；delight；lively atmosphere

例：明星的到来给晚会添了不少的彩儿。

The movie star's appearance enlivened the party.

踩 cǎi

指诽谤、侮辱。slander；calumniate；libel；insult

例：他这种小人只会靠踩别人或拍马屁来向上爬，自己一点儿真才实学也没有。

He is a villain who depends on slandering others and licking boots to get himself promoted. Actually he has no real ability or knowledge at all.

踩道 cǎi dào

指探路。explore the way；search for the way

例：你在考试前应先踩踩道看如何去那所学校。

You'd better find your way to the school before you go to take an examination.

踩点儿 cǎi diǎnr

1.指事先对要去的地点的情况和环境进行周密的调查。

step on the spot; make a thorough and careful investigation of a place a person intends to go to

例:明天我们去承德春游。老王昨天就踩点儿去了。

Tomorrow we will have a spring outing to Chengde. Lao Wang went to step on the spot yesterday.

2.指跳舞时跟上舞蹈音乐的节拍。to follow the rhythm while dancing

例:她的节奏感太差了,这么简单的舞蹈就是踩不到点儿上。

Her sense of rhythm is so poor that she can't keep up with all rhythm of such a simple dance.

踩乎 cǎi hu

欺负;压制;贬低。bully; oppress; depreciate, tread upon; disparage

例1:我可不是那么容易被人踩乎的人。

I'm one who is not easily trodden upon by anyone.

例2:她想踩乎别人来抬高自己。

She wants to put down others so as to build up herself.

菜 cài

1.指人或事窝囊、丢人。也指土气、愚昧(骂人话)。sb. or sth. that is good for nothing; hopelessly stupid; humiliating; rustic; countrified; ignorant

例1:你也真够菜的。这么简单的事情也做不好,还能做些什么。

You are so stupid. You can't do such an easy thing. What else can you do?

例2:你整个一个菜,连手机都没见过。

You are a complete ignoramus. You haven't ever seen a mobile phone before.

2.打输;打败。lose; be beaten

例:你没见过他被菜的时候是啥模样,真让人可怜。

You didn't see what he looked when he was beaten, very pitiful.

菜了 cài le

失败;不成功;完蛋了。fail; be unsuccessful; fall through

例:这次我算是彻底菜了。

I totally failed this time.

菜鸟 cài niǎo

讥指傻瓜,也指新手。fool; blockhead; simpleton, also refers to new hand; greenhorn; rookie

例:他这个人真是个菜鸟。人家跟他开个玩笑,他还真的当真了。

He really is a fool. Someone was only teasing him, but he took it seriously.

菜色 cài sè

指青绿色或黄色。通常指人由于营养不良而造成的脸色不好,面色难看。dark green or sallow yellow/A term to indicate someone who has a colorless complexion or looks famished.

例:她面带菜色。

She looks famished.

残 cán

残废;受伤。maim; wound

例:他的手让机器给残了。

His hand was wounded by the machine.

残废 cán fèi

比喻身高在一米六以下的小个子男人。

crippled man/A metaphor for men shorter than 160 cm.

例:她逗她丈夫说他是个残废。

She teases her husband by calling him a "cripple".

惨 cǎn

1.尴尬;倒霉;可怜;狼狈。awkward; pitiful; miserable

例:别把这事告诉我妻子,否则我可要惨了。

Don't tell my wife about it or I'll be in a very awkward position.

2.(长相)差,不好。(looking) bad; poor

例:他的模样确实惨点儿。

He is really looking down and out.

糙 cāo

1.没礼貌;粗野。rude; rough; boorish; uncouth; impolite

例:别跟他制气。他是个糙人。

Don't be angry with him. He is a rough fellow.

2.(指做工)不细致;粗糙。crudely made; of poor work manship

例:这床做得真够糙的。

The bed is crudely made.

3.非技术性的。unskilled

例:他这个壮工,只能做些糙活儿。

As a hod carrier, he can only do a little unskilled work.

草鸡 cǎo jī

形容人遇事懦弱不敢向前。hen / A metaphor for one who is weak and coward.

例:现在是最关键的时候,谁也不许当草鸡。尽快把我们的销售额搞上去。

Now is a most crucial moment, no one should be a coward.
We will increase our sales as soon as possible.

操 cào

骂人用的下流话。fuck

操蛋 cào dàn

坏的；差劲的；不怎么样的（骂人话）。(swearword) damn;
bad; no good; disappointing

例：你真操蛋。我等了你一小时，可你根本就没露面。

Damn you. I waited for an hour, but you didn't show up.

操行 cào xing

1.样子；品行；行为（骂人话）。(swearword) behavior; look,
appemance; conduct

例：看他这副操行，有谁会信他是出身名门呢？

Who would have thought from his shoddy manners that he's
from a noble family?

2.德行（骂人话）。(swearword) shameful; disgusting;
damn

例：你真操行。

You are disgusting.

瓸 cěi

讥讽人长得难看。a scornful term for bad looking; ugly

例：她长得够瓸的，但她却自我感觉良好。

She doesn't look so great, but she feels okay.

瓸 cèi

1.打（人）。strike; hit; knock; beat

例：我让我哥来甂他。

I'll get my brother to knock him flat.

2. 砸（东西）；打碎；摔碎。break；smash

例：盘子甂了。

The plate is broken.

蹭 cèng

指不花钱白享受，跟着别人沾光。get sth. free from assoication with sb. or sth.；benefit from association with sb. or sth.

例：他昨天蹭了一顿饭。

He got a free meal yesterday.

蹭车 cèng chē

指不花钱坐车、搭车。get a lift；take a bus or train without pay

例：她训斥儿子不该蹭车。

She scolded her son for not paying the bus fare.

蹭儿 cèngr

1. 指不花钱白享受的东西。something one gets for free

例：他常到我家吃蹭儿。

He often comes to get a free meal at my home.

2. 指不花钱白占别人便宜的人。freeloader

例：大家都知道他，因为他有个蹭儿的名声。

Everyone knows him because he has a reputation for being a freeloader.

插一杠子 chā yī gàng zi

指中途参与或干涉。interfere；interrupt

例：不管人家干什么或说什么，他总爱从中插一杠子，生怕人家把他忘了或把他当哑巴卖了。

No matter what others do or say, he always interrupts lest they forget him or consider him dumb.

碴 chá

指打架。fight; come to blows; scuffle (with)

例:楼前有两个人碴起来了。

Two men are fighting in front of the building.

碴架 chá jià

指打架或打群架。fight; engage in a gang fight

例:想碴架,你可不是我的对手。

You're no match for me if you want a fight.

碴霹 chá pī

指跳霹雳舞。break dance

例:他最爱碴霹。

He likes break dancing most of all.

碴舞 chá wǔ

跳舞,多指青年人比赛跳霹雳舞、迪斯科(的士高)等现代舞。dance (refers to an informal competition between break dancers or disco dancers)

例:课后学生们喜欢在一起碴舞。

Those students like to dance after class.

茶钱 chá qián

指小费。tip

例:她几年前离开出版社干起了导游。这几年可发了,光茶钱就挣了不少。

She left the publishing house and worked as a tourist guide several years ago. She has made a fortune in recent years and earned a lot only from tips.

柴 chái

1. 质量太差。poor quality

例：这鞋做得太柴了，刚穿了三天就破了。

The quality of these shoes is so bad that they were worn out in only three days.

2. 指肉太瘦，不松软。tough；thin；hard；lean meat(quality of meat)

例：当牛肉烤过火时，其肉就变得特别柴。

When the roast beef is overdone, it becomes too tough.

柴禾妞儿 chái he niūr

1. 讥指土里土气的农村姑娘。country girl（scornful）

例：他爱上了一个柴禾妞儿。

He's in love with a country girl.

2. 指瘦弱的女孩。thin or skinny girl

缠 chán

对付。deal with；cope with；handle

例：我讨厌见他。这人太难缠。

I dislike to see him. He is too much of a handful.

铲 chǎn

指解决、处理。solve；handle

例：别怕，有事尽管找我，我帮你铲。

Don't be afraid. Come to me if you have difficulties. I'll help you to solve them.

猖 chāng

指猖狂；放肆；厉害。savage；furious；unbridled

例：走私犯够猖的，敢和警察交手。

The smugglers were so unbridled that they fought furiously with the police.

长假 cháng jià

指春节、"五一"国际劳动节和"十一"国庆节放的七天假。a long holiday，mainly referring to the three seven-day holidays of Spring Festival，May 1st International Labor Day，and October 1st National Day

例：A：十一长假你打算干什么？

What are you going to do for the October 1st holiday?

B：我打算同家人一起去日本玩。

I'm going to Japan with my family.

长舌妇 cháng shé fù

指爱说闲话、搬弄是非的女人。gossip monger；garrulous woman

例：一件不起眼的事能让长舌妇说破了天。

A gossip monger can make a small thing into a big event.

吵吵 chāo chao

指许多人乱说话。twitter；talk rapidly at the same time；make a noise

例：别跟他吵吵了。咱们还是听听老师是怎么说的。

Stop talking over him. Let's listen to what the teacher says about it.

抄肥 chāo féi

指看有油水的买卖就捞一把或半路把货截走。reap profit in business；block goods and take them away；waylay；profit reaping

例:他真倒霉。今天碰上一个抄肥的家伙截走了他一池塘的鱼。

He was unlucky today. He met some profit reaping guys, who took away all his fish from the pond.

抄上了 chāo shàng le

指赶上好事了;走好运。be in luck; have good luck

例:今天他真是抄上了,中了个头彩。

Today is his lucky day. He won the first price in the lottery.

潮 cháo

1.时髦;新潮。fashion; fashionable

例1:今年真皮茄克特潮。

Leather jackets are fashionable this year.

例2:如今什么最潮?

What's in fashion now?

2.成色低劣。inferior; low grade; poor; bad

例:潮金 low grade gold

3.技术不高。unskillful; incompetent; awkward

例:他的写作技巧太潮。

His writing style is very poor.

炒 chǎo

1.反复倒买倒卖,从中获利。buy and resell at a profit

例:这张邮票的价钱被炒得越来越高。

The price of the stamp has risen considerably through continual buying and reselling.

2.反复筛选,留取精华。to select

例:从出版者书目中炒出了十本畅销书。

Ten best sellers were selected from the publishers' lists.

3.解聘;开除。dismiss; fire; sack

例:她被老板炒了。

She was sacked by her boss.

炒更 chǎo gēng

指夜间出外活动者，多指演员从事正式工作以外的另一个工作。moonlighter；a spare-time job for extra money/A term that mainly refers to people, mainly actors or actresses, who have another job besides their formal one.

例：如今不像头几年，炒更的人是越来越多。不然怎么有那么多人买房子和汽车呢？

Today, unlike a few years ago, more and more people have another job at night. Otherwise, how could so many people have bought houses and cars?

炒股 chǎo gǔ

从事股票买卖。engage in speculation in stocks；buy and re-sell stocks at a profit

例：他把所有的钱都拿去炒股了。

He speculated all his money in stocks.

炒汇 chǎo huì

反复倒买倒卖外汇，从中获利。arbitrage；buy and resell foreign currency at a profit

例：他整日忙着炒汇。

He is busy all day buying and reselling foreign currency.

炒冷饭 chǎo lěng fàn

重复地做。do sth. again and again；repeat doing the same things

例：编导们年年不辞辛苦地在除夕夜的餐桌上添一道炒冷饭。

Every year directors spare no effort to add a repeat program for the New Year Eve's show.

炒买炒卖 chǎo mǎi chǎo mài

指反复倒买倒卖,从中获利。to speculate; resell at a profit (used mostly for stocks, foreign currency, real estate or other goods in exceeding supply demand)

例:他最早靠炒买炒卖股票发家的。

At the very beginning he built up his family fortune by re-selling stocks.

炒明星 chǎo míng xīng

指利用宣传报导手段吹捧明星。to make a person famous; to create a star through publicity

例:如今越来越多的人明白了炒明星的重要。

Now more and more people have realized the importance of publicity when creating a star.

炒鱿鱼 chǎo yóu yú

解聘;开除。sack; dismiss; fire

例:如果再迟到,你就要被炒鱿鱼了。

You'll be fired if you come to work late again next time.

炒友 chǎo yǒu

指专门从事各种倒买倒卖并从中获利的人。speculator; profiteer

例:他认识许多炒友,可以帮你介绍一下。

He knows many speculators and is willing to introduce them to you.

车本 chē běn

驾驶证。driver's license

例:张小姐上午刚拿到车本,下午就直奔车行去买车。

Ms. Zhang got her driver's license in the morning, and went directly to the car lot to buy a car in the afternoon.

车虫 chē chóng

指爱玩自行车的人。bicycle fanatic (refers to those who enjoy buying, cleaning and repairing bicycles)

例：京城里有不少的车虫。

Beijing is full of bicycle fanatics.

车倒儿 chē dǎor

指倒买倒卖各种车辆从中牟利的人。a person who resells vehicles; second-hand dealer

例：如果你愿意我能通过一个车倒儿帮你弄辆德国车。

I can help you buy a German car through a second-hand dealer if you want.

车匪路霸 chē fěi lù bà

指在公共汽车或火车上抢钱，或拦路向过往汽车司机和行人强行收钱的人。highwaymen or road bandits who rob bus or train passengers or block the road and demand road fare

例：政府近来严厉打击了一批车匪路霸。

The central government has recently cracked down on a group of highwaymen.

扯淡 chě dàn

指闲扯；闲聊；胡说（骂人话）。(swearword) talk nonsense; bullshit

例：我认为他在扯淡。实际上他比任何人都清楚事实的真相。

I think he's talking nonsense. Actually he is aware of the facts better than anyone else.

扯了 chě le

指极多。plenty; too much; excessive; a lot

例:他挣的钱扯了。

He makes a lot of money.

扯平 chě píng

使对等或相等;不亏欠(某人)。be(get)even with sb.;
make even

例:这样就扯平了。

This will make it even.

撤傍 chè bàng

指断绝与朋友、情人的来往。break off a friendship; break
with sb.

例:当得知他被警察通缉的消息后,他的哥儿们都纷纷撤傍。

His friends broke with him after hearing that he was wanted
by the police.

撤火 chè huǒ

1.打击(某人)的积极性;泄气;泼冷水。dampen the enthusiasm
of; discourage; pour cold water on

例:她丈夫不喜欢她干这工作,所以总是给她撤火。

Her husband dislikes her to do this job, so he often pours
cold water on her efforts.

2.停止供暖;不生火。stop heating; extinguish a fire in a
stove

例:每年三月十五日撤火。

The heating stops on the fifteenth of March every year.

趁 chèn

指富有;拥有。be rich in; possess; well-off

例 1：趁钱

have pots of money

例 2：这里数他最趁。

His is the richest man here.

例 3：她趁三百双鞋。

She possesses three hundred pairs of shoes.

撑 chēng

1. 支撑；负责；维持。prop up; maintain; hold out; support

例：这个家全靠我父亲撑着。

The family is supported by only my father.

2. 吃得过饱。eat too much; fill up; make a pig of oneself

例：今天我不该吃得太撑了。

I shouldn't eat too much today.

3. 自找麻烦；没事找事。look for trouble; ask for it

例：我多次告诉你别动刀。现在你出了事，这不是你撑的吗？

I told you many times not to touch that knife. Now you hurt yourself. You simply asked for it.

撑死了 chēng sǐ le

1. 到头；最终（表示达到极点或顶点）。at the utmost; to the end; finally

例：这块表撑死了只值二十美元。

This watch costs only twenty dollars at the utmost.

2. 指吃得太饱，肚里一点儿余地也没有了。too full; stuffed to the gills

例：我吃得快撑死了，连路也走不了了。

I'm too full to walk.

成 chéng

1. 可以；好（表示同意或赞同）。OK; good; all right

例：成，就按你说的办。

OK，act up to your word.

2.能干；有本事（用于夸别人时）。capable；able；skillful

例：你真成！这样复杂的机器你也能修。

You're great. You can repair this kind of complicated machine.

成气候 chéng qì hòu

指人得势，走红。be in power；gain the upper hand；make good；become popular

例：谁也没想到两年后他的歌能成气候。

No one expected he could become popular with his songs in two years.

秤砣 chèng tuó

1.指秤锤。the sliding weight of a steelyard

例：你这个秤砣有多重？

How heavy is the sliding weight in the steelyard?

2.比喻胖人。a fatty or heavy weight

例：我说这车怎么开不动呢，原来后面坐着一个秤砣。

I wondered why I could not make this car move, in fact there was a heavy weight sitting on the back seat.

痴 chī

1.傻；蠢笨。foolish；stupid；idiotic

例：一副痴相。

a stupid look

2.极度迷恋某人或某事。be crazy about（sb. or sth.）；have a fancy for（sb. or sth.）

例：他对她简直痴得不行了。

He's crazy about her.

吃不了兜着走 chī bù liǎo dōu zhe zǒu

1.承受不起；使某人陷入极其困难的处境。get more than one bargained for; land oneself in serious trouble

例：仓库重地你必须要小心，否则失了火你可是要吃不了兜着走。

You should be very careful in the warehouse. If a fire starts, you will be in serious trouble.

2.指（自己）将吃剩下的饭菜打包带回家。ask for a doggy bag; take one's leftovers back home

例：你干吗叫那么多的菜？我想这次你要吃不了兜着走了。

Why have you ordered so many dishes? I guess you'll have to take the leftovers home.

吃错药了 chī cuò yào le

指某人的言行、举止反常，粗暴无礼。take the wrong medicine/A term that infers a person's behavior is a bit strange or rude and impolite.

例：他不是吃错药了吧？我从未见他对我这么凶过。

I haven't seen him so rude to me. Has he taken the wrong medicine today?

吃大户 chī dà hù

原指旧社会灾民聚众前往有钱人家强迫其施舍或分其财，食其粮。今指让最富有或有钱的人请客。to eat at the great households/A term that refers to peasants who got together and went to the rich households for food or to force them to share their wealth and grains during famine in old China, now refers to letting the person with more money pay for the meal; eating at the expense of the rich.

例：听说他一夜之间发了，他那帮哥们儿决定先吃他这个大户一次。

Upon hearing that he had become rich overnight, his friends decided to eat at his expense first.

吃刀 chī dāo

指吃亏,被人欺骗或耍弄。意同"挨宰"和"活宰"。suffer losses; get the worst of it; be cheated or fooled

例:她就是因为心太软脸皮薄,所以上街买东西没少吃刀。

She is often cheated when she buys things in the street because she is too faint-hearted and feels ashamed of bargaining.

吃豆腐 chī dòu fu

1. 指男子对女子(妻子以外)的轻薄行为,引申为男子占女子的便宜。(lit.) eating beancurd; (men) take advantage of women; find sexual satisfaction in touching women apart from one's wife

例:嘿,你们这帮家伙,别打算吃她的豆腐。

Hey, you fellows. Don't try to take advantage of her.

2. 指朋友(同性)之间的寻开心。take advanrage of/A term used between male friends to make fun of each other.

例:你吃我啥豆腐?

How could you take advantage of me?

吃货 chī huò

1. 指无能的人。good for nothing; worthless wretch

例:我怎么养了你这么一个吃货,还总给我惹麻烦。

How could I bring up such a worthless wretch as you? You always give me trouble.

2. 指进货或购买货物。stock (a shop) with goods; lay in merchandise; buy in goods

例:这个店地段好,客人多,所以吃货量也大。

This shop has a good location with large flows of customers, so it buys up a huge stock of goods.

吃价 chī jià

指受欢迎。to be very popular; to be well-liked

例：这种牌子的空调机现在在市面上蛮吃价的。

This brand of air conditioner is very popular now.

吃偏饭 chī piān fàn

指吃别人吃不到的饭,形容接受特殊的待遇或帮助。have particular meal for someone or receive (give sb.) a particular treatment or help

例：我们在这儿人人平等,谁也不能吃偏饭。

We are equal here. No one will receive a particular treatment.

吃枪药 chī qiāng yào

指责某人出言不逊,没有礼貌,不讲道理。to swallow gunpowder; to speak rudely or use insolent and impolite language

例：我怀疑你是吃枪药了,否则你不会那么对我说话。

I wonder if you have swallowed gunpowder, otherwise you wouldn't speak to me like that.

吃请 chī qǐng

1. 别人请自己吃饭。to be invited to a dinner

例：你自己吃吧,我今晚去吃请。

Go ahead and have supper yourself. I've been invited to a dinner tonight.

2. 用公款请客。to treat sb. to a meal at public expense

例：他总找借口带他的朋友们去吃请。

He always find an excuse to take out his friends for dinner

at public expense.

吃软饭 chī ruǎn fàn

指（男人）靠女人养活（含贬义）。(of men) live off women rather than working for a living; (of men) be supported by women

例：如今有些漂亮的小伙子们专门喜欢吃软饭。

Some good looking guys prefer to live off women these days.

吃素的 chī sù de

指简单的,好对付的（人或物）。(of a person or sth.) easy; easy going; easy to deal with

例：你最好当心点儿,他可不是吃素的。

You'd better play it carefully. He's not easy to deal with.

吃香 chī xiāng

指受欢迎,受人喜爱。be very popular; find favor with sb.; be well-liked

例1：现在电脑吃香。

Now computers find favor with customers.

例2：国内懂英语的人到哪儿都吃香。

People who speak English are well-liked everywhere in China.

吃相 chī xiàng

指进食的样子。table manner, generally only referring to eating

例：你要注意你的吃相,特别是在客人面前。

You should be careful of your table manners, especially in front of guests.

吃小灶 chī xiǎo zào

指单独为一个人做饭,多形容得到特殊的服务或待遇,通常用于单独辅导或教某人做事。have a special meal for sb. or receive (give sb.) a special treatment or service/Often it refers to giving someone individual tuition or training.

例1:她父亲是老师,所以常给她吃小灶,还让她做大量的习题。

Her father is a teacher, so he often teaches her alone, making her do many exercises.

例2:他不喜欢上大课,就喜欢吃小灶。

He prefers to be taught alone than to go to a lecture.

吃心 chī xīn

指疑心或多心。become suspicious; be oversensitive

例:我无论说谁她都容易吃心。

She easily becomes suspicious about whatever I say to anyone.

赤佬 chì lǎo

1.指死鬼(骂人话)。devil (used as a swearword)

例:你这个赤佬,大声喊什么?

You devil, what are you yelling about?

2.指亲朋好友之间的互相称呼,有玩笑亲昵之意。devil (a joky way of addressing friends)

例:赤佬,你跑到哪里去了,我几天都没见到你的面。

You devil, where have you been? I haven't seen you for days.

充大个儿 chōng dà gèr

指本身没有能力却硬要干;逞能;蛮干。show off; be foolhardy; to force oneself to do; be braggart/A term refers to one who insists on doing sth. which is beyond his ability or one who tries to impress others.

例：既然你不行，你就不该充大个儿。

You shouldn't show off about something you can't do.

充壳子 chōng ké zi

讥指不懂装懂的人。A scornful term for sb. who doesn't know sth. but pretends to be an expert.

例：这里所有的人都是行家。你小子可别在这儿充壳子乱说，当心让人笑话。

All the people here are experts. You shouldn't pretend to be a dab hand or talk nonsense and be careful not let them laugh at you.

冲洋画片 chōng yáng huà piàn

指一种自动售洋画片的机器，只要投入硬币，然后转动旋钮或拉下扳手就可得到一张精美的卡片。pull the card out of an automatic selling machine

例：我三岁的女儿坚持要自己冲洋画片。

My three-year-old daughter insisted on pulling out the card herself.

冲头 chòng tóu

指单纯老实，容易上当受骗的人。simple, unsophisticated, honest person easily fooled or taken in

例：他那套把戏只能骗骗那些冲头，可蒙不了我。

His tricks only can fool simple-minded people, not me.

抽立 chōu lì

全部输光；战败。lose money (in gambling); be beaten; be defeated

例：在牌桌上他第一个被抽立了。

He lost all his money at the card table.

丑八怪 chǒu bā guài

指相貌很难看的人。very ugly person；very bad-looking person

例：我弄不明白你怎么能嫁给他这样一个丑八怪。

I can't understand how you could marry anyone as hideous as him.

臭 chòu

1. 低劣；愚蠢。stupid；bad；disappointing；inferior

例：这是谁写的字？真够臭的。

Whose handwriting is this? It's really bad.

2. 指败坏某人的名誉。ruin one's reputation；discredit；defame

例：即使我打不赢这场官司，也能臭臭他。

Even though I can't win the lawsuit, I can use it to defame him.

臭大粪 chòu dà fèn

形容拙劣；愚蠢；蠢笨。low-grade；no good；stupid

例："臭大粪"，你连这么简单的棋都下不好。

How stupid! You can't even play the simplest game.

臭狗屎 chòu gǒu shǐ

骂人话。dogshit；shit

臭街了 chòu jiē le

形容东西很多，到处都是。literally stink the street；a fad or craze

例：如今 BP 机都臭街了，所以我改用大哥大了。

C 最新中国俚语 New Slang of China

At present pagers are a fad, so I changed to using a cellular phone.

臭美 chòu měi

1. 打扮，美化自己。make up; dress up; beautify

例：她喜欢照着镜子臭美。

She likes to make herself up in front of the mirror.

2. 自我感觉良好；自鸣得意，高兴。give oneself airs; be stuck on oneself; be swell-headed.

例：别臭美了。没人喜欢跟你去。

Don't be too swell-headed yourself. Nobody likes to go with you.

臭美妞 chòu měi niū

指特别爱打扮、重外表的女孩子。a girl who is fussy about her appearance

例：她是我们班有名的臭美妞。

She is well known in our class for being the fussiest about her appearance.

臭棋篓子 chòu qí lǒu zi

讥讽棋艺很差的人。a scornful term for a bad chess player; an unskilled chess player

例：别跟那小子玩儿，他可是个十足的臭棋篓子。

Don't play with him. He's a very bad chess player.

臭子儿 chòu zǐr

指失效的子弹；没有出枪膛的子弹。dumb fire; faulty cartridge; (of bullet) lose efficacy

例：在起跑线上，他放了三枪，可全是臭子儿。

At the start of the race, he shot the gun three times, but it wouldn't go off because of the dumb fire.

出彩儿 chū cǎir

指搞出精彩的东西；推出好戏。make a good show；put on a good play；do brilliant things；brilliant；exciting；splendid

例：北京人艺近来频频出彩儿，深受观众的欢迎。

The Beijng People's Theater Troupe has recently put on many good plays, which have been well received by audiences.

出菜 chū cài

指出产品；出成果。produce a product；make sth.；achieve sth.

例：多数人都想在中年时出菜。

Most people hope to have achieved something by the time they reach forty.

出道 chū dào

开始从事某种职业（多指娱乐性行业）。to begin a career (usually in show business)

例：吉米出道很早，13 岁就在一部影片中担任男主角。

Jimmy went in for show business very early. He played a leading role in a film when he was only thirteen.

出格 chū gé

1.行动言语与众不同。(speech and action) be out of the ordinary；differ from others

例：他这人很奇怪，办什么事都出格。

He is quite odd. He often does things out of the ordinary.

2.过分；过火；超出常规。overdo sth.；go too far；exceed proper limits for speech or action

例：她能把握自己的言语，从不说出格的话。

She knows what she should say and never gets carried away.

出更 chū gēng

指（公安人员）外出执行任务,巡逻。（policeman）go on a tour of inspection; patrol; make one's rounds

例:小李刚刚从警校毕业。这是他当干警后的第一次出更。
Xiao Li has just graduated from a police school. This is his first time he has made his rounds after becoming a policeman.

出镜 chū jìng

指出演（影片）。come（appear）on the camera; play a role (in a film)

例:一家电影厂花上万美元请她出镜。

A movie studio spent ten thousand dollars on inviting her to appear on camera.

出局 chū jú

指被淘汰出比赛。be knocked out or eliminated in a competition

例:今天下午进行的初赛中红队有两名选手出局,有三名选手进入复赛。

Two players from the Red Team were eliminated in the preliminary contest this afternoon. The other three have entered the semi-finals.

出溜 chū liu

1.滑;滑行。slide; ship
例:她喜欢在冰上出溜。
She likes to slide on the ice.

2.下降;变坏;堕落。degenerate; sink low; so downhill
例1:你不能再这样出溜下去了。

You can't sink low like this any more.

例 2：这学期他的学习成绩一直往下出溜。

His study has been going downhill this semester.

出圈儿 chū quānr

指行为或言语超出规范或界限。(of behavior or words) to go beyond the limit or bounds; to overstep the bounds; to go too far

例：他拿公款去炒股这件事做得太出圈儿了。

Using public money for speculation in the stocks absolutely overstepped the bounds.

出摊儿 chū tānr

指摊主开始营业。(of vendors) do business; open for business

例：昨天下大雨，所以他没有出摊儿。

He didn't open his stand yesterday because of the heavy rain.

出血 chū xiě

指拿出大笔钱。shed blood; squander; plunk down/A metaphor for paying a large sum of money for sth.

例：如果你想买好房就得肯出血。

You'll have to plunk down a large sum of money if you want to buy a spacious house.

储 chǔ

指演员走穴所得的酬金。renumeration for a performance

例：演员的储是由穴头和演员事先谈妥的。

Renumeration for a performance will be negotiated by an agent.

触电 chù diàn

接触电视或电影表演，在电视剧或电影中扮演角色或担任电视主持人。to have one's first experience on TV or in a movie; to play a role in a TV drama or a film, or to be a host/hostess on TV

例：歌星谈到他第一次触电经历时，感受颇多。

The pop star was very moved when he recalled his first experience playing a role in a TV series.

臁 chuái

指人肥胖而肌肉松弛。plump; fat; chubby

例：瞧他多臁，连道儿都走不好了。

How chubby he is! He can't walk properly.

川妹子 chuān mèi zi

称四川的女孩子。a Sichuan girl

例：这名歌手是个川妹子。

The singer is a Sichuan girl.

穿帮 chuān bāng

露馅；把事情搞砸；使内情败露。to let the cat out of the bag; to give oneself away; to let the whole world know

例：这事差点让我给穿帮了。我不知道他没把丢自行车的事告诉他爱人。

I very nearly let the cat out of the bag. I didn't know he hadn't told his wife about his bicycle being lost.

穿水晶鞋 chuān shuǐ jīng xié

比喻暗中刁难或为难别人；比喻约束或限制别人，意同穿小鞋。make sb. wear crystal (or small) shoes/A metaphor for one who makes things difficult for others, or stops others from doing things (generally used to refer to working relationship specially boss and subordinate).

例：我不怕她给我穿水晶鞋。

I'm not afraid of her making my life difficult.

串游 chuàn yóu

闲逛；散步。saunter；stroll；amble

例：我想在附近串游串游。

I would like to stroll around the neighborhood.

窗户纸 chuāng hu zhǐ

糊窗户所用的很薄的纸，比喻用来掩盖、隐藏事实真相或秘密的手段、伎俩等。thin paper used on windows/A metaphor for screen，cover-up or camouflage.

例：他试图以谎言来掩盖事实，但他那层窗户纸最终还是被人捅破了。

He tried to cover up the facts by telling lies. But his screen was torn off at last.

床头柜 chuáng tóu guì

1.床前两边的柜子。night stand

例：他给新卧室添置了两个床头柜。

He bought two night stands for his new bedroom.

2.指怕老婆，经常被罚跪床头的丈夫。hen-pecked husband；uxorious man/A metaphor for a husband who is afraid of his wife and has to kneel beside the bed.

例：他是他们单位有名的床头柜。

He is well known in his work unit for being a hen-pecked husband.

雏(儿) chú(r)

指稚嫩、毫无经验的新手。greenhorn；tyro；new hand；raw recruit

C 最新中国俚语 New Slang of China

例:他是个雏儿。他不知如何应付这种局面。

He's a new hand at this. He doesn't know how to handle the situation.

吹 chuī

1.说大话。talk big; boast

例:他跟我吹他会讲七种语言。

He boasts to me that he can speak seven languages.

2.(事情、友情)失败,破裂,关系断绝。break up (of sth. or friendship); break down; be over; cut off; fail

例1:这个计划最后还是吹了。

The plan failed at the end.

例2:他跟女友吹了。

He broke up with his girlfriend.

吹边哨 chuī biān shào

指在一旁起哄、煽风点火。to blow whistle at a side/A metaphor for someone or a crowd of people who create a disturbance; incite; stir up trouble; inflame or agitate people.

例:有些人每当看见别人遇到点儿什么事,就爱在一旁吹边哨,惟恐还不够热闹。

Someone who likes to exacerbate others' troubles by blowing a whistle at a side when he sees that other people are encountering difficulties.

吹灯拔蜡 chuī dēng bá là

1.比喻事情不成,失败。(literally) blow out the candle and remove it; (figuratively) go fail; fall through

例:我想如果他们不肯帮忙,这件事情迟早得吹灯拔蜡。

I think this matter will fall through sooner or later if they don't give us a hand.

2.比喻人死亡。to die

例：那老家伙早就吹灯拔蜡了。

The old fellow died a long time ago.

戳 chuō

1.竖立。erect; stand sth. on end

例：你能帮我把竹竿戳起来吗？

Would you please help me erect the bamboo pole?

2.支撑；撑腰。back up; support

例：有我给你戳着，你尽管去干你想干的事。

I'll back you up. You simply go ahead and do what you like.

3.站立。stand

例：他个头大，戳在那儿像个电线杆子。

He is so tall that he stood there like a pole.

呲嘚 cī de

指申斥；训斥；批评。

talking-to; tongue-lashing; dressing down

例：她常呲嘚她儿子。

She often gives her son a talking-to.

呲儿 cīr

申斥或斥责。scold; give a talking-to; give a tongue-lashing

例：昨天老板把我呲儿了一顿，说我不该擅自降价处理这批货物。

Yesterday my boss gave me a good talking-to. He said that I shouldn't have sold these goods at a cheaper price without authorization.

瓷(磁) cí

1.指关系非常好，关系特别亲密。(of a relationship) intimate; close; good

例：你无法拆散他们。他们特瓷。

You have no way of breaking them up. They are very close friends.

2. 指关系亲密、特别好的朋友。crony; chum; sidekick; intimate friend

例：我们是瓷。

We are cronies.

瓷公鸡 cí gōng jī

比喻十分吝啬、小气，不出一分钱的人。(of sb.) china rooster; porcelain rooster/A metaphor referring to a mean person or miser.

例：我不指望他能给我钱，因为他是有名的瓷公鸡。

I don't expect that he will give me any money because he is a notorious miser.

瓷器 cí qi

指关系非常好、非常亲密的朋友。intimate friend; close friend; crony

例：他是我的瓷器。

He's my good friend.

次毛 cì máo

指（产品）质量差。(of product) poor in quality; inferior; bad

例：这台机器太次毛，那么容易坏。

The machine is really pool. It breaks down easily.

凑份子 còu fèn zi

1. 各人拿出部分钱合起来送礼或办事。club together (to

present a gift to sb. or do sth.); get together

例:同事们凑份子给我买了个结婚礼物。

My colleagues clubbed together to buy me a wedding present.

2.指添麻烦。to bother sb.

例:请别再凑份子了,你们没见我忙得不亦乐乎吗?

Don't bother me any more, please. Can't you see that I'm very busy now.

醋溜儿小生 cù liūr xiǎo shēng

指多愁善感、说话酸溜溜的青年男子。sentimental wimp; a young man easily moved by emotion

例:我需要的是能支撑我的男人,而不是醋溜儿小生。

I need a man to support me, not a sentimental wimp.

醋坛子 cù tán zi

指非常爱嫉妒的人（多指男女关系上）。vinegar jar/A metaphor for a jealous person.

例:我老婆是个醋坛子,她总是盯着我。

My wife is a jealous woman. She always keeps a close eye on me.

攒 cuán

1.编;写。compile; write

例:今天晚上我攒了一篇文章。

I wrote an article this evening.

2.杜撰;捏造。invent; make up; fabricate

例:别信他。他就喜欢攒故事。

Don't believe him. He likes to make up stories.

3.组装;拼凑。assemble; piece together

例:他自己攒了一辆自行车。

He assembled a bicycle himself.

攒瓣儿 cuán bànr

原指旧社会大伙儿一起动手收拾一个人,现用于折腾、折磨某人或某物。Originally it refers to a group of people who treat one harshly or ruthlessly, now used to refer one who tramples, tortures or toys with sb. or sth.

例:我女儿可喜欢她那个泰迪熊了,每次回到家都先要攒瓣儿它一通。

My daughter likes her Teddy bear very much. Every time she gets back home she plays with it the first thing.

蹿 cuàn

指(价格)突然上涨。(of price) rise quickly; hike up; go up suddenly

例:一个阑尾手术两年前花一千元,可今年年初却一下蹿到五千元。

An appendectomy costed 1,000 *yuan* two years ago, but the price was hiked up to 5,000 *yuan* early this year.

催本儿 cuī benr

受人指使干杂事,跑腿的人。errand-boy

例:我小时候是我姐姐的催本儿。

I used to be my sister's errand-boy when I was young.

村姑 cūn gū

指农村姑娘。a country girl; girl from the country

例:这是她头一回在影片中扮演村姑。

This is the first time for her to play the role of a girl from the country in a film.

寸 cùn

巧;刚好。coincidentally; just; exactly

例:你来得真寸,我正要走。

You've come just in time as I'm about to leave.

寸劲儿 cùn jìnr

1.凑巧的事。coincidence; accident

例:瞧这寸劲儿。只剩两张票了,正好你们一人一张。

What a coincidence! There are only two tickets left, making precisely one for each of you.

2.微妙的力量;巧妙的力量。just the right strength

例:你打乒乓球得学会掌握打球的寸劲儿。

You have to learn how to play ping-pong by hitting the ball with just the right strength.

搓板(儿) cuō bǎn(r)

比喻非常瘦的人。washboard/A metaphor for a skinny person or a girl with a flat chest.

例:别看她长得像搓板,可她的力气比你大。

She may look like a washboard, but she's stronger than you.

搓麻 cuō má

指打麻将牌。play mahjong

例:他正在家里搓麻。

He's playing mahjong at home.

搓火 cuō huǒ

使生气;使着急。get angry; worry; feel impatient

例:遇上这样的麻烦事谁能不搓火?

Who wouldn't worry in such a mess?

撮 cuō

吃。eat; have a meal

例：咱们找个地方撮一顿。

Let's eat out somewhere.

撮堆儿 cuō duīr

指剩下不太好的东西或人；便宜货。goods of lower quality; left over/A metaphor for people or things not chosen in the first lot.

例：她爱上街买撮堆儿的菜。

She likes to buy second quality vegetables in the market to save money.

婑 cuó

指人的个子矮。be short (of stature)

例：他这个人可不算婑。

He is not at all short.

婑子 cuó zi

指个子矮的人。a short person

例：那个婑子是他的父亲。

That short man is his father.

D

搭车 dā chē

1.顺便乘别人的车。give sb. a lift；get a lift；hitchhike

例：我能搭车跟你们一起进城吗？

Could you give me a lift downtown?

2.附带着做某事。do sth. at the same time；do sth. along with someone else

例：这本书我们要印四千本。他们想搭车为他们印一千本。

We'll print 4,000 copies of this book. They would like us to print 1,000 copies for them at the same time.

搭错线了 dā cuò xiàn le

指搞错了；弄错了。have one's wires crossed；make a mistake；misunderstand

例：很抱谦，我真不该给你预约。这事是我搭错线了。

I'm sorry. I shouldn't have made that appointment for you. I had my wires crossed.

搭档 dā dàng

1.协作。cooperate；collaborate

例：我将与他搭档创作一本小说。

I'll collaborate with him to write a novel.

2.协作人。partner；collaborator

例：他是我的老搭档。

He is my old partner.

打八刀 dǎ bā dāo

指离婚。divorce

例:老王上个月刚与老婆打八刀,这个月就要和他的新女友结婚了。

Lao Wang divorced his wife just last month. But this month he will marry his new girlfriend.

打镲 dǎ chǎ

起哄;开玩笑;耍弄。make fun of sb. ; make a fool of sb. ; jeer

例:我就知道看见我这身新衣服,你们准会拿我打镲。

I know you'd make fun of me when you saw my new clothes.

打车 dǎ chē

指乘坐出租汽车;叫出租汽车。hail cab; take a taxi; by taxi

例:由于下雨我就打车过来了。

I came here by taxi because of the rain.

打的 dǎ dí

乘出租汽车。take a taxi; travel by taxi

例:我要是你,我就打的去,不傻等公共汽车了。

If I were you, I would go by taxi instead of waiting for the bus.

打点 dǎ diǎn

1.准备。get one's belongings ready

例:你先把出国所需的东西打点一下,然后我再帮你装箱。

You'd better first get ready the things you'll need abroad, then I'll help you pack them up.

2.行贿;送礼。offer a bribe; present a gift

例:你若办事就得处处打点,否则你的事情准难办成。

If you want something done, you have to offer a bribe; oth-

D

erwise it cannot be done smoothly.

打工仔 dǎ gōng zǎi

指外出干活挣钱的男青年。male employee; male worker

例：他雇了一个新打工仔。

He hired a new male worker.

打工妹 dǎ gōng mèi

指外出干活挣钱的女青年。female employee; female worker

例：这里有不少外地来的打工妹。

There are lots of female workers from other parts of the country here.

打哈哈 dǎ hā ha

指开玩笑。poke fun at; joke about

例：我可没打哈哈，我是认真的。

I'm not joking. I'm serious.

打喷嚏 dǎ pēn tì

指对某事的回应。response; answer

例：你这个人动作也太慢了。我两星期前就把资料给你了，可你今天才打喷嚏，就不怕这笔买卖让别人抢了去。

Your reaction is too slow. I sent you the information two weeks ago, but you answered only today. Are you not afraid that the business will be taken away by someone else?

打水漂儿 dǎ shuǐ piāor

徒劳无获；无结果；(指钱财)一去不复返。play (make) ducks and drakes(with sth.); spend in vain; with no result; pay out, but get nothing in return

例：他的全部资金都打水漂儿了。

He played ducks and drakes with all his money on that business deal.

打小报告 dǎ xiǎo bào gào

指到领导面前告某人的状或说某人的坏话。write small reports/Refers to those who blow the whistle on or slander sb. to a leader.

例：她最善于打小报告。

She's very good at informing on others.

打眼 dǎ yǎn

1. 指惹人注目。attract attention; catch the eye

例：红颜色最打眼，离老远你就能看见。

Red can easily attract attention. You can see it from afar.

2. 指长相好；漂亮。beautiful; good looking

例：这个女孩在孩子们中最打眼。

This girl is the most stunning among the children.

打一枪换一个地方 dǎ yī qiāng huàn yī ge dì fang

指经常移动（位置、工作等）。go job-hopping; move regularly (from one place to another); change frequently (job, things)

例：年轻人总喜欢打一枪换一个地方，寻找更好的工作。

Young people are always moving around looking for a better job.

打游击 dǎ yóu jī

指没有固定的工作或住处。work (live, etc.) at no fixed place

例：他现在还在打游击。对他来说找一个很好的工作真是太难了。

He is not working at one particular place at the moment, so

it's very difficult for him to find a good job.

打住 dǎ zhù

停止；到此为止。stop; hold on; bring to a halt

例：到此打住！我们不要再讨论下去了。

Hold on! We can't discuss this any longer.

大放送 dà fàng sòng

指播出时间长的电视连续剧。a long running TV drama series or a lengthy drama

例：中央电视台影视频道在春节期间有三部国产电视剧大放送。

The Movie Channel of CCTV showed three homemade TV dramas over several hours during the Spring Festival.

大巴 dà bā

大型公共汽车。large bus; coach

例：昨天学校租了三辆大巴带学生去了一趟世界公园。

The school hired three large buses and took the students to the World Park yesterday.

大瓣儿蒜 dà bànr suàn

比喻装模作样的人。意同"大尾巴狼"。big clove of garlic/A metaphor for someone who behaves in an affected way or puts on an act.

例：你不了解他，他就是一个大瓣儿蒜，总爱用领导的口气跟人说话。

You don't know him. He is really a big clove of garlic, and always likes to talk in the tones of a boss.

大比拼 dà bǐ pīn

指对抗赛。dual meet; a meeting between two competing

D

最新中国俚语

New Slang of China

teams or two competitors

例：比赛现场热闹非凡，场内运动员激烈竞争，而场外各路记者也在进行大比拼，纷纷抢发赛事消息。

The scene of contest was extremely hot. The athletes competed fiercely. There was also a competition between journalists, trying to be the first to send the latest news of the results of the competition.

大鼻子 dà bí zi

指洋人；外国人。high-bridged nose; big nose/A metaphor for foreigners.

例：那儿过来了两个大鼻子。

There came along two foreigners.

大兵 dà bīng

讥指士兵；军人。G. I. (impolite term); soldier

例：我曾当过大兵和工人，但如今我开了一家私营公司。

Before, I was a G. I. and a worker, but now I have my own company.

大出血 dà chū xiě

形容降价出售商品。sell goods at a very low price; have a grand sale

例：她在那家商店年底大出血时买了一件大衣。

She bought an overcoat from that shop when it had its grand sale at the end of the year.

大喘气 dà chuǎn qì

指说话时故意先说前一半，停顿一会儿再说后一半来捉弄人。take a deep breath before finishing a sentence or phrase (on purpose); make fun of or tease

例:别大喘气,快点儿告诉我那里发生了什么事。

Don't take a deep breath. Please tell me immediately what happened there.

大大咧咧 dà da liē liē

形容随随便便,满不在乎。careless; casual

例:他太大大咧咧,总是忘带钥匙。

He is very careless. He often forgets to take the key with him.

大吊车 dà diào chē

指未婚的大龄男子,或光棍。big crane/A metaphor for a single man of around thirty; unmarried man; bachelor.

例:你都三十好几的人了,怎么还不急哪,真想当大吊车呀。

You're over thirty. How come you don't worry? Do you really want to be a big crane?

大跌眼镜 dà diē yǎn jìng

指非常吃惊和意外。very surprising, unexpected

例:我从没有想到这部由著名导演拍出来的电影会令人大跌眼镜。

I've never thought that film directed by famous directors could really show people something unexpected.

大发 dà fa

指超过了适当的限度;过度。excessive; over the top/Refers to one who overdoes sth. or exceeds a limit.

例:我今天亏大发了。

I suffered a great loss today.

大哥大 dà gē dà

1.无线电蜂窝移动电话。cellular phone

例：他随身带着大哥大以便随时与头儿联系。

He takes a cellular phone around with him so he can get in touch with his boss at any time.

2.大哥，多指某一团体或帮会内有威望的中青年男子。

older brother/Refers to the head of a gang or a person with the highest prestige in a group.

例：谭咏麟被誉为香港歌坛的大哥大。

Alan Tan is an older brother to many pop singers in Hong Kong.

大红大紫 dà hóng dà zǐ

指某人的名气很大或某人非常出名。(of a person) very famous; well-known; celebrated

例：她已是国内大红大紫的歌星了。

She has become one of the most famous singers in the country.

大伙儿 dà huǒr

指大家。everybody; you all; we all

例：大伙儿都不赞成你干这种事。

We all don't agree that you do this kind of things.

大件 dà jiàn

指二十世纪八十年代价钱比较贵的家庭消费品（电视、电冰箱、洗衣机、收录机等）。

expensive consumer goods (television, refrigerator, washing machine, tape recorder)in the 80s of the 20th century

例：除非他置齐那四大件——电视、冰箱、洗衣机、收录机，否则他的女友就不跟他结婚。

His girlfriend won't marry him until he's bought the four items.

大姐大 dà jiě dà

大姐，多指某一团体或帮会内有威望的中青年女子。

older sister/Refers to the head of a gang or a woman who has the highest prestige in a group.

例：在你们那片儿谁是大姐大？

Who is the older sister in your town?

大块头 dà kuài tóu

胖子；身材高大的人。a hefty person；a tall person；a tall and strong person

例：他的对手是个大块头。

His opponent is tall and hefty.

大款 dà kuǎn

1. 有钱的人。rich person；big wheel

例：我们这儿的人都是吃皇粮的，没有大款。

We are government officials, so there is no rich person here.

2. 指暴发户；新贵族（多含贬义）。parvenu；nouveau riche

例：他哥哥两年前还从广州倒腾服装呢，可如今成大款了，买了两辆汽车。

His brother used to deal in clothes from Guangzhou two years ago. Now he's part of the nouveau riche and owns two cars.

3. 指一笔钱；大数额款项。big sum of money

例：他愿出大款买我那张珍贵的邮票。

He would like to pay me a lot for that rare stamp.

大佬 dà lǎo

1. 大哥 eldest brother
2. 黑社会老大 gang leader

大礼拜 dà lǐ bài

指星期六、日两天休息的星期。"big weekend"（Saturday and Sunday）In 1994, the Chinese government passed the official 44-hour work week. This means that Chinese who work in companies that follow this guideline have alternating weekend — "big" and "small" weekends. "Big weekend" means people get Saturday and Sunday off. "Small weekend" means they must work on Saturday (a full day).

例：这个星期是大礼拜，所以星期六很多人会去香山。我不想去，人一定很多。

This week is the "big weekend", so a lot of people will go to the Fragrant Hills on Saturday. I don't want to go because there will be too many people.

大路菜 dà lù cài

指普通的常见的蔬菜。common vegetables

例：大白菜是北方人冬季爱吃的大路菜之一。

Cabbage is one of the common and popular vegetables in winter in the north of China.

大路货 dà lù huò

1. 指一般价格便宜的货物。goods at ordinary or low price; cheap goods

例：街角那个商店主要经销大路货。

The store at the corner of the street mainly sells cheap goods.

2. 指质量好，信得过，来路正的普通商品。popular goods of

fine quality

例：最好买大路货，不买水货。

It is better to buy popular goods of fine quality rather than smuggled ones.

大面儿 dà miànr

1. 指外表；外貌；表面。outlook；appearance；surface

例：这所学校大面儿还可以。

The outlook of the school is agreeable.

2. 指面子；脸面。face

例：在外人面前她从不顾及我的大面儿。

She never saves my face in front of others.

大拿 dà ná

1. 掌大权的人。person with power；head；boss

例：在我们家我老婆是大拿。

My wife wears the trousers at my home.

2. 在某方面有权威的人；能人。expert；able person

例：在服装设计上她可是大拿。

She is an expert in dress designing.

大排档 dà pái dàng

指由许多私人经营的餐馆组成的一大排饮食场所，通常以大众化食谱为主，价钱比较便宜，有露天和室内两种。stalls selling food normally in the street but can also be indoors, normally very cheap

例：昨天晚上我们在大排档吃了一顿饭。

We had dinner at the food stalls last night.

大片 dà piān

指电影制作投入成本很高，票房很高的影片。high investment, high cost and high box-office success films

例:今年又将有七部美国大片与国人见面。

This year there will be seven American high cost and high box-office success films shown in China.

大头朝下 dà tóu cháo xià

1. 指头朝下,反过来。head over heels; upside down

例:他被人大头朝下地扔出了窗外。

He was thrown out of the window head over heels.

2. 指体操倒立。handstand

例:让我们打赌,谁输谁就来个大头朝下。

Let's bet, the loser will have to do a handstand!

大团结 dà tuán jié

票面值为十元的人民币。a ten-*yuan* bill

例:我一个月只拿五十张大团结。

I only get fifty ten-*yuan* bills a month.

大腕儿 dà wànr

大人物;名人;权威。famous person; big shot; expert; celebrity

例:如今在中国多数大腕儿置了房、买了车而且开了自己的公司。

Now many celebrities in China have their own houses, cars and companies.

大尾巴狼 dà wěi ba láng

比喻装模作样的人。意同"大瓣蒜"。"big tailed wolf" similar with the meaning of the "big clove of garlic"/A metaphor for someone behaves in an affected way or puts on an act.

例:你初来乍到的,不知道我们这里有个大尾巴狼。时间长了,你就了解了。

You're a newcomer, and don't know that we have a "big tailed wolf" here. You'll get to know him well when you work here longer.

大仙 dà xiān

指算命、占卜的高手。a professional fortune teller, or sorcerer/sorceress

例:他冒充大仙,到处招摇撞骗。

He passed himself off as a sorcerer, and went about cheating people.

大修 dà xiū

原指对机器车辆进行全面检修,现比喻动手术。(lit.) overhaul/A metaphor for having an operation or a surgery.

例:我的病不严重,还没到大修的地步呐。

I'm not so seriously ill that an operation is needed.

大战 dà zhàn

1. 指激烈的竞争(商业产品)。fierce competition

例:今年空调大战已经开始。

A fierce competition over air conditioners has begun this year.

2. 指大规模的战斗。a large-scale fight; big clash

例:这是场决定性的大战。

It was a decisive big clash.

大周 dà zhōu

指星期六、日两天休息(参见"大礼拜")。"big weekend" (Saturday and Sunday)/(see the definition of the entry dà lǐ bài)

例:这个大周你想干点儿什么?

What will you plan to do in this weekend?

带把儿的 dài bàr de

指小男孩。boy

例:他高兴地看到他老婆给他生了个带把儿的。

He was happy to see that his wife had given birth to a baby boy.

带子 dài zi

指录像带;录像片。video tape; video film

例:我想借几盘好带子回家看。

I want to borrow some good videos to watch at home.

DIY dài

指自己动手动脑做事情。do it yourself

例:如今世面上出现了很多各种各样 DIY 方面的书,据说卖得还不错。

There have been quite a variety of books on DIY on the market recently. It's said that they are selling pretty well.

单车 dān chē

指自行车。bicycle; bike

例:她每天骑单车上班。

She goes to work by bicycle everyday.

单飞 dān fēi

1.指已婚的人独自出国留学或工作。solo flight/A married person who goes to work or study abroad alone without his or her spouse.

例:你近来怎样? 还在单飞吗?

How have you been doing? Are you still abroad without your spouse?

2.单帮。a traveling trader on his or her own; to travel around and do business by oneself

例:他厌倦了单飞的生活,如今在一家外企工作。

He got tired of the life of being a traveling trader on his own, so he now works in a foreign company.

单练 dān liàn

1.一对一的比试高低。fight one to one; have a contest

例:如果你不服,咱们再单练一次。

If you are not convinced, let's have another contest.

2.指独自从事某种活动或工作。do sth. alone; do sth. by oneself or single-handed

例:这里没人懂怎样修这台机器,所以恐怕这活儿我得单练了。

No one here knows how to repair the machine, so I'm afraid that I will have to do it alone.

单挑 dān tiǎo

指独自一人干(某事)。do sth. by oneself; work on one's own

例:由于他的伙伴病了,这一摊活儿都靠他单挑。

He does all the work by himself since his partner is ill.

单元儿 dān yuánr

指一元人民币。one-*yuan* note

例:你有单元儿吗,给我几张?

Do you have any one-*yuan* notes? Can you give me some?

担砖的 dān zhuān de

指没有权势、地位的普通人。brick carrier/A metaphor for

ordinary people with neither authority nor status.

例：他的眼睛只会向上看,哪里会理睬我们这些担砖的呢?

His eyes can only look up. How could he pay attention to us ordinary people?

蛋白质 dàn bái zhì

是笨蛋、白痴和神经质的简称,多用来指人(含贬义)。a fool, idiot or neurotic/ a derogatory term which mostly refers to people

例：听说你们班有一个蛋白质女孩,还是文学发烧友,经常在网上发表一些文章。

They say there's a girl in your class who's a real idiot. But she's also a literature fanatic, and often publishes articles on the Internet.

淡出 dàn chū

指悄悄离开或慢慢地消失。leave (a career) without notice; gradually disappear

例：自从她淡出歌坛以后,人们很少见过她。听说她移民去了加拿大。

People have seldom seen her since she left the circle of singers. It's said that she has immigrated to Canada.

弹子 dàn zǐ

指台球。billiards

例：弹子房。billiards room

挡横儿 dǎng hèngr

阻碍(或妨碍)行动;挡路。get in the way; block; hinder

例：别在这儿给我挡横儿。

Don't get in my way.

挡镜头 dǎng jìng tóu

1. 阻碍拍摄。to be in view of the camera

例：您挡镜头了，请往那边站一点儿，好吗？

Would you please stand over there for you are in view of the camera?

2. 指人爱出风头，爱炫耀自己。be in the limelight；show off

例：不管别人做什么她总喜欢挡镜头。

No matter what anyone else does, she always wants to be in the limelight.

党票 dǎng piào

指中国共产党党员证，意指党员。card carrying member of the Communist Party

例：他年年都在十分努力地工作，以求有一天能拿到党票。

He works very hard year after year, hoping to join the Party one day.

档次 dàng cì

水平；水准。level；standard

例1：你怎么能穿这种鞋呢？这鞋对你来说档次太低了。

How can you wear these shoes? They fall short of your standards.

例2：这顿晚餐档次够高的。

This is a high-class dinner.

捯 dáo

1. 用手交替地把线或绳子拉回或绕好。pull back thread or rope；wind thread

例：你能帮我把线捯一下吗？

Would you please wind the thread for me?

2. 追查；找出；查出。find out；trace

例：这个案子是根据线索一点一点地捯出来的。

The case was unfolded little by little according to the clues.

捯饬 dáo chi

修饰；打扮。dress up; make up; doll up

例：她每天早晨都要捯饬一番。

She gets all dolled up every morning.

倒 dǎo

转手；转进转出。make money through business transactions

例：最近那小子倒了不少香烟。

That guy has made a lot of money recently through selling cigarettes.

倒儿 dǎor

倒买倒卖从中获利的人。speculator; profiteer/Refers to individual retailers who buy things at a low price in one place and sell them for a profit elsewhere.

例：京城有不少外地来的倒儿。

Speculators from other parts of the country come to Beijing to make cash.

倒汇 dǎo huì

指倒买倒卖外汇，从中牟利。speculate in foreign currency; resell foreign currency at a profit

例：国家禁止非法倒汇。

Speculation in foreign currency is forbidden by law.

倒腾 dǎo teng

1. 翻腾；移动。turn sth. over and over; remove; move from here to there

例:她把所有的抽屉倒腾了个遍,也没找到那份合同。

She turned all her drawers inside out and couldn't find the contract.

2.买进卖出;贩卖。engage in buying and selling (goods or foreign currency) for profit

例:目前他正倒腾钢材。

He is engaged in buying and selling steel materials at present.

倒胃口 dǎo wèi kǒu

1.破坏食欲;恶心。ruin one's appetite; feel sick; feel like vomiting; make one nauseous

例:我在菜中看见一只苍蝇,真倒胃口。

Seeing a fly in the dish completely ruined my appetite.

2.比喻对某事厌烦,失去兴趣。have no interest in sb. or sth.; get tired of sb. or sth.

例:别再跟我谈那人,一提到他我就倒胃口。

Don't talk to me about that person. I'm tired of him.

倒儿爷 dǎor yé

倒买倒卖从中获利的人。speculator; profiteer

例:他决定辞职干倒儿爷去。

He decided to quit his job to become a speculator.

捣浆糊 dǎo jiàng hu

指不安分,瞎折腾的行为。act restlessly or recklessly; run wild

例:这孩子整天捣浆糊,不好好学习,谁也管不了他。

This boy acts restlessly all day long. He doesn't study hard. Nobody can control him.

导游虫 dǎo yóu chóng

非法从事导游的人。illegal tourist guide

例：如今旅游市场挺火，每逢节假日，出行的人都不少，而导游虫也多了起来。

Nowadays the tourism market is extremely busy. Whenever there are holidays many people travel and illegal tourist guides are becoming more and more common.

道 dào

量词，表示次数。classifier; measure word

例：他才学棋一年就想灭我一道。

He's just learned playing chess for one year and he wants to win me a game once.

倒插门 dào chā mén

指结婚后，男方住到女方家。bolt the door in a back to front way/A metaphor for a man who goes to live in his wife's parents' home after marriage.

例：小张家在外地，独自一人在北京工作。他希望能找个北京的女孩，倒插门也没关系。

Xiao Zhang is from another part of the country and works alone in Beijing. He hopes to have a Beijing girlfriend. He doesn't care if he goes to live with his girlfriend in her parents' home after marriage.

德行 dé xing

一种表示不喜欢或瞧不起他人的仪容、言行、举止、作风等时所用的话（含有骂人的语气）。(a curse of anger) disgusting; shameful; damn

例：真德行，那司机开车溅我一身水。

How disgusting! The driver splashed water on me with his car.

84

登 dēng

穿（鞋、裤等）。wear（shoes or trousers）

例：小男孩从床上爬起来，登上鞋就跑出了房间。

The boy got up，clad in his shoes and ran out of the room.

低能儿 dī néng ér

1. 指智力和能力都很差的人。retarded child/A term often used to indicate someone who is unclever and incapable or even idiotic.

例：他连自己的衣服都不会洗，真可算是一个低能儿了。

He is really like retarded child! He doesn't even know how to wash his clothes!

2. 指成绩好，能力低的人。incapable people/A term often used to describe someone who gets high marks in school, but is incapable in life.

例：家长应防止孩子成为低能儿。

Parents should prevent their children from becoming incapable people.

的 dí

出租汽车。taxi；cab

例：别傻站在这儿看着我，你还不快到马路上叫辆的去呀！

Don't stand here like an idiot looking at me. Quickly go out and call a taxi.

的哥 dí gē

称男性出租汽车司机。taxi driver；cabman/An affectionate form of address to taxi driver.

例：他的朋友大多是的哥。

Most his friends are taxi drivers.

最新中国俚语

New Slang of China

D

的姐 dí jiě

称女性出租汽车司机。female taxi driver

例：夜晚运客不安全，所以许多的姐晚上都不出车。

It's dangerous to carry passengers late at night, so many female taxi drivers don't work at night.

的票 dí piào

即出租汽车司机给乘客开的收费票据。taxi receipt

例：你最好明天一早打的去机场，别忘了跟的哥要张的票，回来我给你报销。

You'd better take a taxi to the airport early tomorrow. Don't forget to ask for a receipt from the taxi driver so that I can submit an expense account for you.

的士 dí shì

指出租汽车。taxi

例：你带着这么多东西，我想我还是给你叫辆的士送你回家。

I think I'd better hail a taxi for you to go home since you've got so many things with you.

的爷 dí yé

称男性出租汽车司机。male taxi driver

例：那家饭馆因为饭菜实惠价低，每天都有不少的爷前去那儿吃饭。

Because of the good food and low prices many male taxi drivers go there for meals every day.

底儿潮 dǐr cháo

指有犯罪前科。have a criminal record

例：只要他对我好，我不在乎他是否底儿潮。

I don't care whether he has a criminal record as long as he

treats me well.

底儿掉 dǐr diào

1.彻底揭露，一点儿不留。turn over；reveal

例：他把他所知的有关帮会的情况向警察来了个底儿掉。

He turned over all he knew about the gang to the police.

2.失去信心；勇气。lose one's confidence or courage

例：如果你的底儿先掉了，那没人能救你了。

No one can help you if you lose your courage first.

地撮儿 dì cuōr

指清扫垃圾的人；环卫工人。street cleaner；scavenger；sanitation worker；rubbish scooper

例：他干了三十年的地撮儿。

He has worked as a rubbish scooper for thirty years.

颠(儿) diān(r)

离开；走开；跑。go away；leave；run

例1：我们遇到困难时，他颠(儿)得比谁都快。

When we meet with difficulties，he runs faster than anyone.

例2：让他们在那儿等吧，我先颠(儿)了。

Let them wait there. I'll leave first.

颠菜 diān cài

离开；走人。leave；go

例：他早就颠菜了。

He left quite a long time.

掂量 diān liang

1.用手托着东西上下晃动来估量轻重。weigh by hand

例：你来掂量一下这本书的分量。

Guess how much this book weighs.

2.考虑;思量。think over; consider

例:这事只能你自己掂量着办。

You have to consider how to deal with this matter yourself.

点卯 diǎn mǎo

原指旧时官厅在卯时（上午五点到七点）查点到班人员,现指到单位报到或露一面后就走。roll call in the morning(in *yamen* originally); check in; make an appearance; show one's face

例:他喜欢先去单位点卯,然后再走开去办自己的事。

He likes first to make an appearance at his office, and then goes off to do his own business.

点水 diǎn shuǐ

告密。inform against

例:这件事背后肯定有人点水,不然他们怎么行动得那么快。

There must be someone who informed against us on this case, otherwise they couldn't have acted so quickly.

点涕 diǎn tì

指小费。tip

例:他做导游有好几年了,最喜欢带的就是老外的团,因为点涕多。

He has been working as a tourist guide for years. He likes to guide foreign tourists because they give more tips.

点子 diǎn zi

本身是不法分子,但负有责任向公安部门提供情况的人。

squealer/A term refers to one who is a criminal himself, but has responsibilities to supply information for the public security organs.

例：警察从点子那儿获悉了这个情报。

The police got this information from a squealer.

点儿背 diǎnr bèi

指运气不好。这里的点是指骰子（俗称色子）上的点,点数的多少代表运气的好坏。bad luck—The word "*dian*" here refers to the dots on dice. Good luck and bad luck are represented by different numbers of dots.

例：这个月我点儿背,刚买的新车就被撞了三次。

I'm having bad luck this month. The new car I just bought has had three fender-benders already.

垫背的 diàn bèi de

代别人受过的人；替死鬼。scapegoat；fall guy

例：即使他死了,他也要拉个垫背的。

He will take a scapegoat with him even if he is going to die.

垫底儿 diàn dǐr

1. 形容最差的；最低的。be the poorest (lowest; bottommost)；be the worst one

例：我知道你们的数学都比我强。我担心我将是垫底儿的。

I know you are all better than me in mathematics. I'm afraid that I'm the worst.

2. 做基础；承担；支撑。base；take responsibility；support

例：有他垫底儿,你还担心什么!

You needn't worry, he will take responsibility.

电灯泡 diàn dēng pào

形容充当他人的陪衬,通常是一对情人中一方的陪衬,为一方遮挡羞涩达到相互见面交流的目的。electric bulb / a vivid expression for someone who accompanies another to see his or her beloved, or who serves as a pretext or foil for a courting pair;a third wheel

例:你们俩还是自己去吧！我可不想当你们的电灯泡。

You two go by yourselves. I don't want to be the third wheel.

电老虎 diàn lǎo hǔ

指供电部门内的贪污腐化分子。power (electricity) tiger/A metaphor for embezzlers from power (electricity) supply units.

例:我们这里的电老虎可厉害,不给他们一点好处,就给你拉闸。

The power tigers in our area very fearsome. They will cut your electricity off if you don't bribe them.

电脑虫 diàn nǎo chóng

从事电脑软件盗版的人。computer worm/A metaphor for software pirate.

例:电脑虫的确让电脑软件开发商们大伤脑筋,最后开发商们不得不用大量低价格的正版软件来打击这些电脑虫。

The software pirates really created a difficult problem for software developers so that they had to hit them with original copies at very cheap prices.

店嫂 diàn sǎo

指已婚的商店女售货员。married saleswoman

例:这家连锁店要招店嫂的消息刚刚传出,便有 300 多名下岗女工前来应聘。

As soon as the news of this chain store hiring married saleswomen spread, over 300 laid off women rushed here to apply for the job.

掉价 diào jià

降低身份，有失体面。lower oneself (socially)

例：他不认为去餐馆洗盘子就使他掉价。

He doesn't think it is beneath him to wash dishes at a restaurant.

掉链子 diào liàn zi

指出问题；犯毛病。break down; have problems; go wrong; make mistakes

例：他平时的学习成绩可好了，但是一到考试他就掉链子。这大概是心理素质不好造成的。

Usually he has good marks, but he always goes wrong in examinations. Perhaps this is caused by a flaw in his psychological make-up.

掉茅坑里了 diào máo kēng lǐ le

形容在厕所里呆的时间太长。to fall into the latrine pit; describing someone who has stayed in the restroom for a long time

例：妮娜还占着卫生间，我怀疑她是否掉茅坑里了。

Nina is still in the restroom. I wonder if she's fallen in.

掉钱眼儿里 diào qián yǎnr lǐ

精于算计。fall into the hole of a coin/A metaphor for someone who is very good with money.

例：现在的人们都掉钱眼儿里了，一说多干点儿活就跟你开口要钱。

At present people are all good at calculating their own worth. As soon as they are told to work more they will ask you for money.

吊死鬼 diào sǐ guǐ

1. 指一种能拉丝从树上悬下于半空中的虫子。hanging looper；caterpillar

例：夏天这种槐树上尽是吊死鬼。

There are many loopers hanging down on the branches of Chinese scholartrees in summer.

2. 指上吊而死的人。one who hangs oneself；hanging devil

例：他上吊自尽了，所以这世上又多了一个吊死鬼。

He committed suicide by hanging. So there is one more hanging devil to the world.

调胃口 diào wèi kǒu

勾起某人的食欲，比喻使用各种方法、手段让人感兴趣。whet one's appetite

例：别光耍嘴皮子来调我们的胃口。

Don't attract us with empty promises.

跌份 diē fèn

丢面子；失尊严。embarrass yourself；cause yourself embarrassment

例：别穿这件破衣服去赴宴，给我跌份。

Don't embarrass me by wearing this shabby clothes to a dinner party.

钉子户 dīng zi hù

拆迁时拒不迁走的住户。a "nailed down" household/A metaphor for those who refuse to move when their house is about to be torn down by the government for a new construction project.

例：这条路下星期就要开工了，可还有两个钉子户不肯搬家。

The construction of the new highway will start next week,

but two "nailed down" households refuse to move out of here.

顶得住 dǐng dé zhù

能够坚持；支撑；抵住。bear；endure；stand up to

例 1：这点儿痛我还顶得住。

I can bear such pain.

例 2：任何困难他们都能顶得住。

They can stand up to any difficulties.

丢份 diū fèn

丢面子。lose face；embarrass oneself；disgraceful

例 1：他不会使刀叉，所以不敢去吃西餐，生怕丢份。

He doesn't know how to use a knife and fork, so he never tries Western food out of fear of embarrassing himself in front of others.

例 2：真丢份！

How disgraceful!

东东 dōng dōng

东西。thing

例：妈妈，今天给我买了什么好东东啊。哇，是我想吃的薯片耶。

Mum, what did you buy for me today? Oh, my favorite potato chips!

懂眼 dǒng yǎn

指懂行；内行。know the business；know the ropes；be an expert；know the ins and outs of

例：我的电脑坏了。你能不能帮我找个懂眼的人来看看哪里出了毛病。

My computer is broken. Can't you find me an expert to see

what's wrong with it?

兜圈子 dōu quān zi

指绕弯,多形容某人说话拐弯抹角,不直接了当。beat about the bush

例:他是个痛快人,说话从不兜圈子。

He is a straightforward chap who never beats about the bush.

抖骚 dǒu sāo

指卖弄风骚,四处招摇。play the coquette; show off

例:大冷天的,别在外面穷抖骚了,快点儿回家休息吧。

Don't show off outside any more in such a cold day. Come back home and have a rest quickly.

斗 dòu

商量;讨论。discuss; talk over; consult

例:今天我让你们来是想把这个问题斗一斗,看如何更好地解决它。

Today I called you here to discuss this matter and see how we can solve it in a better way.

斗富 dòu fù

有钱的人互相比赛花钱以炫耀财富。show off one's wealth by trying to spend more money than someone else/A term usually used to describe the competition between business-men, nouveau riche, etc, in trying to spend more at restau-rants, karaoke bars, etc.

例:我最看不惯那些在歌舞厅斗富的人。

I don't like to see people showing off their wealth by trying to spend more money than everyone else in the karaoke bar.

豆腐块 dòu fu kuài

指报刊上发表的版面很小的文章。beancurd cube/A tiny article published in a periodical or newspaper.

例：她很高兴看到自己写的豆腐块发表在一家报纸上。

She is happy to see her small piece in a newspaper.

逗 dòu

1. 荒唐；可笑。absurd；ridiculous

例：这事的确够逗的，这么一条假消息竟能登在报纸上。

This is really ridiculous! How could this bogus news appear in the newspaper?

2. 引人发笑；有趣。funny；amusing

例：这影片真逗。

What an amusing film!

逗咳嗽 dòu ké sou

斗气；找碴儿。be at each other's throats；quarrel with someone on account of a personal grudge；pick a fight；find fault

例：她闲得无事就跟丈夫逗咳嗽。

Whenever she has nothing to do, she picks a fight with her husband.

逗闷子 dòu mèn zi

指开玩笑。make fun of；tease in a playful way；joke with

例：我现在很忙，没有工夫跟你逗闷子。

I'm too busy to joke with you.

独食 dú shí

指得到的东西自己单独吃，不让他人分享。比喻自私，专横。

selfish；domineering/A term used to describe someone who

gets something and does not share it with others.

例：我女儿不独食。她喜欢与其他小朋友一起分享她的好吃的。

My daughter is not selfish. She enjoys sharing her goodies with other kids.

短拖 duǎn tuō

讥指身材矮小的人。short person (scornful)

例：在今天的社会中，择偶标准已经不再局限在身材的高矮上。只要你有金钱或权势或有一个聪明的头脑，即便你是个短拖也照样能赢得漂亮女孩的喜欢。

In today's society choosing a spouse is no longer limited by the height of a person. Even if you are short you can win the love of a beautiful girl as long as you have money, power or a smart head.

断档 duàn dàng

1. 指（人员）中间出现空缺，使前后无法衔接上。(of people) break off in the middle; miss a link

例：由于"文革"的影响，我们研究所已经出现了研究员严重断档的现象。研究员不是老的老，就是小的小，中年的廖廖无几，整个缺了一代人。

As a result of the "cultural revolution" there has been a severe shortage of researchers in our research institutions. All our researchers are either too old or too young. We have simply lost a generation of middle-aged researchers.

2. 指脱销。(of goods) to be out of supply or stock

例：这本书快卖完了，赶紧再版，千万别让它断档。

This book is going to be sold out. We'd better reprint it again. Don't let stocks run out.

断码 duàn mǎ

指货物的品种不全，号码尺寸短缺。no all sizes of goods are available; a shortage of some sizes

例：这个店里所有断码的鞋都半价处理。

All the shoes which don't have a full range of sizes in this shop are sold at half price.

断尾 duàn wěi

以某一规定的时刻排在最后队尾的人作为结束的标志。

tail end; end up with the last person who stands at the tail of a scheduled queue

例：到时我会派人去断尾。

I'll send a person to end the line on time.

对表 duì biǎo

指设计上相同，但大小不同的男女配套手表，也称为情侣表。

a pair of watches for a couple

例：小韩这个周末结婚。咱们选一款对表送他做新婚纪念吧。

Xiao Han will get married this weekend. Let's choose a pair of watches for them as a wedding present.

对路子 duì lù zi

适当；恰当；合适。be in line with; be correct

例：你提的建议与我们想的不对路子。

The proposal you put forward is not in line with what we have in mind.

对衫 duì shān

指设计上男女配套的衬衫。a set of shirts designed for a couple wear; matching shirts

例：今年夏天青年人都流行穿对衫。

It's fashionable for young people to wear matching shirts this summer.

吨 dūn

指一千元人民币。thousand-*yuan* bill

例：今天他挣了七吨。

He made seven thousand-*yuan* bills today.

蹲点 dūn diǎn

1. 上厕所大便。defecate; have a bowel movement; shit

例：他每天早上这个时候都要去蹲点。

Every morning he has a bowel movement at this time.

2. 警察埋伏在一处等候抓坏人。at a selected waiting spot for catching criminals

例：这几天总有警察在这周围蹲点，说是要抓一个逃犯。

Policemen have waited here for several days for arresting an escaped criminal.

蹲坑 dūn kēng

埋伏在某处，等待坏人出现或进行侦察。stake out; station (police, detectives, etc.) for surveillance of a suspected criminal, a place, etc.

例：他被派到罪犯家附近蹲坑，监视罪犯的活动。

He was sent to stake out the house and keep an eye on the criminal's activities.

E

恶心 ě xīn

使某人难堪。put someone in an awkward situation; make sb. embarrassed; make someone uncomfortable

例:你干吗非要将此事闹大？是不是要恶心恶心他？

Why do you insist on making this known to the public? You want to make him embarrassed, don't you?

耳朵根子软 ěr duo gēn zi ruǎn

指容易听信别人的话而改变自己的主意。soft ear/A person who is easily swayed by other's words.

例:他耳朵根子软,所以时常改变主意。

He's vulnerable to talk, so he often changes his mind.

二百五 èr bǎi wǔ

1.讥称有些傻气,做事莽撞的人。idiot; rash person

例:他是个二百五。如果冒犯了你,别往心里去。

He is a rash young man. Don't be upset if he wrongs you.

2.对某事一知半解的人。smatterer

例:论法语他只不过是二百五,但他却装出一副知之甚多的样子。

He only has a smattering of French, but he pretends to know a lot.

二道贩子 èr dào fàn zi

指做转手生意从中获利的人。resale monger; middle-man profiteer/A term to indicate someone who buys goods and then resells them at higher prices.

例：菜农实际挣不到多少钱，大部分钱让二道贩子挣了。

Vegetable farmers don't make a lot of money. Actually middlemen take most of the money away from farmers.

二等公民 èr děng gōng mín

指移民；非在他国出生的公民。second-class citizen/A term that refers to migrants or citizens not born in the country.

例：他从美国回来了，因为他不愿在那儿做二等公民。

He came back from the United States because he doesn't like to be a second-class citizen there.

二锅头 èr guō tóu

原为一种白酒，借指第二次结婚的人。Originally it is a strong liquor which is distilled twice / A term for a person (usually a woman) who gets married for the second time; divorcee

例：我才知道她是二锅头。

I've just learned that she has got married for the second time.

二乎 èr hu

1.害怕；退缩。withdraw；retreat (because one is scared)

例：他遇到困难从不二乎。

He never retreats when he is in trouble.

2.犹豫不决，拿不定主意；疑惑不定。hesitate

例：别再二乎了，否则东西就卖光了。

Don't hesitate any more or it will be sold out.

3.希望不大。have little hope；be hopeless

例：我看这件事二乎了。

I think it's hopeless.

二婚 èr hūn

指第二次结婚。remarriage

例：那男孩是她二婚后生的孩子。

That boy was born after her remarriage.

二进宫 èr jìn gōng

指第二次违法被公安部门收押。take into custody for the
second time; put in prison for the second time

例：在释放三个月后他因抢劫二进宫了。

Three months after he was set free, he was jailed again for
robbery.

二奶 èr nǎi

指小老婆。通常指与已婚男子在异地另成非法夫妻的女子。
mistress; illegal spouse

例：她成了老板的二奶，因为她一点儿也不知道老板另有妻
子和儿女之事。

She became her boss' mistress because she didn't know anything about his wife and children.

二十一遥 èr shí yī yáo

指二十一英寸，直角平面，带遥控的彩色电视机。21-inch remote control color television

例：她把二十一遥卖了，又买了一台更大的彩电。

She sold her 21-inch remote control color television and
bought a bigger one.

二手货 èr shǒu huò

1.指别人用过以后转卖的货物。second-hand; used; worn

例：这个相机是个二手货。

This is a second-hand camera.

2.指已失去贞节的女性（含贬义）。girl who has lost her virgini-
ty; divorced woman; defiled woman; sullied woman (derogatory)

例:我对二手货没有兴趣。

I have no interest in divorced women.

二叔 èr shū

指专占别人便宜的人。second uncle/A term that refers to someone who likes to take advantage of others.

例:我们厂里没有人愿意跟他来往,都知道他是出了名的二叔。

Nobody in our factory wants to deal with him because we all know that he likes to take advantage of others.

二五眼 èr wǔ yǎn

1.(人)能力差;(物品)质量差。of inferior ability or quality

例:买衣服我可是个二五眼。

I'm no good at buying clothes.

2.能力差的人,对事物的判断力差或眼力差的人。an incompetent person; someone with a poor sense of judgment

例1:你要买车可别找他。他是有名的二五眼,找他帮忙准砸。

Don't ask him about buying cars. He's famous for his poor judgment. You're doomed to fail if you ask him for help.

例2:你找谁帮忙都行,就是不能找他,他是个二五眼。

You can ask anyone for help but him, as he is totally incompetent.

F

发 fā

1. 发财；发家。make a fortune; get rich; build up a family fortune

例：他玩股票可发了。

He made a fortune by speculating in stocks.

2. 发配，指把某人转介绍给别人。introduce; recommend someone to others; pass someone onto someone else

例：当他玩腻了一个女人时，他就把她发给他的朋友。

When he gets tired of a girl, he passes her onto his friend.

发憷 fā chù

胆怯；畏惧；害怕。feel timid; fear; shrink

例：她见到陌生人就发憷。

She feels shy of strangers.

发福 fā fú

指人长胖（委婉表达方式）。put on weight; get fat; plump (a euphemism)

例：自从一年前见过你以后，你又发福了。

You've swelled out again since I saw you a year ago.

发愣 fā lèng

指发呆。stare blankly; be in a daze

例：他望着天花板发愣。

He is staring blankly at the ceiling.

发毛 fā máo

1. 害怕；惊慌。be afraid of; be terrified; be scared

例:夜里的尖叫声让我听了直发毛。

I was terrified when I heard the shriek at night.

2.发脾气。lose one's temper

例:他即使是遇到最恼火的事也从不发毛。

He never loses his temper even when faced with the most ir-ritating problem.

发蒙 fā mēng

糊涂;弄不清楚。be confused; be at a loss; get into a muddle

例:当他问我这个问题时,我还真有些发蒙。

I got into a muddle when he asked me the question.

发难 fā nàn

指用言词对某人进行批评或攻击。attack (in speech or writ-ing); assail (with words); lash out at sb.

例:当头儿的也确实不容易,经济效益搞不好,群众就会向你发难。

It's not very easy to be the boss of a company as for people will attack you if you don't keep up a good economic per-formance.

发烧友 fā shāo yǒu

1. 指现代音乐设备酷爱者。video fever/Someone who is crazy about stereo equipment and music, particularly those intent on buying the latest hi-tech equipment.

例:京城有一家发烧友俱乐部。

There is a video fever club in Beijing.

2. 泛指非常热衷于某物的人。fanatic

例:我父亲可以称得上是个京剧发烧友。他不仅爱看,而且爱唱。

My father can be called as a Peking Opera fanatic. He not

only enjoys watching but also singing.

发烧音响 fā shāo yīn xiǎng

指最先进的音乐设备。the latest, most hi-tech sound system

例:他很了解发烧音乐的市场行情。

He knows a lot about the prices of the latest and most hi-tech sound systems.

翻白眼 fān bái yǎn

1. 表示不满、愤恨、无可奈何时的表情。show the whites of one's eyes/Refers to one's dissatisfaction, hatred or helplessness.

例:跟我翻白眼也白搭,我不会放你走。

It's useless to look helpless. I won't let you go.

2. 指人快要死亡或处于十分危险的境地。show the whites of one's eyes/Refers to one who is dying or is at a very dangerous situation.

例:我看他翻白眼就马上送他上医院了。

I sent him to the hospital immediately when I saw the display in the whites of his eyes.

翻眼猴 fān yǎn hóu

指不领情,不知感谢别人帮助的人;忘恩负义的人。意同"白眼狼"。ingrate; treacherous and ruthless person

例:我要是早知道他是这么一个翻眼猴,才不会把钱借给他呢。

If I had known earlier that he was such an ingrate, I wouldn't have lent him any money at all.

反炒 fǎn chǎo

指不做正面宣传,利用批评的形式引起人们的注意,逗起人们的兴趣。quick-fry something in a backward way/Drawing public attention with negative spiel in the mass media.

例：这本小说是因为反炒才一跃成为畅销书的。

This novel jumped to be a best seller because it was plugged dammingly.

反动 fǎn dòng

指坏；不该这样做。bad/A term used mostly in a joking manner to criticize someone for doing something wrong.

例：你这家伙真够反动的，昨天说得好好的，但今天就变卦了。

You're really bad. Yesterday you agreed，but today you've changed your mind.

犯不着 fàn bu zháo

指没有必要；不值得；多余。unnecessary；not worthwhile

例：算了，我们自己修这辆自行车。为这点儿小毛病犯不着跟他生气。

Well，let's repair the bicycle by ourselves. It's pointless to get angry with him for such a small problem.

犯各 fàn gě

1. 出花样；搞别的；干新鲜事。act differently；do things in a strange or unusual manner

例1：你按着我的要求在这儿站直了，别犯各。

Stand still here as I ordered. Don't do anything else.

例2：他总在我面前犯各，不听我的命令。

He always acts differently in front of me and doesn't listen to what I say.

2. 跟某人过不去；找麻烦。make trouble for sb.；mess with

例：你要再跟我犯各，我就揍你。

I'll knock you down if you mess with me anymore.

犯傻 fàn shǎ

1. 干蠢事；干不明智的事。be foolish；do an unclever or unwise thing

例：他发觉他又犯傻了，把所知的情况都告诉他的朋友了。

He realized he did a foolish thing again by telling his friend everything he knew.

2. 发呆；发木。stare blankly；be in a daze；be in a trance

例：你在那儿犯什么傻呢？

What are you doing there staring blankly?

饭点儿 fàn diǎnr

指吃饭的时间。meal time；time to have meals

例：今天咱们好好讨论一下这个问题，别着急走。中午到了饭点儿，咱们一起去食堂。

We will discuss this matter thoroughly so don't worry about leaving. At lunch time we will go to the dining hall together.

饭局 fàn jú

指宴请；应酬。dinner party；fete

例：今晚我有饭局，回来要晚一些。

I have been invited to a dinner this evening，so I will come back a bit late.

饭碗 fàn wǎn

比喻工作；职业。rice bowl/A metaphor for secure job guaranteeing social welfare benefits.

例：她砸了自己的饭碗，干起了个体经商买卖。

She gave up her job as a govement employee and started

her own business.

范儿 fànr

1. 款式;样式。style; design; pattern; form

例:今年新潮范儿的高宽跟鞋开始风行起来。

The new style of high- and broad-heeled shoes has come into fashion this year.

2. 标准;风度。distinguished graceful manner; standard

例:我就爱看他跳舞,那范儿无人能比。

I enjoy watching him dance. No one has a more distinguished manner than he.

方 fāng

指一万元人民币。ten thousand *yuan*

例:光买一套沙发他就花了一方。

He spent ten thousand *yuan* all for one set of sofa.

方便 fāng biàn

指大小便(委婉说法)。(polite expression for) go to the bath room; go to the bathroom to tidy up

例:我想先方便一下,然后再跟你出去。

I want to tidy up before going out.

房倒儿 fáng dǎor

通过帮助他人换房或买卖房屋从中牟利的人。real estate speculator/A person who profits by helping people sell their houses.

例:那小子是个房倒儿,这几年倒了不少房,发了。

That fellow is a real estate speculator. He's bought and sold many houses and made a pile of money in recent years.

放电 fàng diàn

指两性间情感迸发四射。(electric) discharge/A metaphor for expressing passion between the sexes.

例:高雨的眼睛会放电,难怪见过他的女孩子都会被他迷住。

Gao Yu's eyes can express strong passion. No wonder all the girls who have ever met him tend to be attracted by him.

放份儿 fàng fènr

显示自己的威风,气派。to demonstrate one's courage and power; display one's arrogance or superiority

例:你算老几,竟敢在这儿放份儿。

What do you think you are doing showing off your power like this here?

放鸽子 fàng gē zi

失约;耍某人。to break an appointment; to stand someone up

例:昨天他竟然放我鸽子,害得我大冷天在车站等了他一个小时。

How dare he stand me up yesterday! He made me wait for an hour in the cold, and he never showed up.

放话 fàng huà

散风;造舆论。spread news or rumors; create public opinion

例:他在工人中放话说工厂不久就要倒闭。

He spread rumors among the workers that the factory would go bankrupt soon.

放空 fàng kōng

1.指无乘客空车行驶。an automobile with no passengers in it, usually it refers to a taxi

例：出租汽车司机都怕回来放空。那个地区人少，所以没人愿意拉人去那儿。

All taxi drivers are afraid of driving back without passengers. Since there are few people living there, no taxi driver likes to take customers there.

2. 放风筝。fly a kite

例：今天天好，广场上放空的人特别多。各种各样的风筝在空中飞舞，好看极了！

It's a nice day today. There are lots of people flying kites on the square. Various kinds of kites are dancing in the air. What a magnificent view!

3. 比喻某物或人处于闲置或不落实、不发挥作用的状态。leave unused; lie idle; set aside

例：这台高级相机在你手上算是被放空了。如果在我手里，怎么也能出它几张获奖作品了。

What a pity! This advanced camera lay idle in your hands. If I had had it, I would have taken some rewarding pictures anyway.

放平 fàng píng

1. 把东西平放在地上。put sth. flat on the ground

例：小心点儿，把行李箱放平。

Be careful. Put the suitcase flat on the ground.

2. 把人打趴在地上。knock sb. down

例：如果下一次你再来给我找麻烦，我就把你放平了。

I'll knock you down next time if you come here and give me trouble again.

放血 fàng xiě

指把人扎伤，使之流血。stab someone with a knife; make someone bleed

例：强盗威胁那女孩，叫她打开保险柜，否则就给她放血。

The robber told the girl to open the safe or he would stab her.

放一码 fàng yī mǎ

饶恕一次；宽容；放手。let a person（usually a criminal）off；
have mercy on；forgive；release

例：小偷求年轻的警察放他一码，并且把全部赃物交给警察。

The thief returned all the stolen goods and begged the young policeman to let him off.

飞着 fēi zhe

指（事情）没有落实，没有处理。float in the air；unsolved；
not decided

例：三个月了，这个问题还飞着呢！

This problem still has not been solved for three months.

匪 fěi

指流里流气，蛮横无礼的样子。rough；loutish；hooliganish；
thuggish

例：那小子虽说蹲了三年的大狱，可看上去还是那么匪。

That fellow，although re-educated in jail for three years，
still has a hooliganish look.

废 fèi

1. 打残废；打伤。cause bodily injury to；injure；maim

例：一群愤怒的人们把小偷给废了。

A group of angry people maimed the thief.

2. 残废；折断；截肢。break；amputate

例：他的命保住了，但那条腿还是废了。

His life was saved，but he had to have his leg amputated.

费 fèi

指费话,多用于斥责人胡说。talk nonsense

例:你别再费了,快回去干活儿。

Stop talking nonsense and quickly get back to work.

粉丝 fěn sī

狂慕者(指影迷、歌迷、球迷等)。fans (of movie, pop music, ball games, etc.)

例:随着"超女"比赛的白热化,无数粉丝变得越来越疯狂。

As the "Super Girl" contest became white-hot, numerous fans became more and more excited.

粉子 fěn zi

指漂亮的女子。beautiful woman; pretty girl

例:人们都说这个城市出粉子,大街上随便碰上一个女孩都特粉。

People all say that this city is rich in pretty girls. Any girl you come across in streets is very beautiful.

份儿 fènr

1. 棒;有本事。good; fine; excellent; capable; skilful; cool; awesome

例:瞧这辆新车,真够份儿的。

Look at this brand-new car. It's really awesome.

2. 地位;座次;位置。place; seat; part

例:我们刚吃完蛋糕。你来得太晚了,没你的份儿了。

We have just finished the cake. You're too late for it. There is nothing left for you.

3. 空余的地方;缝隙。room; gap; space

例:把桌子放在墙边,但注意留点儿份儿。

Put the table beside the wall, but be sure to leave a gap.

112

4.地步;程度。to the extent of; at the utmost

例:他累得都到站不起来的份儿了。

He was exhausted to the extent that he could not stand up.

风光 fēng guāng

指铺张;有名望;有地位。have fame; have status; enjoy a luxury life

例:荣获拳击冠军之后,他的确风光了一阵子。

After he won the boxing championship, he really became a man of the hour for a period.

封杀 fēng shā

1.指为了惩罚某人而不给其机会。prohibit sb. from doing sth. or provide sb. no chance as a punishment

例:约翰逊因服用兴奋剂而被封杀两年不得参加任何世界比赛。

Mr. Johnson was given no chance of attending any world competition for two years because he had taken dope.

2.禁止。ban; stop sth. from

例:她最新拍的一部电影尚未上映便因有太多裸戏而遭封杀。

One film she recently acted in has been banned for show because it includes too many nude scenes.

佛爷 fó ye

指小偷儿。pilferer; thief

例:他看上去特别单纯无邪,但谁会相信他竟是个佛爷。

He looks so innocent no one can believe he's a thief.

福分 fú fen

指福气;好运气。good fortune; happy lot

例:有这么一位好老婆是你的福分。

It's your stroke of luck to have such a good wife.

F 最新中国俚语 New Slang of China

服软 fú ruǎn

认输；承认错误；退让一步。admit defeat；ask pardon；knuckle under；compromise

例：即便被人打得很惨，他也从不服软。

He never asks throws in the sponge even if he is badly beaten.

富姐 fù jiě

很有钱的女人。a rich woman

例：如今在独身主义者中有相当一部分人是富姐，自己有房子有车，还有一份高薪的工作。

Nowadays, there are quite a few rich women among the bachelors. They have their own apartments, cars, and a highly paid job.

富婆 fù pó

指十分富有的已婚女子。rich or wealthy married woman

例：她是国内影视圈中有名的富婆，也由此引来了不少官司。

She is well known as a wealthy married woman in film and TV circles of China. However her high income and investments have resulted in many lawsuits.

富态 fù tai

（委婉地指人）身体胖。plump；stout；fat/A polite way to address someone who is overweight.

例：你越来越富态了。

You're getting chubbier and chubbier.

G

嘎嘣脆 gā bēng cuì

形容说话、办事干净利索,不拖泥带水。crisp and neat; clear-cut; prompt; to act or speak nattily and promptly

例1:他回答我的问题真是嘎嘣脆。

He gave me a swift answer.

例2:她喜欢做事嘎嘣脆。

She likes a neat job.

乍 gǎ

1.脾气不好;古怪。bad tempered; odd; eccentric; peculiar

例:这家伙有点乍。

This fellow is a queer specimen.

2.逗;顽皮。funny; interesting; naughty

例:他是个乍小子。

He is a scamp.

该着 gāi zháo

应该;理所当然。ought to; certainly; naturally

例:我听说你最近升官了,所以这顿饭该着由你请。

I heard you got a promotion recently, so you certainly should treat me to this meal.

盖 gài

指极棒,超过所有其他的。extremely good; the best; marvelous; excellent; ace out

例:他的英语把这儿的所有人都盖了。

He aces out all of his colleagues in English.

盖了面积 gài le miàn jī

指极棒,在一定范围内超过所有其他的。be the best within a certain field of expertise

例:她的手工艺品在这一带真是盖了面积了。

Her handicrafts are the best in the region.

盖帽儿 gài màor

本指蓝球盖球动作,后指极棒,超过所有其他的。cream of the crop; superexcellent; the best of all/A term originally used in basketball referring putting the ball through the hoop.

例:中国女子排球队盖帽儿了。

The Chinese women volleyball team is the best.

丐帮 gài bāng

指专门以行乞为职业的人组成的团伙或集团。group of beggars/A term that refers to a group of people who live off begging.

例:现在在车站行乞的人来自不同的丐帮。

Now most beggars in railway stations came from different beggar groups.

干巴 gān ba

1.变干;干枯。dry up; wither; shrivel

例:你最好勤浇花,否则花儿就干巴了。

You'd better water your flowers frequently, otherwise they will wither.

2.皮肤干燥;瘦。thin; skinny

例:她身体不错,就是有点儿干巴。

She is in fine health, but a little skinny.

干巴瘦 gān ba shòu

指(人)瘦,没有脂肪。thin; skinny; lean

例:五年了,我的体重一点儿没长,还是这么干巴瘦。

I haven't put on any weight for five years and remain as skinny as before.

干货 gān huò

指有价值,高昂的东西。dried goods/A metaphor for high value or expensive things.

例:这次我老爸从日本回来带了不少干货。有时间你就过来看看。

This time my father brought back many expensive things from Japan. Come over and have a look if you have time.

肝儿颤 gānr chàn

指十分害怕;畏惧;恐惧。have a shaken liver; be scared; tremble with fear; be terrified

例1:一听说明天要考试,他就肝儿颤。

He is scared stiff to hear that he will take an examination tomorrow.

例2:只要别人一请他做报告,他就有点儿肝儿颤。

He trembles with fear at the thought of being asked to give a speech.

赶趟儿 gǎn tàngr

来得及;能赶上。have time for; be in time for

例:如果我们现在去火车站还赶趟儿。

We can be in time for the train if we leave right now for the railway station.

敢开牙 gǎn kāi yá

本指蟋蟀咬斗，后指敢开大价钱，敢说大话，敢胡说。dare to ask a high price/A term that originated from cricket fighting.

例：你可真敢开牙！这么一个台灯要一千块。

How dare you ask for such a high price—one thousand *yuan* for a lamp like this!

感冒 gǎn mào

感兴趣。be interested in; have interest in

例：她喜欢言情片，对恐怖片不感冒。

She is fond of romantic movies and is not interested in horror movies.

钢蹦儿 gāng bèngr

硬币。coin

例：这个存钱罐里全是钢蹦儿。

This piggy bank is full of coins.

港 gǎng

指时髦。fashionable; stylish

例：两年不见你变了，比以前港多了。

I haven't seen you for two years. You're even more fashionable than before.

港姐 gǎng jiě

对香港女明星的昵称。female (movie or pop) star from Hong Kong/An affectionate term of address for famous Hong Kong actresses.

例：他特别喜欢听港姐唱的歌。

He likes to listen to the songs sung by female pop stars

from Hong Kong the most.

港客 gǎng kè

指去大陆的港澳同胞。compatriots in Hong Kong and Macao who come to the mainland

例:他请港客吃饭去了。

He invited his Hong Kong friends for a meal.

港星 gǎng xīng

指香港的明星。Hong Kong movie or pop star

例:她不仅买了很多港星的照片,而且还能告诉你许多关于他们的事情。

She not only buys a lot of prints of Hong Kong movie stars, but also can tell you a great deal about them.

港仔 gǎng zǎi

指香港的小伙子。Hong Kong lad

例:我刚刚认识了一个港仔,他教了我几句广东话。

I've just met a boy from Hong Kong, who taught me a little Cantonese.

港纸 gǎng zhǐ

指港币。Hong Kong currency; Hong Kong dollar

例:这件皮大衣在香港要一千九百元港纸,比在北京买便宜多了。

This leather jacket costs HK＄1,900, much cheaper than it would be in Beijing.

杠头 gàng tóu

指办事头脑不灵活,教条;死心眼儿。stubborn person; person with a one-track mind

例：你可真是个杠头，你就不会先做这个后做那个吗？

You really have a one-track mind. Why don't you do this first and that later?

高 gāo

1. 表示非常好；高明。excellent；brilliant

例1：A：你们觉得我的主意怎么样？

What do you think of my idea?

B：高，高，实在是高。

It's a brilliant idea，indeed.

2. 表示酒喝多了。having drunk to excess

例2：今天他喝高了，所以话特别多。

He drank too much today, that's why he was so talkative.

高价老头儿 gāo jià lǎo tóur

指退休或离休后另任他职，拿高额工资的老人。rich old man/A term that refers to older man who has a high salary or earns a lot from a second job after retirement.

例：他可是个高价老头儿。许多公司请他去当顾问。

He is a rich old man. Many companies have invited him to be their consultant.

高宰 gāo zǎi

指狠命地向买方多要钱。charge an exorbitant price（so as to swindle）

例：街头小贩通常喜欢高宰有钱的人。

Street vendors usually charge the rich exorbitant prices.

搞错 gǎo cuò

弄错；做得不好。mistake；make a mistake；confuse

例：你把日期搞错了，你这张票是明天的。

You confused the date. Your ticket is for tomorrow.

搞定 gǎo dìng

指把事情办好或落实下来。settle; fix; decide; ascertain; make sure

例：今天总经理不在，所以这个计划无法搞定。我们只有等到明天再说了。

The general manager is not in today so this plan can't be settled. We have to wait till tomorrow.

搞什么飞机 gǎo shén me fēi jī

（年轻人用语）表示不明内情或埋怨。What on earth...? an expression used among young people to ask an unknown detail or express a complaint to someone

例：你们昨天搞什么飞机？为何瞒着我。

What on earth were you doing yesterday? Why did you hide it from me?

搞笑 gǎo xiào

指通过语言和形体产生的幽默来逗大家笑。(words or actions) meant to amuse or to cause laughter

例：这部新片中有许多搞笑的镜头，吸引了不少观众，票房收入跃居第一。

This new film is full of amusing scenes that it has attracted many viewers and its box-office value has leaped to first place.

哥们儿 gē menr

兄弟（男青年之间见面时的一种称呼）。brother

例1：嘿，哥们儿，小心点儿。

Hey brothers, be careful.

例2:如果你有什么好事,可别忘了我们哥们儿。

If you've got good stuff, don't forget our friends.

各 gè

指人性格十分特别;与众不同;各别。out of the ordinary; peculiar; different from others; odd/A term mostly used to describe one's character or disposition.

例:他特别各,从不让别人碰或借他的书。

He is very peculiar. He never lets others touch his books or borrow them.

各村有各村的高招儿 gè cūn yǒu gè cūn de gāo zhāor

指各有各的办法、经验。everyone has his or her own way; everyone has his or her own style or experience

例:在展览大厅你可以看到在展台布置上各村有各村的高招儿。

In the exhibition hall, you can see that every exhibit has its own style by the way the stalls are decorated.

各色 gè sè

与众不同;古怪(含贬义)odd, eccentric

例:我丈夫特别各色,别人很难与他相处。

My husband is quite eccentric, others find him hard to work with.

各漾 gè yang

恶心;不舒服。feel sick; feel uncomfortable

例:他最各漾别人用他的饭碗吃饭。

He feels very uncomfortable if someone uses his bowl.

给脸上鼻梁 gěi liǎn shàng bí liáng

又可称为登鼻子上脸,指得寸进尺。give him an inch and he'll take a mile

例:这人给脸上鼻梁。对他你千万不能客气。

You should never treat him too well. He is the sort of person who, you give him an inch, will take a mile.

给他一大哄 gěi tā yī dà hòng

让大家一起发出声音哄笑某人。boo someone; gather together to jeer at someone; hoot at someone

例:她唱得真难听,让我们给她一大哄。

She sings so bad. Let's boo her.

跟风 gēn fēng

指赶时髦。to follow the trends; do as others do

例:自从《哈里·波特》系列书问世并畅销全球以来,许多出版社纷纷跟风随后出版了不少有关魔法故事的图书。

Since the Harry Potter series were published and became a global success, many publishers have followed the trend and published books about magic stories.

跟屁虫 gēn pì chóng

1. 指没有主见、完全听从别人的人。someone who is obsequious and has no definite views of his or her own; one's shadow

例:我女儿是我的跟屁虫。我走到哪儿她跟到哪儿。

My daughter is my shadow. Wherever I go she follows me.

2. 指爱谄媚奉承的人。flatterer; boot licker; ass-kisser; brown-noser

例:我可不想当跟屁虫,整天看老板的脸色过日子。

I don't want to be someone who has to kiss up to the boss

every day.

跟着感觉走 gēn zhe gǎn jué zǒu

不加思索地、顺其自然地行事。follow one's heart; do what comes naturally; do something without thinking

例：他很少听医生的意见，喜欢跟着感觉走。

He likes to do whatever he pleases and seldom listens to the doctor's advice.

根儿正 gēnr zhèng

"文革"时说人的出身成分好，现多指人的思想本质好。have a good family background/A metaphor for those who have a good political and spiritual nature. A term widely used during the "cultural revolution". Workers, peasants, soldiers and cadres are considered as good family background, while anti-revolutionaries, landlords, capitalists and rightists are not.

例：他根儿正，入党不成问题。

There won't be any problems for him to join the Party since his character is good and he has high moral standards.

根儿硬 gēnr yìng

有背景；背后有人撑腰；有后台。be backed up; have strong support; have connections

例：我知道我比不上他，因为他根儿硬。

I know I can't compare with him because he has strong support (connections).

哏 gén

1.滑稽；有趣；逗。funny; amusing; comical

例：他戴着那顶帽子显得挺哏。

He looks very funny with that hat.

2.逗乐有趣的言行。clownish speech or behavior

例:他喜欢逗哏。

He likes making clownish speech.

艮 gěn

1.性格直爽,固执;(说话或态度)僵硬,不委婉。straightforward;stubborn;blunt;forthright

例:他这人太艮,不好与人相处。

He is too blunt to work with other people.

2.(食物)硬而不脆。(of food) tough not crisp; hard to chew

例:你把海鲜炒过头了。它们都变艮了。

You have overcooked the sea food. It turned tough.

工农兵 gōng nóng bīng

指五十元人民币。a fifty-*yuan* bill/There are three figures on a fifty-*yuan* note:a worker, farmer and soldier.

例:今年给孩子压岁钱的红包中工农兵少了,老头票多了。

This year few people gave red envelopes containing only one fifty-*yuan* bill to children at Chinese new year, most gave them one hundred-*yuan* instead.

公了 gōng liǎo

指通过正当的渠道解决;由官方按规章办理,如起诉、打官司等。solve or settle sth. in a proper manner or according to public regulations/Usually refers to resolution of a problem or dispute by going to court or according to official principles.

例:他不想公了,因为交通民警会扣他的驾驶执照。

He doesn't want to solve the problem in the proper way because the police will take away his driving license.

公鸭嗓子 gōng yā sǎng zi

形容嗓子粗、哑、扁。drake's voice; raucous voice/A voice which is husky and flat.

例:我想没人喜欢听你这个公鸭嗓子唱歌。

I don't think people like to hear you sing since you've got a raucous voice.

拱火 gǒng huǒ

使生气。annoy; irritate

例:我尽量保持平静,但她还继续在一边拱火,说些不受听的话。

I tried to keep calm, but she continued to irritate me with her unpleasant words.

够档次 gòu dàng cì

够水平;够格。reach a certain (high) level; be up to standard; be up to par

例:你这房子装修得真够档次,跟宾馆相差无几。

The house you decorated is up to hotel standards.

够劲儿 gòu jìnr

1.够重的;(分量或味道等)很重;很费力气。heavy; strong (in taste, strength, etc.); strenuous

例:你能把这箱书搬上楼吗? 它可够劲儿的。

Can you carry this box of books upstairs? It's pretty hefty.

2.指程度深,或力不所及。almost too much to cope with

例:这么多活儿都让我一人干够劲儿。

It's too much for me to handle all the work alone.

够呛 gòu qiàng

难以忍受或承受;困难较大。terrible; hard; difficult; unbearable

例1：今天交稿我看够呛。

I think it is difficult to meet my deadline today.

例2：今年冬天冷得够呛。

It's terribly cold this winter.

够味儿 gòu wèir

指水平高；味道浓；地道的。pretty good；well done；strong (in taste, flavor)

例1：她英语说得够味儿。

Her spoken English is pretty good.

例2：这菜不够味儿，请再加一点儿盐。

Put more salt in the dish please. It's not strong enough.

例3：这汤做得够味儿。

The soup is well done.

鼓捣 gǔ dao

1. 反复拨弄；移来移去。tinker with；fiddle with

例：他喜欢鼓捣电视机。

He likes to tinker with the television.

2. 背后说坏话，使坏；怂恿；煽动。egg on；incite；play a dirty trick；speak ill of sb.

例1：她总是鼓捣别人提意见。

She always eggs on others to make a suggestion.

例2：他爱在背后鼓捣人。

He likes to speak ill of others behind their backs.

骨头轻 gǔ tou qīng

指不自重、不自爱、轻浮的人（多指女人）。light bones/A term describing women who are not self-possessed and behave frivolously.

例：她这人骨头轻，总爱招引男人。

She's got light bones and likes to flirt with men.

呱呱叫 guā guā jiào

形容非常好。tiptop; extremely good

例：他那活儿干得呱呱叫。

He is doing a tiptop job.

挂 guà

盯上；注意；盯梢。shadow; tail; follow

例：一个富翁被两名抢劫犯挂上了。

A wealthy man was tailed by two robbers.

挂号 guà hào

指有犯罪前科的人的档案已在公安部门有记录。establish a criminal record

例：你该格外小心，因为你已在公安局挂过号了。

You should be very careful because you have already established a criminal record with the police.

挂拍 guà pāi

泛指（多指网球、乒乓球、羽毛球）运动员退役。hang up one's racket; retire from (professional) athletics (mostly refers to tennis, ping-pong or badminton); give up an athlete's life

例：著名网球选手王红宣布她将在下月挂拍，年底出国留学。

Wang Hong, the famous tennis player, announced she would hang up her racket next month and go to study abroad at the end of the year.

挂着 guà zhe

指事情还没有处理或解决，被搁在一边。leave aside; hang; shelve

例：我的住房问题三年来一直挂着。

My housing problem has been hanging for three years.

怪才 guài cái

指有令人不可思议、奇特才华的人。one with outstanding artistic talent; a talented person

例：红高粱的导演张艺谋被誉为中国电影界的怪才。

Zhang Yimou, director of the film "Red Sorghum" is known for his extraordinary artistic talent in Chinese film circles.

官倒(儿) guān dǎo(r)

指担任政府公职而又从事倒买倒卖，从中获取私利的人。government official who engages in speculation/A term that refers to government officials who illegally use their status or political or economic clout to make a profit.

例：政府下决心要严肃惩办官倒。

The government has decided to inflict heavy penalties on corrupt government officials.

官盖 guān gài

绝好的；最棒的。the best of all; extremely good

例：你若系上这条皮带，官盖。

It would look the best if you wore this belt.

关板儿 guān bǎnr

指倒闭。close down; go bankrupt

例：那家饭店上星期关板儿了。

That restaurant closed down last week.

灌水 guàn shuǐ

（网络语言）自己充当网民给自己的网站写吹捧性文章。to pour water; to fill web pages with exaggerated content or articles (an Internet term meaning to write articles praising one's own web site)

例：你们网站的文章大多是你写的吧？好小子，真不少灌水啊！

Most of the articles published on your website were written by you, aren't they? Buddy, you've poured a lot of water!

光溜 guāng liu

滑溜；平滑。smooth; slippery

例1：这块丝绸真光溜。

This silk is really smooth.

例2：脚下留神。这种大理石地面太光溜了。

Be careful when you walk on the marble floor. It's very slippery.

广告人 guǎng gào rén

指从事广告专业的人。advertising man; adman

例：他们是新一代的广告人。

They are the admen of the new generation.

逛街 guàng jiē

1. 购物；买东西。go shopping

例：大多数人在周末逛街。

Most people go shopping on weekend.

2. 在街道上散步。go window shopping; stroll in the street

例：她爱在阳光明媚的日子里逛街。

She enjoys window shopping on sunny days.

归置 guī zhì

收拾;摆放整齐;整理干净。tidy up; put in order; clear away

例 1:她把书架上的书归置得整整齐齐。

She put her books in good order on the shelf.

例 2:咱们把房间归置一下。

Let's tidy up the room.

鬼 guǐ

指（小孩或动物）机灵;聪明。smart; clever

例:这孩子鬼着呢,总钻我们的空子。

This boy is very smart. He always exploits our loopholes.

鬼扯 guǐ chě

胡说八道。talk nonsense; rubbish

例:他们三个到一块儿就鬼扯,根本就没有什么正经的话。

The three of them only talk nonsense, nothing serious can occur as long as they get together.

鬼佬 guǐ lǎo

称外国人(含贬义)。foreigner (impolite term)

例:你不知道鬼佬最爱吃中国菜,所以中餐馆的生意在海外总是那么兴隆。

Don't you know that foreigners like Chinese food? That's why business in Chinese restaurants is always so prosperous.

鬼市 guǐ shì

指天黑时进行交易的非法自由市场。black market; illegal trading center (usually opened at dusk)/A term that refers to unlicensed peddlers who trade illegally after sunset when all tax collectors have gotten off work and gone home for the day.

例：他常去鬼市买便宜货。

He often buys cheap goods on the black market.

鬼子烟 guǐ zi yān

指外国进口的香烟；洋烟。imported cigarette (mainly from the United States and Britain)

例：他爱抽鬼子烟，喝威士忌酒。

He likes to smoke imported cigarettes and drink whisky.

滚大包 gǔn dà bāo

指偷行李。steal luggage

例：他在火车站候车室闲逛，伺机滚大包。

He lingers in the railway station waiting room looking for an opportunity to steal luggage.

滚刀肉 gǔn dāo ròu

原指不易剁烂的肉，现比喻不好对付、胡搅蛮缠的人。hard meat to be chopped up/A metaphor for those who are difficult to deal with or harass others with unreasonable demands.

例：与他共事一段时间后，我发现这家伙真是个滚刀肉。

After working with him for a period of time I realized he is really hard to deal with.

国际倒儿爷 guó jì dǎor yé

指从事跨国倒买倒卖，并从中获利的人。transnational goods speculator；international goods profiteer

例：大多数国际倒儿爷都到秀水街买服装，所以这条街的生意就变得格外红火。

Most international traders come to buy clothes in Xiushui Street, which has resulted in a great boom for business.

国脚 guó jiǎo

指国家足球队的运动员。player on national soccer team

例：中国国脚将于明日迎战伊朗队。

The Chinese soccer team will play the Iran team tomorrow.

过 guò

过分；过度。overdo sth. ; go too far

例：我认为在这个剧中你的表演有些过了。

I think you overdid your part in the play.

过电 guò diàn

1. 触摸异性时所产生的感觉（亲吻等）。have an electric shock/A metaphor for feeling sexual excitement on touching someone of the opposite sex (kiss, etc.).

例：当他碰到她的手时，他第一次尝到了过电的滋味。

He could feel the electricity between them when he touched her hand for the first time.

2. 指酒席上用酒杯轻敲桌面以表示相互碰杯的一种形式。to knock the table with one's glass instead of clinking glasses

例：她觉得过电这种形式很有意思。

She thinks the way that they knock the table with their glasses is very interesting.

过气 guò qì

名气已经过时。to be old or out of date (of a famous person)

例：很多 80 年代过气的歌星如今纷纷想杀回歌坛，不幸的是时过境迁，没有几个能成功的。

Many pop singers from the 1980s, who are now past their prime, have tried to get back on stage. Unfortunately few of them have succeeded, because things have changed with time.

H

哈韩族 hā hán zú

喜欢韩国流行歌曲或电视剧的年轻人。young people who love Korean pop songs or TV dramas

例:你知道吗?这次参加青年歌手大赛的人当中有相当一部分人是哈韩族。

Do you know, most of the people who participated in this Young Singers' Contest are young people who love Korean pop songs?

哈日族 hā rì zú

喜欢日本流行歌曲或电视剧的年轻人。young people who love Japanese pop songs or TV dramas

例:A:你们学校也有哈日族吗?

Are there any young people who love Japanese pop songs or TV dramas in your school?

B:当然了,还不少呢!

Of course, a quite a few.

孩子王 hái zi wáng

1.指孩子中的头。head of children

例:他小时候就是孩子王。

He was the children's leader when he was young.

2.指教师。teacher

例:她当了近四十年的孩子王。

She has worked as a teacher for nearly forty years.

海 hǎi

1,形容多极了或大极了。plenty；extremely large

例 1：海口。big talk

例 2：海碗。big bowl

例 3：这两年他挣的钱海了去了。

He's made a pile of money in these two years.

例 4：论喝酒,他可有海量。

He is a heavy drinker.

2.没有目标地。willy-nilly；without a goal

例 1：她不知谁拿了她的外衣,只是一个劲儿地海骂。

She didn't know who took away her overcoat，but ranted willy-nilly and incessantly.

例 2：我忘了把钥匙放在哪儿了,只得海找一气。

I forgot where I put my key and made a blind search for it.

预 hān

指粗。thick

例 1：他用这么预的棍子打我。

He beat me with a stick this thick.

例 2：这棵树真够预的,五个人都抱不住。

The tree trunk is so massive that five people cannot get their arms around it.

号贩子 hào fàn zi

指专门倒卖医院挂号单并从中牟利的人。someone who scalps registration tickets

例：医院明知这些号贩子的身份却因无执法权而难以将他们驱逐出医院。

Hospitals know exactly who these registration-ticket scalpers are，but they're unable to drive them out of the hospitals because they don't have the legal right to do so.

喝水 hē shuǐ

指（在工作或生活中）受挫折或（在生意上）亏本,吃亏。

to drink water/A metaphor for those who suffer setbacks (in work or life) or suffer losses (in business).

例:当你初下海经商时免不了要喝水。

It's quite common to suffer losses when you are first starting out in business.

盒饭 hé fàn

指盛有饭和菜的盒子。boxed meal/A meal of rice and aside dish in a box.

例:我出差或外出旅行时常在火车上吃盒饭。

I usually eat boxed meals on the train when I go on business or trips.

黑 hēi

1. 指人贪心;心狠;心黑。greedy; avaricious; evil-minded; crafty

例:那个小贩太黑,所以我从不在他那儿买东西。

That peddler is so crafty that I never buy things from him.

2. 欺骗;敲诈;坑害。extort; extract

例:那群团伙黑了他一大笔钱。

The gang extorted a large sum of money out of him.

3. 算计。scheme; plot; plan in a deceitful way

例:我知道你们暗中黑我。

I know you secretly schemed against me.

黑车 hēi chē

无出租牌照,非法进行载客运营服务的汽车。illegal taxi; a car that carries passengers illegally and without a business license

例:因为白天查得严,所以多数黑车都在晚上出来拉活。

To avoid the daytime inspections most illegal taxis work in the evening.

黑单 hēi dān

假账,指收银员收顾客钱后不全入账,扣下一部分据为已有。
unreported bill; false accounts; the practice of cooking the books (American slang)/A term that refers to the practice of an accountant or employee of not entering bills, receipts, charges, etc, in the account book, but instead pocketing the money for himself of herself.

例:她靠做黑单发了起来.

She has gotten rich by making false accounts.

黑道 hēi dào

指黑社会或专干违法犯罪勾当的地下活动组织。gang (of criminals)

例:这事一定是黑道上干的。

This must be the work of the gang.

黑点 hēi diǎn

指劣迹。black dot/A metaphor for a misdeed or evil act.

例:一旦你受过处分,你的档案中就会有一个一生也无法抹掉的黑点。

Once you are punished, your file will be marked throughout your life with an indelible black dot.

黑哨 hēi shào

指因受贿或偏袒等原因而导致裁判员裁判不公。black whistle/A metaphor for an unfair decision of a judge (referee) who is partial or who has been bribed.

例:在近来的几场足球赛中,经常发生裁判员吹黑哨的事情,这已引起了人们的关注。

Recent unfair referee's decisions on the football field have attracted considerable attention.

黑着干 hēi zhe gàn

指无执照私自营业或不公开地、偷偷摸摸地做某事。do something covertly and illegally or without a license

例:中国禁止买卖武器,可有些走私犯却黑着干。

It is forbidden to sell weapons in China, but some smugglers sell them illegally.

横插一杠子 héng chā yī gàng zi

1.从中添麻烦;生事;捣乱。make trouble; create a disturbance

例:她妒忌我的才能,所以总要对我的工作横插一杠子。

She is jealous of my ability, so she always disturbs me in my work.

2.从中阻碍,阻拦。hinder; bar the way

例:每次我想干些自己有兴趣的事时,我丈夫就横插一杠子,使我十分扫兴。

Each time I want to do something I like, my husband bars the way and makes me unhappy.

横路静二 héng lù jìng èr

源自日本影片《追捕》中一角色。在此片中该角色服用一种药物而变成呆傻。现用于比喻呆傻、有神经病的人。

idiot/A term made popular by the Japanese film, "Chasing". In the film, one character, whose Chinese name is Heng Lu Jing Er, lost his memory and became an idiot after taking a pill. The term is now used to describe an idiot or stupid person.

例:他没想到他的朋友会赢。所以当他输了这场比赛时,他那副样子就像横路静二。

He didn't think his friend would beat him, so he looked like an idiot after losing the game.

横是 héng shi

大概;可能;也许。maybe; probably; perhaps

例:他横是又改变主意不来了。

Perhaps he changed his mind not to come again.

横竖 héng shù

反正(表示一种肯定的语气)。anyway; anyhow

例:我们横竖是死,还不如跟那些匪徒拼了。

We should fight with those hoods to the end since we're destined to die anyway.

横着出来 héng zhe chū lái

指人说话办事不加思考、修饰,直来直去。go horizontally out/It refers to someone who does or says sth. directly without thinking or modifying his words or actions; speaking frankly or doing sth. in a straightforward way.

例:你今后说话得注意点,别总让话横着出来,别人没法接受。

You should mind what you say. Don't let your words out horizontally because nobody likes to hear them.

红包 hóng bāo

用红纸包着,作为贺礼或酬金送人的钱,也泛指赠款。

red envelope filled with money that is usually given to someone as a bonus, gift, reward or donation

例:春节她女儿收到很多红包。

Her daughter received a lot of red envelopes at the Spring

Festival.

红火 hóng huo

形容兴旺,繁荣,热闹。having a run of luck; prosperous

例:她的生意真够红火的。

Her business is really striking it rich.

红眼病 hóng yǎn bìng

1.传染性结膜炎;眼炎。pinkeye (an acute eye disease)

例:我儿子患了红眼病。

My son has pinkeye.

2.嫉妒。jealousy; resentment

例:只要见别人比她拿钱多,她便害红眼病。

She is full of jealousy when she sees someone earning more than she does.

餿 hōu

1.因太甜或咸使人感到不舒服。sickeningly sweet or salty

例:这是什么糖呀? 真够餿的。

This candy is too sweet.

2.非常。very; awfully

例:这菜餿咸没法吃。

This dish is awfully salty.

后娘养的 hòu niáng yǎng de

指不受人重视或喜爱。to be raised by a stepmother/A metaphor for one who receives little attention or ill treatment or who is out of favor.

例:在单位里咱是后娘养的,所以总是得不到提升。

I'm out of favor with the boss so I can hardly get a promotion.

后生 hòu shēng

指青年男子。young man; lad

例：这后生真是个善良的人。

This young man is a really kindhearted person.

呼 hū

指通过 BP 机与某人联系。page

例：如有事可随时呼我。

If any thing comes in, please page me at any time.

忽悠 hū you

1. 晃动 flicker; wave

例：秋千一上一下，我感到心也跟着忽悠。

I felt my heart wavering as the swing went up and down.

2. 花言巧语地鼓动诱惑，使人轻信。Persuade someone to believe what one says (usually by means of honeyed words).

例：他这个人最擅长销售，没有几个人能经受得住他忽悠的。用不了多长时间他就能把顾客忽悠得掏钱。

He is good at sales. Almost no one can withstand his persuasion. He can talk a customer into buying his products in no time.

胡同串子 hú tòng chuàn zi

指走街串巷的小商小贩。peddler; hawker

例：如今胡同串子比过去多了，你总能听到他们的吆喝声。

There are more peddlers now than before. You can hear their shouts all the time.

唬人 hǔ rén

吓人；蒙骗人。bluff; scare; frighten; cheat; deceive

例:别拿湖怪这样耸人听闻的消息来唬人。我们不信真有其事。

Don't frighten us with the sensational story of the Lake Monster. We don't believe it is real.

护犊子 hù dú zi

比喻庇护自己的孩子(含贬义)Originally referring to an adult cow or ox protecting its calf, this is now a metaphor to refer to shielding the shortcomings or faults of one's child.

例:在学校老师最感头疼的就是与那些护犊子的家长谈话,他们总认为他们的孩子没有错。

School teachers feel that the hardest thing is talking with parents who shield the faults of their child, and always insist that their child is right.

糊弄 hù nong

1. 骗人;蒙骗;蒙人。fool; cheat; deceive

例1:我知道你在糊弄我。

I knew you are kidding.

例2:他这人可不好糊弄。

He is not easily fooled.

2. 敷衍了事;不认真去做;应付。do sth. lackadaisically of carelessly; go through the motions

例:今天轮到她打扫厕所,可她在那儿糊弄了几下就回家了。

It's her turm to clean the toilet today, but she only did it lackadaisically and left for home.

花 huā

好色的。randy; lecherous

例:他六十多岁了,可是还很花。

He is over sixty, but he is still randy.

花花肠子 huā huā cháng zi

比喻某人的主意或点子很多。many ideas; fertile imagination

例:别看他年纪小,肚子里花花肠子可不少。

He is an ideas wizard though he is quite young.

花花哨 huā huā shào

花言巧语哄骗人。to cheat one with sweet words

例:他这个人没有别的本事,就会花花哨。

He can do nothing, but cheat one with sweet words.

花活 huā huó

鬼把戏,新花招。也指华而不实的事情。dirty or wicked trick; sinister plot; new tricks/It also refers to something flashy and without substance.

例:你能不能踏实点儿,别总耍花活。

Can't you do things seriously? Don't always play wicked tricks.

花老头 huā lǎo tóu

爱好女色的年长的男子。dirty old man

例:她那个老板一定是个花老头,因为他常请年轻女子吃饭。

Her boss must be a dirty old man because he often invites young girls to dinner.

花了 huā le

把人打得头破血流。wound; make someone bleed

例:强盗威胁那妇人如果她喊叫就花了她。

The robber threatened to wound the woman if she shouted.

划拉 huá la

1. 随便找来或移来移去。pick；move to and fro；get casually or easily

例1：这种东西太一般，我随便到一家商店就能给你划拉来一个。

This stuff is very common. I can get you one easily from a store anywhere.

例2：站好了，别用脚在地上乱划拉。

Stand still. Don't move your foot to and fro on the floor.

2. 不用心地写字；不认真地涂抹。scrawl

例：这是我的书，别在上面瞎划拉。

It's my book. Don't scrawl on it.

滑溜 huá liu

1. 光滑。smooth；slippery

例：溪中的鹅卵石挺滑溜的。

The cobblestones in the stream are very slippery.

2. 滑落。slip

例：她突然从山坡上滑溜下来。

She suddenly slipped from a hill slope.

话痨 huà láo

形容好说话，而且一说起来就没完没了的人。one who is talkative，who won't stop talking

例：我真不敢相信在大学时沉默寡言的他，做了几年销售后如今也成了话痨。

He was a man of so few words in college, I can hardly believe that he's turned into such a talkative person after working as a salesman for a few years.

话由 huà yóu

可以作为开始说话的事或借口。a pretext or an excuse to

start a conversation with someone

例：与人交往可有学问，首先要懂礼貌，还要会找话由。

Communication with other people takes a lot of studying. You have to learn to be polite, and to be able to find a pretext to start a conversation.

坏菜 huài cài

指坏事或完蛋。多用于口语表示惊叹"完了，大事不好"的意思。bad thing；be done for；be finished

例1：这件事不能告诉他老婆，否则准坏菜。

We can't tell this to his wife, otherwise, we will be finished.

例2：坏菜了，这下可真的坏菜了。我把钥匙锁在家里了。

Something terrible has happened. I locked my keys in my home.

坏了醋了 huài le cù le

糟了；事情办坏了。things go wrong

例：哎呀，坏了醋了。我私下找工作的事让老板知道了。

Oh, my god. Things went wrong. The boss heard about me finding jobs privately.

黄伯伯 huáng bó bo

指说话不算数，为个人目的信口开河的人。（lit.）Uncle Huang/A form of address to a person who wags his tongue too freely or makes irresponsible remarks.

例：别人叫他黄伯伯，可见他说的话不能信。

He is known for making irresponsible remarks. That's why we don't take him seriously.

黄虫 huáng chóng

"蝗虫"的谐音,指黄色的出租汽车(主要指面的)。"yellow bugs"/ The same tones as the word for locust. An expression used in early 1990s of the 20th century to describe the plethora of yellow taxis (particularly *miandi*, the yellow taxi minivans) in the city—like a swarm of locusts.

例:没有人确切知道黄虫何时出现在京城的大街小巷,并且其数量增加得如此之快。

No one knows exactly when or how the swarm of yellow taxis appeared and increased so quickly on the streets of Beijing.

黄花闺女 huáng huā guī nü

指处女。virgin

例:她今年十八岁,还是个花黄闺女呢。

She is eighteen years old this year and still a virgin.

黄花后生 huáng huā hòu sheng

指处男。celibate man

例:没人相信他会是个黄花后生。

No one believes that he is celibate.

黄了 huáng le

失败;完蛋了;无结果;化为泡影。come to nought; go through without result; be finished; fall through

例:这个计划再拖下去就黄了。

The plan will fall through if it is put off any more.

黄脸婆 huáng liǎn pó

指已婚的中年妇女。middle-aged married woman

例:如今的她早已成了黄脸婆,失去了往日的光彩。

She's already a middle-aged married woman and has lost her

past beauty.

黄牛 huáng niú

1. 非法从事倒买倒卖外汇的人。(lit.) yellow ox/A term refers to a black market dealer who buys foreign currency in the street; scalper

例:随着B股的上市,私下倒汇的人略有增加。美元兑人民币的黑市价格从1比8.36涨到了8.4。为了达到赚黑钱的目的,"黄牛"们大谈炒B股的好处,追着人直至进银行大门。

With the opening of B share, scalpers have increased a little bit. In the black market, dollars to RMB rose from 8.36 *yuan* up to 8.4 *yuan* per dollar. In order to make more money, scalpers exaggerated the advantages of purchasing B shares to people and even followed them to the entrance of the bank.

2. 指不承担、无力或拒绝赔偿经济损失的人。a person who will not or cannot take responsibility and pay for their debts

例:我要早知道你是黄牛,才不会跟你做这笔生意呢!

If I had known earlier that you were so irresponsible, I wouldn't have done business with you.

皇历 huáng lì

指历书。比喻旧的规章制度或过去的事情。(lit.) almance; old hat/A metaphor for old system, regulations or things in the past.

例:A:你们买粮食还要粮票吗?

Do you still need coupons to buy grain?

B:不要,这是老皇历了,早就取消了。如今你想买多少就买多少。

No, that is an old hat. They have been abolished for ages. You can buy as much as you want now.

回放 huí fàng

指重播。review; show again; rebroadcast a program

例：让我们一起看一下这场比赛中几个精彩镜头的回放。

Let's have a review of some of the best scenes from this game.

回头客 huí tóu kè

指两次以上光顾某一个地方的顾客。多用于形容某个地方的生意好，信誉好或者价廉物美，能吸引顾客再来。

returned customer/Refers to customers who return to a place once or more often. A metaphor for a place that has built up a prosperous business, has a reputation for good quality goods at cheap prices and which attracts customers back.

例：这个小饭馆的生意好极了，来吃饭的大多是回头客。

This small restaurant's business is booming. Those who come to dine here are mostly returned customers.

会会 huì huì

见面，会面。常用于将来时。meet (often used in future tense)

例：听说你的女朋友很漂亮。什么时候带我去会会她，看看她到底有多漂亮。

I've heard that your girlfriend is very pretty. Take me to meet her someday, and we'll see how pretty she really is.

会来事儿 huì lái shìr

指会看人脸色行事；会投其所好；善解人意。

know how to cater to someone's tastes; good at getting along with others; butter someone up

例：她特别会来事儿，总是捡好听的话对我说。

Saying all those good things about me — she really knows

how to butter me up.

会油子 huì yóu zi

指经常举办各种会议的人。someone who often convenes various kinds of conferences or meetings; conference (meeting) organizer

例：我们单位的领导整天跑东跑西，在会海里忙着。如果没有这么多的大会小会，这些会油子不是要下岗了吗？

The heads of our unit are very busy for showing up at all kinds of meetings. These meeting organizers would be laid off if there were no so many meetings, wouldn't they?

荤的 hūn de

下流的；黄色的。常指骂人话或脏话。obscene; pornographic; obscene language; swearword; abusive language

例：这帮小子一见面，说的全是荤的。

These boys can't speak without swearwords when they get together.

浑球儿 hún qiúr

不明事理，胡搅蛮缠的人（骂人话）。也可写成混球儿。(swearword)blackguard; wretch; scoundrel; bastard

例：你这个小浑球儿，今天又惹你爸生气了，是吗？

You little bastard, you made your Dad angry again today, didn't you?

混车 hùn chē

指乘公共汽车不买车票。take a free ride (take a public bus without paying the fare)

例：他坐车进城时总混车，从不买票。

Whenever he takes the bus to go downtown he always gets a

free ride and never buys a ticket.

混混儿 hùn hunr

指不干正经事、苟且生活的人；游手好闲的人。idler；loafer；slacker/A term that refers to those who idle about and lead an ignoble existence.

例：他外表长得就像个混混儿，所以每逢一部影片有这样的角色，他便是导演眼中的最佳人选。

Since he looks like a slacker, the film director always chooses him to those type of rolls.

活份 huó fèn

灵活；不古板；开朗；活泼。flexible；quick；lively；open

例1：他处理问题很活份，所以他的工作效率很高。

Because he is very flexible at handling affairs, he works very efficiently.

例2：她这个人十分活份，也容易与人共事。

She is very open and easy to work with.

活该 huó gāi

就该如此（用于表示气愤）。serve you right

例：活该！谁叫你当时不听我的劝告呢？

It served you right. Why didn't you listen to my advice then?

活宰 huó zǎi

意为受骗上当，多指在购物时被人坑骗。be killed alive/A metaphor for being cheated (mostly used in shopping).

例：在这里买东西你得特别小心，一不留神就会被人活宰了。

You ought to be extremely careful when you come to buy things here. You will be cheated unless you give it your full attention.

火 huǒ

火爆；红火；热烈。prosperous；flourishing

例：他的生意越做越火。

His business is growing more and more prosperous.

火爆 huǒ bào

形容生意特别好，或演出非常受欢迎。extremely hot/A metaphor for business, a show or something that is lively, prosperous, or very popular.

例：今年买房的人多，所以家装市场异常火爆。

A lot more people bought houses this year so that made the house decoration market extremely active.

火柴盒 huǒ chái hé

指报刊上发表的版面很小的文章。match-box sized article in a newspaper or a magazine

例：她写的一些火柴盒常登在一家妇女杂志上。

She often has tiny articles published in a woman's magazine.

火箭干部 huǒ jiàn gàn bù

指晋升迅速的人。(lit)"a rocket cadre"; a fast riser/A term used to describe someone who gets promotion quickly and rises quickly in the ranks.

例：他是个火箭干部，三十四岁就当上了局长。

He is a fast riser. He became director of the bureau at the age of thirty-four.

火星 huǒ xīng

很出名的身价高的明星。very popular, famous or highly rated star

例：几位火星的临场表现令人不敢恭维。

Some very popular stars' performances did not come up to the requirements, which made it hard for people to compliment them.

火穴 huǒ xuè

指红火、收人多的走穴演出。profitable show

例：许多歌星从火穴中收益非浅,发起来了。

Many pop singers benefited from profitable shows and got rich.

和弄 huò nong

1. 来回拨弄；搅拌。move to and fro (with hand, foot or stick); mix; stir

例：请你帮我把锅里的粥和弄一下,好吗?

Would you please help me stir the porridge in the pot?

2. 挑拨离间。incite; foment dissension

例：她为这事在你我之间和弄来和弄去。

She incited you against me over this thing.

3. 捣乱。make trouble

例：你最好到外面去玩儿,省得在这儿和弄我们。

You'd better go to play outside instead of making trouble for us here.

J

鸡 jī

此为"妓"的谐音。指妓女。prostitute

例:这条街晚上有不少的鸡。

There are many prostitutes in this street at night.

犄角旮旯儿 jī jiǎo gā lár

1.角落;僻静处。corner; nook; quiet and secluded place; out-of-the-way place

例:我不知道那只猫躲在哪个犄角旮旯儿里。

I don't know in which corner the cat is hiding.

2.不常用的;不重要的。uncommon; trite; rare

例1:他把犄角旮旯的词从他的字典中删去。

He cut out the rarely used words from his dictionary.

例2:她喜欢问犄角旮旯儿的问题。

She likes to ask trite questions.

急茬儿 jí chár

1.紧急的事情。urgent matter

例:每次他来找我,我就知道又是急茬儿,否则他才不会大驾光临呢。

Every time when he visits me, I know there must be something urgent, otherwise he wouldn't come himself.

2.急(性子)。quick-tempered; hot-headed

例:他干什么事情都是急茬儿。

He is hot-headed at everything.

急赤白脸 jí chi bái liǎn

指心里着急,面色难看。形容十分着急的样子。burning with impatience; looking pale with worry; extremely pressing

例1:她急赤白脸地找到我,问我是否看到过她的钥匙。

She came to me in an extreme hurry and asked whether I saw her keys。

例2:看他那副急赤白脸的样子,仿佛谁抢了他的钱似的。

He looked hyperanxious, as if someone had taken away all his money.

挤兑 jǐ dui

1. 逼迫使屈从;欺负。force to; bully

例:如果她自己不愿意学钢琴,你就别挤兑她了。

You shouldn't force her to learn the piano if she doesn't want to.

2. 贬低(人);看不起;嘲讽挖苦。insult; belittle

例:他们挤兑我,说我什么事都干不了。

They insulted me by saying I'm good for nothing.

加傍 jiā bàng

参加;加盟;加入;入伙。take part in; join; participate

例:由于这位明星的加傍使这部电视连续剧的收视率大大地提高了。

The viewership of the TV series greatly increased because of the participation of the movie star.

加盟 jiā méng

参加进来;加入。take part in; join; participate

例:他离开山东篮球队加盟北京篮球队。

He left the Shandong basketball team and joined the Beijing team.

加塞儿 jiā sāir

指不按秩序排队。jump a queue; push into a queue

例：她不让他加塞。

She stopped him from jumping the queue.

家庭号 jiā tíng hào

指体积和容量较大的冰淇淋盒子。family-size box of ice-cream

例：我想买一个家庭号冰淇淋。

I'll buy a family-size box of ice-cream.

假活儿 jiǎ huór

1. 骗子。swindler; con man

例：如今假活儿太多，你一不留神就会上当。

There are too many con men now. If you are not careful you'll be fooled by them.

2. 假冒事物。fraud; fake

例：这盘 CD 这么便宜。我想它一定是假活儿。

This CD-ROM is so cheap. I'm afraid that it must be a fake one.

甲壳虫 jiǎ ké chóng

指体积比一般汽车还小的私人汽车。beetle/A type of private car smaller in size than ordinary cars.

例：许多人拥有豪华轿车，甲壳虫已经过时了。

Many people have their own fancy cars. Beetles have become a thing of the past.

架秧子 jià yāng zi

指参与挑拨离间或唆使别人聚众生事。(of a crowd of people) create a disturbance; make trouble

J

最新中国俚语

New Slang of China

例：你们都回去,该干嘛就干嘛去。别围在这儿跟着起哄架秧子。

All of you go back and do what you should do. Don't stand here and make troubles.

奸 jiān

指人自私、小气、滑头。selfish；mean；petty；crafty

例1：她特别奸,从不让别人借用她的电话。

She is so mean that she never lets others use her phone.

例2：这家伙是又奸又滑又馋。

This fellow is mean，crafty and greedy.

拣软的捏 jiǎn ruǎn de niē

专门欺负胆小、懦弱的人。choose the weak to bully；take advantage of the coward

例：谁都爱拣软的捏。

Everyone likes to take advantage of the weak.

见数就晕 jiàn shù jiù yūn

指不善长计算；数学不好。be poor in mathematics or accounting

例：你最好帮我核一下账。我这个人见数就晕。

You'd better help me check this account. I'm not good at math.

矫情 jiáo qing

强词夺理；无理取闹。use lame arguments；resort to sophistry；wilfully make trouble

例：我再也不跟他打交道了。他就爱跟人矫情。

I'll never have any dealings with him. He likes to use lame arguments.

脚底板抹油 jiǎo dǐ bǎn mǒ yóu

形容溜得很快；逃跑。hotfoot；clear out；go fast；flee quickly

例 1：当他看到对手比他强壮时,便脚底板抹油踪影全无了。

He cleared out when he found his opponent was stronger.

例 2：贼一听到有人喊来人便脚底板抹油。

The thief hotfooted it out of the building when he heard someone calling for help.

叫板 jiào bǎn

原为戏曲开唱前的咏叹,现为向某人挑战或滋事。challenge；ask for trouble；pick a quarrel

例：他才从武术训练班毕业,你怎么敢跟他叫板。

How dare you challenge him! He has just graduated from martial arts school.

叫彩儿 jiào cǎir

受欢迎；得到喝彩。appealing；welcome；appeal to；with the applause of；be warmly welcomed

例：张艺谋执导的影片大多在海外叫彩儿。

The films directed by Zhang Yimou are usually warmly welcomed abroad.

叫倒好 jiào dào hǎo

指观众起哄表示对表演的不满。hoot

例：一些观众不喜欢那位歌手,于是他们就不停地吹口哨,叫倒好。

Some of the audience didn't like the singer, so they whistled and hooted endlessly in the theater.

叫(较)劲儿 jiào jìnr

1. 比试;较量。 challenge; have a competition

例:他们俩叫上劲儿了,看谁能把这块大石头搬走。

The two have a competition to see who can move this heavy rock away.

2. 作对。 oppose; dispute

例:他处处跟我叫劲儿。

He opposes me in everything.

叫(较)针儿 jiào zhēnr

1. 指争辩。 argue; wrangle

例:她就爱跟人叫针儿。

She likes to argue with people.

2. 形容某人说话做事一丝不苟,十分认真;死板;不灵活。

be finicky; be conscientious and meticulous; be inflexible

例:对你的工作别那么叫针儿,差不多就行了。

That's good enough. Don't be so meticulous about your work.

叫座 jiào zuò

指戏剧,电影,演出等受欢迎,观众多。 (of a play, movie, show) very popular; a box-office success; draw a large audience

例:真没想到这部电影居然这么叫座。

No one expected that this movie would be such a great box-office success.

窖 jiào

1. 储藏。 deposit (in the bank); save; store

例:大多数人宁愿将钱窖起来,也不愿玩股票。

Most people prefer to save their money rather than buy stocks.

2. 藏。hide; conceal

例：我不知他把钱窖到哪儿去了。

I don't know where he hid all the money.

教头 jiào tóu

指教练。coach

例：他们足球队请了一个洋教头执教。

They hired a foreign coach for their football team.

结了 jié le

用于结束谈话的时候，表示同意。有"得了"、"行了"、"成了"、"完了"的意思。All right! That's it! (used to end a discussion and to express agreement)

例：A：这事本来就跟我无关。

It's none of my business at all.

B：这不结了。那你还不马上回家去？

That's it! Why don't you go home immediately?

姐们儿 jiě menr

称关系比较好的年轻女性。sisters; sister; pals; close female friends/A term used among women to address close friends.

例：你的姐们儿都很想你。她们决定明天来看你。

Your sisters (female friends) are missing you a lot. They have decided to come and see you tomorrow.

进局子 jìn jú zi

被公安局收押；被抓起来。be taken into custody by police; go to prison; be taken to prison

例：直到邻居告诉他，他才知道儿子进局子了。

He didn't know his son was taken into custody by police

until his neighbor told him.

警花 jǐng huā

指女警察。policewoman

例：她也想像姐姐一样成为一名警花。

She aspires to be a policewoman like her elder sister.

酒蜜 jiǔ mì

指陪酒的女友。girl who accompanies someone to drink in a bar or restaurant

例：老板去酒吧喝酒时总忘不了带一个酒蜜。

That boss always takes a girl to accompany him when he drinks in a bar.

九曲十八弯 jiǔ qū shí bā wān

形容花费很大力气或经过许多曲折磨难。strenuous; hard; difficult; complicated; complications; twists and turns; hardship; tribulations/A term used to describe something that is done only through many trials and tribulations.

例：他经过了九曲十八弯，最后才找到了失散多年的妹妹。

He went through many twists and turns before finding his long lost sister at last.

局子 jú zi

指公安局。police station; cop shop

例：我听说那家伙又进局子了。

I was told that the fellow was taken to the cop shop again.

巨 jù

即极为；特别；非常。extremely; very; so

例：前天我们爬了一次香山，巨累，直到今天这腿还疼哪。

We climbed the Fragrant Hills the day before yesterday and felt extremely tired. My legs are still sore today.

卷地 juǎn dì

收摊 pack up the stall

例：今天生意不好，他早早地就卷地，回家去了。

There wasn't much business today, so he packed up the stall early and left for home.

卷铺盖 juǎn pū gài

原指把被褥卷起来。Originally referred to rolling up one's bedclothes. Later it came to mean：

1. 撤退。withdraw, retreat; quit; leave

例：杰克不喜欢这工作，于是他卷铺盖走了，去了深圳。

Jack didn't like this job, so he quit and left. He went to Shenzhen.

2. 被辞退、开除。be fired, be sacked

例：他已经迟到过两次。如果再迟到一次，就要被老板卷铺盖了。

He has been late for work twice. If he's late one more time, the boss will fire him.

绝 jué

1. 拒绝。refuse; turn down; reject

例：她看上去没精打采的，我想她一定是让作者给绝回来了。

She looked unhappy. I think she must have been rejected by the writer.

2. 不尽人情；不留一点儿情分。heartless; merciless

例：虽然她是个女人，但办任何事都很绝。

Although a woman, she does everything mercilessly.

3. 妙；高明。unique; excellent; brilliant

例：你这主意真绝。

Your idea is extremely clever.

绝代佳人 jué dài jiā rén

原指特别漂亮的女人，也用来戏称没有生儿子而只生女儿的年轻女子。Originally it means a woman of matchless beauty. Now by playing with the words people jocularly use it to refer to a young woman of beauty who does not produce a male heir，only a girl，for her husband.（According to an old custom only a male heir can continue a family line.）

例：老赵跟他老婆戏言说他这辈子是难圆儿子梦了，因为他娶了一位绝代佳人。

Lao Zhao said jokingly to his wife that he could never make his dream of having a son come true because he had married a woman of beauty who will not produce a male heir.

绝活 jué huó

独特的或独一无二的技术或本领。special skill；unique ability

例：她的绝活是刻萝卜花儿。

Her special skill is carving garnishes out of turnip.

倔驴 juè lü

比喻固执、性子直的人。bullheaded mule/A metaphor for someone who is stubborn and straightforward.

例：他是头倔驴。

He is as stubborn as a bullheaded mule.

军蜜 jūn mì

指军人的女朋友。soldier's girlfriend

例：他们不知如何请那两位军蜜跳舞。

They don't know how to invite those two soldiers' girlfriends to dance.

军嫂 jūn sǎo

指军人的妻子。soldier's wife

例：她被誉为好军嫂。

She is regarded as a model soldier's wife.

K

咔 kā

切；切换；切掉。cut, cut off

例：这首歌太长了。我不唱了。咔了换首歌吧。

This song is too long. I give up! Please stop it and switch to another one.

咔哧 kā chi

1. 用刀子刮。scrape off with a knife

例：他们打扫房间并把墙上的字都咔哧干净了。

They swept the house and scraped all the letters off the wall.

2. 撤职；撤换（人或物）。

dismiss; discharge someone from office; fire; replace

例：由于失职他被头儿咔哧了。

He was fired by his boss for not doing his job well.

撬油 kā yóu

占便宜；搜刮好的或有用的东西。take advantage of someone; profit at someone else's expense; abuse a privilege

例：她常跟父亲逛商场，撬父亲的油。

She often goes shopping with her father and takes advantage of his money.

卡哇依 kǎ wā yī

源自日本语，用于形容人或物的可爱。A Japanese expression for (someone or something) cute or lovely

例：妈妈，我喜欢这个娃娃，多卡哇依呀！

Mummy, I love this doll. It's so cute!

开国际玩笑 kāi guó jì wán xiào

1. 开很大的,不同一般的玩笑。make a big joke; kid

例:A:我离了。

　I got divorced.

　B:开什么国际玩笑,你一个月前才结的婚。

　Are you kidding? You just got married a month ago.

2. 胡说;胡闹。act without thinking; kid

例:你不是开国际玩笑吧? 一件衬衫卖这么高的价。

What were you thinking? How could you sell this shirt at such a high price?

开练 kāi liàn

1. 开始工作;开始干活。start working

例:等东西一到我们就开练。

We'll start working as soon as the materials arrive.

2. 打架。fight; scuffle; come to blows

例:他性子急,常跟人开练。

He's got a quick temper and often fights with people.

开溜 kāi liū

指逃跑;趁机溜走。escape; run away; sneak away; slink off

例:今天下午有个重要的会,谁敢开溜呀。

We'll have an important meeting this afternoon. Who dares to sneak off?

开瓢 kāi piáo

指头被打破了。break one's head

例:他小时候三天两头跟别人打架,开瓢是常事儿。

He used to fight with others almost every day so it was quite common for him to have his head broken.

开涮 kāi shuàn

拿人耍着玩儿。make fun of; make a fool of

例：他跟这帮朋友太熟了，所以他们拿他开涮他从不生气。

He knows his friends very well, so he never gets angry when they make fun of him.

开牙 kāi yá

1.指提出过分的要求或索取过高的价钱。make excessive demands or ask a high price

例：你可真敢开牙，这活儿我还是找别人来干吧。

How dare you ask such a high price. I'll get someone else to do this work for me.

2.指吹牛皮。boast; brag; talk big

例：别信他的话，他就会到处开牙。

Don't believe what he says. He is good at boasting.

开眼 kāi yǎn

见世面。see the world; enrich one's experience

例：参加国际书展真让我开眼。

I enriched my experience by attending the International Book Fair.

开洋荤 kāi yáng hūn

享受洋人的生活或洋人的食品。enjoy a foreign lifestyle; enjoy foreign food

例：多数中国人喜欢开洋荤，难怪美国的快餐食品在中国卖得这么火。

Most Chinese people like foreign food. That's why American fast food is booming in China.

开夜车 kāi yè chē

比喻在夜里加班干活(通常指读书、写作)。to burn the midnight oil, usually meaning to stay up late reading, studying or writing

例:今天你看上去很疲倦,是不是昨晚又开夜车了?

You look very tired today. Were you burning the midnight oil last night?

看堆儿 kān duīr

看守东西;照顾(某物)。keep an eye on sth.; watch over sth.

例:她父母把买来的水果放下,让她看堆儿,然后转身又去买衣服了。

His parents asked her to keep an eye on the fruits they just bought and then went shopping for clothes.

看走眼 kàn zǒu yǎn

指看人或看事没有看准。to misjudge or fail to recognize someone or something

例:A:我昨天在一家商店看到你和你女友了。

I saw you with your girlfriend in a shop yesterday.

B:不会。昨天我哪儿都没去。你一定是看走眼了。

No. I didn't go anywhere yesterday. You must have thought someone else was me.

侃 kǎn

1. 开聊。chat

例:晚饭后他们常凑在一块儿侃,直到深夜。

After dinner they often get together and chat late into the night.

2. 吹牛。boast

例：他总跟我们侃他多能挣钱。

He always boasts about how good he is at making money.

3. 能说会道。smooth talk

例：你瞧他，又能侃又精明。

Watch him. He's a smooth talker and is very clever.

侃大山 kǎn dà shān

1. 开聊。chat

例：他整天不干事，只知道侃大山。

He does nothing but sit around and chat.

2. 吹牛。boast

例：我最不喜欢听他侃大山。

I have a strong dislike for his boasts.

侃价 kǎn jià

讨价还价，多指买方往下压低价钱。bargain；haggle with a peddler

例：你得学会如何在自由市场上侃价，否则就要吃亏。

You have to learn how to bargain in the free market or you'll be ripped off.

侃星 kǎn xīng

1. 指非常能开聊的人。chatterbox

例：我的这位朋友真是个侃星。你和他一起工作不会感觉乏味的。

My friend is a real chatterbox. You won't get bored working with him.

2. 指特别能吹牛、说大话的人。a great boaster；a really boastful person

例：我很少把侃星说的话当真。

I seldom take what a great boaster says seriously.

侃爷 kǎn yé

能说或善吹牛的男人。big talker; someone who is good at boasting; someone full of hot air（American slang）

例：他是这楼里的几位侃爷之一。

He is one of the biggest talkers in the building.

砍价 kǎn jià

使价格降低。cut down the price; beat down the price

例：上街买东西时你最好带上她。她可是砍价的好手。

You'd better take her with you if you want to buy something on the street. She is good at cutting down the price.

坎儿 kǎnr

1.关；劫数；障碍。barrier; obstacle; inexorable doom; predestined fate

例：他病得很重。我担心这次他过不了这个坎儿。

He is seriously ill. I'm afraid he won't surmount this obstacle this time.

2.隐语；暗语。code; enigmatic language

例：他们说的都是他们自己的坎儿，你当然听不懂了。

You certainly can't understand them. They are talking in a code of their own.

看好 kàn hǎo

有发展希望；有前途。have a bright future; stand a good chance of success; have good prospects

例：专家预测今年夏天空调的销售市场看好。

Experts predict that sales of air conditioners will stand a good chance of success this summer.

看西洋镜 kàn xī yáng jìng

1.指偷看别人的私生活或秘密。get a glimpse into one's personal life or secrets

例:别在这儿吻我,我可不愿让人看咱们的西洋镜。

Don't kiss me now. I don't like other people to see our private life.

2.指在公众场合围观。circle around and watch

例:那儿一定出事了,否则不会有那么多人看西洋镜。

There must have been an accident over there, otherwise there wouldn't be so many people circled round and watching.

看涨 kàn zhǎng

指行情上涨,价格上升。(of market prices)expected to rise

例:前几天他没有想到这种邮票会看涨。

Several days ago he didn't expect that the value of this stamp would rise.

康师傅 kāng shī fu

1.指一种名为"康师傅"牌的即食面。Chef Kang — a brand of instant noodles

例:我早餐吃了一碗康师傅。

I had a bowl of "Chef Kang" instant noodles for my breakfast.

2.此为"糠"的谐音。指人无能软弱。(of a person) weak, coward, hopeless

例:他整个是一个康师傅,不敢面对这种挑战。对他我算是完全失去信心了。

He's really a coward and doesn't dare to face up to this kind of challenge. I've lost all my confidence in him.

扛 káng

1. 承受;忍受。stand; bear; tolerate; endure

例:这活再苦我也得扛着。

I have to stand it no matter how hard the work is.

2. 对付;应付。deal with; cope with; handle

例:这事太复杂,我担心你扛不住了。

I'm afraid this matter is too complicated for you to handle.

CALL 机 kāo jī

即"呼"机(流行于 20 世纪 90 年代)。pager; beeper (used mostly in the 1990s of the 20th century)

例:他只给我留了个 CALL 机号,说有事就 CALL 他。

He only gave me a pager number and told me to call him when I needed to find him.

靠谱 kào pǔ

指说话办事有准确性。to be accurate or reliable in speech or action

例:听说今年我们能涨工资。你觉得这事靠谱吗?

I heard that we'll be getting raises this year. Do you think it's true?

棵 kē

称面值为一百元的人民币。a hundred-*yuan* bill

例:那个小贩每天至少挣三棵。

The street vendor makes at least three hundred *yuan* a day.

呵碜 kē chen

样子难看。也可以用寒碜。ugly

例:这是你包的饺子呀,真够呵碜的。

Did you make this dumpling? It's so ugly.

磕 kē

拼;硬碰。risk one's life (to fight for sth.); go all out

例:如果今天他不把我的手稿还回来,我就跟他磕到底。

If he doesn't return my manuscript today, I'm going to go all out after him.

磕蜜 kē mì

追求;寻找女友。chase after girls; look for a girlfriend

例:他们找不到他,也许他去磕蜜了。

They couldn't find him. Perhaps he went out girl chasing.

可气 kě qì

指令人气愤、生气。annoying; irritating

例:真可气!我又白跑了一趟。

How irritating! I made a fruitless trip again.

可圈可点 kě quān kě diǎn

原本指在书或文稿上加圆圈或点,作为记号,或用来标出认为值得注意的语句。后形容某人或某事有好有坏,或值得注意或探讨分析。Originally this referred to making circles or dots on a manuscript as notation, or to draw attention. Later it was used to mean that something has both good and bad points, or that something is worth noticing and making further study.

例:不要把小王说的一无是处。他这个人还是有可圈可点的地方嘛。

You shouldn't make Xiao Wang out to be completely lacking in redeeming qualities. He's got his good points.

可心 kě xīn

使人满意;使人喜欢。satisfying; likeable

例 1：我终于找到了可心的工作。

I found a satisfying job at last.

例 2：她买了些她可心的东西。

She bought something she really likes.

剋 kēi

训斥；责骂。scold

例：这件事本来是你做的不对。怎么，还不许人家剋你几句呀？

Actually you didn't do it right. How come you wouldn't let them scold you.

啃 kěn

亲吻。kiss

例 1：他们一见面就啃。

They kiss each other when they meet.

例 2：这小孩多可爱！我真想在她脸上啃几口。

What a lovely child! I really want to kiss her on the cheek.

肯节儿 kèn jiér

事情的一个重要转折点。at the critical moment，at a turning point

例：马上就要高考了，可他偏偏在这个肯节儿上病了。

The college entrance exams are around the corner, but he became sick at the critical moment.

空姐 kōng jiě

民航客机上的女服务员。stewardess

例：高中毕业后她当上了空姐。

She became a stewardess after graduating from high school.

空嫂 kōng sǎo

指已婚的民航空中女服务员。married stewardess

例：每次乘坐民航，你都能享受到空嫂为你提供的热情而周到的服务。

Every time you fly you can enjoy the warmth and good services given by the married stewardesses of CAAC.

空少 kōng shào

指民航空中男服务员。steward

例：她的男友是空少，可帅了。

Her boyfriend is a steward, very handsome.

空手道 kōng shǒu dào

1. 指小偷。petty thief; pilferer (a term originally used in karate)

例：乘坐公共汽车要当心，提防着那些空手道对你下手。

Be careful when you take a public bus for you might be the target of those petty thieves.

2. 指买空卖空，倒买倒卖。Literally it means doing things empty handed or without capital or investment. / A metaphor for a person who buys, sells or exchanges merchandise, etc, without using his own money.

例：张三最早是靠空手道发起来的，如今在市中心开了一家快餐厅。

Zhang San made his fortune by trading on credit at the very beginning. Now he has opened a fast food restaurant downtown.

空调 kōng tiáo

原本指空调机，后引申比喻说出或决定的事情不落实；光说不做，特指许诺调工资，可又不落实，意指空谈。

air-conditioner/A term used to describe an empty talker or someone who simply pays lip service. The term, which also means "empty adjustment" emerged during the teacher salary reform. The department concerned announced the rise in teacher salaries but took a long time before actually implementing the change, hence the term.

例：我听说今年十月又要调工资了。这次不会又是"空调"吧？

I heard that we will have a salary rise this October. It won't be an empty promise again this time, will it?

恐龙 kǒng lóng

（贬义词、起初为网络语言）形容女孩子相貌丑陋。(derogatory term first used on Internet) a dinosaur, a metaphor for an ugly girl

例：这就是你说的美女呀，什么眼力啊！分明是恐龙嘛！

This is the beautiful girl you told me about? What terrible taste you have. Obviously she is an ugly girl.

控办 kòng bàn

控制购买办公用品（多指 20 世纪 80 年代的大件贵重商品）。commodities purchased for office use are controlled/The government controls the purchase of many expensive household commodities（furniture，television，tape recorders，etc. in the 1980s of the 20th century）for office use.

例：几年前家具还是控办商品。

Furniture was listed as a controlled commodity for office use several years ago.

抠门儿 kōu ménr

指小气；吝啬。stingy; mean; closefisted

例：他特别抠门儿。如你问他要一角钱，他多一分都不给你。

He is very stingy. He won't give one more cent if you want a dime.

口碑 kǒu bēi

名声。reputation; fame

例：这个品牌的电视机在这里已经卖了好几年了，口碑不错，顾客都认它。

This brand of television has been sold here for several years and had a good reputation. It has a good market in this city.

口彩 kǒu cǎi

指口头表扬，称赞。praise; extol; acclaim; commend

例：她出色的表演赢得了不少口彩。

Her outstanding performance won much acclaim from the audience.

口头禅 kǒu tóu chán

指常挂在嘴边的话或词句。pet expression

例：A：你还记得七十年代人们流行的口头禅是什么吗？

Do you still remember the most popular expression used in China in the 1970s?

B：怎么不记得，"向毛主席保证"。

Of course I do. "In Chairman Mao's name." How could I ever forget it!

酷毙 kù bì

指人的外表非常冷俊、孤傲，风度不凡；也指最好或最棒。
very or extremely cool; the coolest; the best

例：他长得的确够酷毙的了，难怪广告商都让他来做产品广告。

He really looks very cool. That's why the advertising agent

wanted him to do the ads for the product.

块儿 kuàir

1. 成疙瘩或成团的东西。lump; chunk; piece; cube

例：她给孩子买了些糖块儿。

She bought some lumps of sugar for her child.

2. 指人的体格高大，体形身材魁梧。built; physically strong

例：他真够块儿的，所以女孩子认为他很有魅力。

He is really square built so the girls think he's sexy.

3. 力量；肌肉。muscular; strong

例：史泰龙浑身都是块儿。

Sylvester Stallone is a muscular man.

4. 地方；处所。place; spot

例：他们在这块儿住了好长时间。

They have been living here for quite a long time.

款 kuǎn

挣大钱的人；有钱的人。rich person; money bags

例：他五年前开始种花，如今也算是这小镇上的一个款。

He started growing flowers five years ago. Now he's considered a rich man in the small town.

款哥 kuǎn gē

对有钱男子的昵称。rich brother/An intimate term for a rich man.

例：她认识不少款哥。

She knows many rich men.

款姐 kuǎn jiě

对有钱女子的昵称。rich sister/An intimate term for a rich woman.

例：如今她是个款姐了，出门就打的。

She is a rich woman now. Every time she goes out, she takes a taxi.

款爷 kuǎn yé

挣大钱的，有钱的男子。rich man

例：他看上去不像款爷，因为他的衣着总是十分简朴。

He doesn't look like a rich man because he always wears plain clothes.

狂 kuáng

指极端自高自大；自视清高谁也看不起。arrogant；over bearing

例：这人没多大本事，可还挺狂。

He is very arrogant, but quite useless.

困难户 kùn nan hù

1. 指经济收入不高的家庭或人。low-income household；someone with a low income

例：与那些在独资企业工作的人相比，我们这些国营厂的人可算得上是困难户了。

Compared with those who work in private firms, we are low-income wage earners who work in a government-run factory.

2. 指人长相很差，很难让人看上。bad looking；ugly；hard for someone to love

例：她可不是困难户，只不过是她不愿结婚罢了。

She's not bad looking; she just doesn't want to get married.

L

拉倒 lā dǎo

算了；别提了；不干了。forget about it; never mind; drop it; let it go at that

例1：我没钱买，所以这事还是拉倒吧。

I don't have enough money for it, so let it go at that.

例2：拉倒吧！反正也不值几个钱。

Never mind. It doesn't cost too much anyway.

拉钩 lā gōu

指发誓；许诺某事不再反悔。pull each others' little fingers/ A term which refers to making a promise or swearing to do sth.

例：我看完这本书就还你，不信咱们可以拉钩。

I'll return this book after I finish it. If you don't believe me, we'll pull fingers on it.

拉饥荒 lā jī huāng

欠债。be in debt; run into debt; owe a debt

例：她爱买衣服，所以常常拉饥荒。

She enjoys buying clothes so she is in debt frequently.

辣妹子 là mèi zi

指性格泼辣、胆子大、性急、嘴巴能说的女孩子。hot girl/A girl who is bold, hot- and quick-tempered with a sharp tongue.

例：跟她打交道要小心点儿，她可是出了名的辣妹子。

Be careful dealing with her. She is known as a vixen.

辣子 là zi

指辣椒。hot pepper

例：他每顿都离不开辣子。

He can't have meal without hot peppers.

来菜 lái cài

有机会；有事干；有买卖（生意）。do business；have a chance；have sth. to do

例：如果再不来菜，这厂子就要关板儿了。

The factory will close down if it runs out of business.

来电 lái diàn

指男女间相互产生好感。(of both sexes) to fall in love with someone

例：我们先后给他介绍了三个女朋友，可都因为他总不来电，所以没成。

We have introduced him to three girlfriends. But none of them succeeded because he has not fallen in love with any of them.

来劲 lái jìn

1. 有劲头；使振奋。get excited；become alive；get pumped up；become full of energy；inspire

例1：听说要与别的队比赛，他们马上来劲了。

They got pumped up the minute they heard about the competition with the other team.

例2：听到中国女排获冠军的消息真让人来劲。

We were inspired by the news that the Chinese women's volleyball team won the world championship.

2. 捣乱；找麻烦。make trouble；find fault with

例：看别人干得好，她就来劲。

She likes to find faults with people who do their work well.

来三 lái sān

1.指人精明能干。smart and capable

例:侬(你)来三。

You are smart.

2.指(某事)可以;可行。all right; OK

例:这样做不来三。

This won't work.

赖 lài

1.不好;坏。bad; no good; poor

例:你的办公条件还不赖。

Your working conditions are not bad.

2.赖皮;不认账。not admit what one has said or done; not acknowledge a debt (or an account); shameful; unsports-manlike

例:你真赖,总是自食其言。

Shame on you. You always break your promises.

揽爷 lǎn yé

1.招揽旅客住旅馆从中得利的人。hotel introducer/People (usually men) who stand outside busy areas (usually rail-way stations) and try to solicit customers often aggressive-ly to stay in hotels, for which they get a cut of the profit from the hotels.

例:在火车站有许多揽爷。

There are many hotel introducers at the railway station.

2.包揽生意,充当中间人,从中获利的人。agent; a middle-man

例:不少公司通过揽爷帮他们扩大财源。

Many companies hire agents to help them to drum up business.

懒汉鞋 lǎn hàn xié

一种布面松紧口、不用系带的鞋。"lazy man's shoe"/A shoe that has a cloth cover and no shoestrings.

例：老年人喜欢穿懒汉鞋，因为它轻松舒适，而且易穿脱。

The old like to wear lazy man's shoes because they are soft and comfortable and easy to put on and take off.

浪 làng

1. 放纵；举止轻浮（多形容女性）。(of women) frivolous; flighty

例：我是个很传统的人，不喜欢我妹妹的那副浪样。

I'm a very traditional person. I don't like my sister's frivolous behavior.

2. 逛。stroll; wander

例：我不知那家伙浪到哪里去了。

I don't know where the fellow has wandered off to.

浪头 làng tou

指说话的口气，多指说话口气大，或说话办事华而不实。

(lit.) wave/A metaphor usually used to describe people who talk big, but don't actually do anything about it.

例：看你浪头不小，可一点儿浪花也不起。

You only talk big, but never bother to take any action.

捞 lāo

顺手拉或拿。to easily bring or take something

例：他每次回家都能捞点东西回来。

He always takes something back whenever he goes home.

捞外块 lāo wài kuài

指追求工资以外的收益;除工资收入外再靠打工或做生意挣钱。make extra money apart from one's salary by doing business or a part time job; moonlight

例1:他每天晚上都不在家,靠到餐馆洗盘子捞外块。

He is always out in the evening making extra money by washing dishes in a restaurant.

例2:他每天下了班就忙着去捞外块。

He is busy making extra money every day after work.

劳模 láo mó

指劳动模范。model worker

例:她是全国十大劳模之一。

She is one of the top ten model workers in the country.

老爸 lǎo bà

对父亲的称呼。father; dad

例:今天我要早回家,因为我老爸病了。

I'm going home early today because my father is ill.

老帮子 lǎo bāng zi

指年纪大的人(含不敬的意思)。old person; old fogy; old fart/An impolite term for the elderly.

例:别烦我,你这老帮子。

Don't bother me, you old fogy.

老鼻子 lǎo bí zi

1. 极多。much more; far more

例:他在抽烟上花的钱老鼻子了,足够买一幢新房子的了。

He spent far more money on smoking, enough to buy a new house.

New Slang of China 最新中国俚语

2.很早;很久以前。long time ago; far back; remote past

例:那都是老鼻子的事情了,提它还有什么意思。

It's a boring to mention it again. It's a story from far far back.

老不死的 lǎo bù sǐ de

称年老的人;老家伙(骂人话或亲昵语)。(swearword or intimate term)old fellow; old folk; old fogy; old fart/An impolite term for the elderly.

例:天快黑了,那个老不死的到哪儿去了?

Where's the old fart gone? It's getting dark.

老插 lǎo chā

指老知青;曾下乡插队后返城的人。old re-educated youth/The generation of Chinese, most now in their 40's, who have returned to the cities after having been sent down to the countryside to be re-educated by farmers during the "cultural revolution" (1966-1976).

例:老插们常聚在一起追忆插队时那段生活。

The old re-educated youth often get together and reminisce about the time they spent in the countryside.

老大 lǎo dà

1.称黑帮中的头领。Literally it means the eldest of sisters and brothers. /A metaphor for a head of a gang or a bandit chieftain.

例:他要见你们老大,有要事相商。

He wants to see your head and has something important to discuss.

2.称国营大中型企业。It refers to large- and medium-sized enterprises run by the state.

例:如今老大的日子不好过。最大的问题就是如何解决下岗职工的生活问题和再就业的问题。

Now state-run large- and medium-sized enterprises are having a difficult time. The biggest problem is how to solve the living problems of laid-off employees and find them jobs again.

老到 lǎo dao

指办事经验丰富,周到细致。experienced; sophisticated; considerate; careful

例:这家伙精明老到。你不是他的对手。

He is very shrewd and sophisticated. You are no match for him.

老东西 lǎo dōng xi

指不被喜欢的老年人。unwelcomed old creature (person)/ An impolite term used to describe some old men not liked.

例:我不喜欢这老东西,因为他总想控制我。

I don't like the old creature, because he always wants to control me.

老赶 lǎo gǎn

1.指不懂行的人。amateur; nonprofessional person; layman

例:论做生意我可是老赶。

I'm a layman in the trade.

2.未见世面的人;愚昧无知的人。ignorant; benighted; hillbilly

例:你真老赶,连这个是干什么用的都不知道。

You're really ignorant, you even don't know what this is used for.

老公 lǎo gōng

指丈夫。husband; old man; hubby

例：她老公是司机。

Her hubby is a driver.

老姑娘 lǎ gū niang

指老处女；未婚女子（常指年过三十岁的未婚女子）。old maid; spinster/Usually refers to an unmarried woman over 30 years old.

例：那个老姑娘不住在这儿。她两年前就搬走了。

That old maid doesn't live here. She moved out two years ago.

老家儿 lǎo jiār

父母。parents

例：出国留学的事最好跟老家儿打个招呼，免得他们为你担心，还以为你找不到工作呢。

You'd better tell your parents about your plan to go abroad to study just in case they are worried about you because they thought you couldn't find a job.

老来俏 lǎo lái qiào

指年纪虽老却打扮入时，穿戴花哨的人。hip older person/ A term to describe an older person who dresses in clothes popular among younger people.

例：别人常逗她说她是个老来俏，可她对此毫不在乎。

Others often joke with her calling her a hip older person, but she doesn't care what they say about her.

老冒儿 lǎo màor

指乡下人；外行；没见过世面的人。country person; layman;

hick; ignorant and ill-informed person

例：你真老冒儿，连什么是 BP 机都不知道。

You're such a hick—you don't even know what a pager is.

老美 lǎo měi

美国人。American

例：那两个老美能说一口流利的中文。

The two Americans can speak fluent Chinese.

老模砢碜眼 lǎo mó kē chen yǎn

形容人年纪大，眼皮下垂，容貌难看的样子（含贬义）。ugly; unsightly; bad looking/A derogatory term that describes those who are old and not good looking any more.

例：她认为自己老模砢碜眼的，穿什么也不会好看。

She thinks she's so old and ugly that nothing will look good on her.

老莫 lǎo mò

北京莫斯科餐厅。the Moscow Restaurant in Beijing

例：她请她父母去老莫吃西餐。

She treated her parents to Western-style food at the Moscow Restaurant in Beijing.

老蔫(儿) lǎo niān(r)

指性子慢，办事不爽快，或不爱说话的人。slowpoke; slow, sluggish, slothful person; taciturn person

例：我那口子可是个典型的老蔫儿。他干起活儿来那叫一个慢，谁看了都着急。

My husband is a typical slowpoke. He does things so slowly that anyone watching feels exasperated.

老娘 lǎo niáng

1. 指老母亲。old mother; old lady

例：她得照顾她的老娘。

She has to take care of her old mother.

2. 中年妇女自称（多用于打架愤怒时）。old biddy/A term of self reference used by middle-aged woman in intense moments.

例：今天你不把这事说清楚，老娘不会放了你。

I won't let you leave this old biddy here unless you make these things clear today.

老人家 lǎo rén jiā

1. 指毛泽东。Mao Zedong; Chairman Mao

例：他时刻铭记着老人家说过的那句话："要全心全意地为人民服务。"

He always keeps Chairman Mao's words about "serving the people heart and soul" in mind.

2. 称年长者。elderly

例：那位老人家多大年岁了？

How old is that elderly person?

老日 lǎo rì

指日元。Japanese Yen（￥）

例：我手上还有点儿老日，你需要就都拿去。

I have some Japanese Yen left. You can take them all if you need them.

老鼠会 lǎo shǔ huì

也称为传销。a mouse meeting（association）/A metaphor for a pyramid sale.

例：前两年全国各地有不少老鼠会。我听说过，但没有参加过。

Two years ago there were many mouse associations all over the country. I heard of them, but didn't join in.

老头儿 lǎo tóur

1. 年老的男子。old man; old chap

例：那老头儿是我的邻居。

The old man over there is my neighbor.

2. 指父亲。father

例：我们家老头儿五年前退的休，如今正在学国画。

My father retired five years ago and is now studying Chinese painting.

3. 指丈夫。husband

老头儿票 lǎo tóur piào

面值为一百元的人民币。a hundred-*yuan* note/So nicknamed because of the four men on it.

例：我今天挣了四张老头票。

I made four hundred *yuan* today.

老外 lǎo wài

1. 外国人。foreigner

例：她嫁给一个老外，跟他出国了。

She married a foreigner and went abroad.

2. 外行。layman; someone unexperienced

例：你真老外，我告诉你如何用这个工具。

You're a layman. Let me show you how to use this tool.

老爷子 lǎo yé zi

1. 父亲。father; dad

例:今天你可以来,因为老爷子不在家。

You can come today because my father's not at home.

2.年老的男子。old man; old chap

例:你得大声跟这位老爷子说话,他的耳朵背。

You have to speak louder to the old man. His hearing is bad.

老油条 lǎo yóu tiáo

形容十分油滑或奸滑的人。a slippery or cunning person

例:他是生意场上的老油条了。

He is very cunning at doing business.

老子 lǎo zi

1.称父亲。father

例:她老子是大官儿。

Her dad is a high-ranking official.

2.指自己;我(表示狂妄,自大)。oneself (in arrogant or conceited tones)

例:老子做事从不半途而废。

This soul never gives up anything midway.

唠 lào

说;谈;聊。chat; talk

例:我们有几年没见面了,今晚咱们好好唠一唠。

We haven't seen each other for years. Let's have a good gab tonight.

唠嗑 lào kē

闲聊;闲谈;聊天。chat; talk

例:晚饭后老爷子就找邻居唠嗑去了。

My father went to chat with my neighbor after dinner.

落忍 lào rěn

指安心;坦实;过意得去;不以为然。feel all right (comfortable or natural); have peace of mind; feel at ease

例:你怎么能落忍让这么小的孩子干这么重的活儿。

How could you feel at ease making the little child do such heavy work?

乐子 lè zi

1.愉快的事;高兴的事。pleasure; delight

例:退休的人通常利用学画、学书法或养鸟来找乐子。

Retired people usually find their pleasure in learning painting or calligraphy or bird raising.

2.引人发笑的事(含有幸灾乐祸的意思)。joke; laughing stock; poke fun at

例:这些坏家伙专门捉弄人来找乐子。

These bad chaps like to make jokes by playing tricks on others.

雷 léi

灾祸。thunder/A metaphor for disaster; calamity; catastrophe

例:对我来说这真是一个不小的雷。

This is really a big calamity for me.

雷子 léi zi

(黑话)指警察;公安人员。cop; policeman; public security man

例:小偷让雷子盯上了。

The thief was tailed by a cop.

累 lèi

处处小心谨慎;拘谨;不洒脱;不快活。overcautious; too restrained

例:她活得真累。她总担心自己的话会伤他人的感情。

She is overcautious. She's afraid anything she says will offend someone.

愣 lèng

1.失神;呆。distracted; stupefied; blank

例:你站在这儿发什么愣呢?

Why are you standing here staring blankly?

2.说话做事不考虑效果,硬来;鲁莽。rash; foolhardy; reckless

例:他是个愣小子,办什么事都不考虑后果。

He's a rash young fellow. He does everything recklessly.

3.(表示惊讶)竟然;认定(语气词,表示坚决、肯定)。definitively; surprisingly

例1:店主愣说我没付水果钱。

The shop owner said definitively that I didn't pay for the fruit.

例2:今天巴西足球队愣输了。

To everyone's surprise, the Brazil Soccer Team lost the game today.

哩咯愣 lī gē lēng

指假装糊涂;故意打马虎眼。pretend not to know; act like a fool; play the fool; act dumb

例:别跟我这儿玩哩咯愣,这事你比我明白多了。

Don't play the fool with me. You understand more about this than me.

里弄 lǐ nòng

1. 巷；胡同。alley；lane

例：上海的里弄又窄又拥挤。

The alleys in Shanghai are narrow and crowded.

2. 街道。neighborhood；residential district

例：去年当地政府建立了里弄活动中心。

The neighborhood entertainment center was established last year by the local authorities.

礼拜 lǐ bài

1. 星期。week

例：一个礼拜有七天。

There are seven days in a week.

2. 星期中的日期。day of the week

例：今天是礼拜一。

Today is Monday.

3. 周末或星期天。weekend

例：中国也有大礼拜（星期六、日休息）。

Now Chinese people have a "big weekend" which includes Saturday and Sunday.

立马儿 lì mǎr

立刻；马上。immediately；at once；right away

例：如事情紧急我立马儿就走。

I will go at once if it is urgent.

利市 lì shì

1. 买卖顺利的预兆。prediction of business prosperity；omen of good fortune to come

例：你们这家书店的利市不错，开张第一天就卖了一千多元的书。

It is a good sign for business that your bookstore made over one thousand *yuan* in sales on its first day.

2. 压岁钱；红包。money given to children as a lunar New Year gift; red envelope; bonus

例：我用春节她爷爷给她的利市为她买了一个洋娃娃。

I bought my daughter a doll with the money given by her grandfather at the Spring Festival.

粒豆 lì dòu

人民币。Chinese currency for RMB

例：只要有粒豆，你想吃什么都能买到。

You can buy anything you want to eat as long as you have RMB.

练 liàn

1. 比试；较量。challenge; have a competition

例：你敢跟我练一练看谁更厉害吗？

Do you dare to have a competition with me to see who is better?

2. 揍；打架。beat; thrash; beating; thrashing

例：你是不是找练呀？

You're looking for a thrashing, aren't you?

3. 从事某种活动或工作。work; engage in sth.

例：由于原料没运来，所以今天我们不练了。

We won't work today because the materials have not arrived.

练摊儿 liàn tānr

摆摊；经营商品。set up a stall to sell goods; run a private stall

例：他辞了工厂的工作，练摊儿卖书去了。

He gave up his job as a factory worker to set up a stall and sell books.

亮报口 liàng bào kǒu

表明身份。to make one's identity known

亮点 liàng diǎn

指引人注目的人或事。(lit.) a bright spot/A metaphor for (sb. or sth.) to be attractive; eye-catching; attract attention.

例：澳门回归无疑会是去年的一个亮点。

The return of Macao to her motherland was no doubt one of last year's attention attracting events.

晾 liàng

把某人放在一旁，不去答理。purposely ignore; intentionally brush aside

例：她只愿同朋友聊天，把我晾在一边。

She talked with her friends and ignored me.

靓 liàng

指漂亮；好看。pretty; good looking; beautiful

例：她长得够靓。

She's very pretty.

靓女 liàng nǚ

指长相漂亮的年轻女子。pretty girl

例：有些杂志选用靓女做封面来吸引顾客。

Some magazines choose pretty girls to appear on the cover of their magazines so that they attract buyers.

靓仔 liàng zǎi

指长相好的年轻男子。good looking man；handsome young man

例：他是影视界最受欢迎的靓仔。

He is the most popular good looking man in the movie and television circles.

蹽 liāo

1. 快速地走。walk swiftly；stride rapidly

例：他蹽开步子就走了。

He took long strides and left in a hurry.

2. 悄悄地走或离开。sneak away；leave quietly

例：这家伙没有跟我招呼一声就蹽了。

The fellow sneaked away without a word to me.

撩人 liáo rén

情绪激昂的，（感官）刺激的，挑逗的。stirring；exciting；hot；teasing

例：刚才那个舞蹈可真够撩人的。

That dance performed just now was really stirring.

了了 liǎo le

结束；解决了；完了；了结。be over；end；finish；settle

例：这事了了之后，我就去海边度假。

I'll take a beach vocation after the task is over.

料 liào

1. 材料。material

例：这点儿料哪够用呢？

Is this little bit of material enough?

2. 适合从事某种事情的条件、素质或材料。makings；material or qualities needed for the development or making of sth.

例：我可不是运动员的料。

I don't have the makings of athlete.

咧咧 liē lie

说(含贬义)。使用时，常与"胡"或"瞎"连用。to talk (often used with '*hu*' or '*xia*')

例：你别跟我胡咧咧了。我还有正事急着要办呢。

Don't talk nonsense to me. I have some pressing business to do right now.

猎头 liè tóu

寻找各行各业中的高级人才。head hunting；look for senior talented people in all kinds of fields

例：猎头公司是一个专门为客户猎头，推荐所需人才的服务公司。

A head hunting agency is a service company which engages in head hunting and recommending required talents to its agents.

临了 lín liǎo

到头；到底；最后。in the end；finally

例：他打算同妻子女儿一起去，可临了还是自己一个人去了。

He planned to go with his wife and daughter, but in the end he went alone.

零碎儿 líng suìr

1.零散杂乱的事物或东西。odds and ends；bits and pieces

例：谁能帮我把这些零碎儿扔出去？

Who can help me throw these odds and ends out of the room?

2.脏话；骂人话。swearword；dirty word；curse words；abusive

language

例：他没有什么教养，说话时常带出不少零碎儿。

He's not well-bred. He often uses swearwords when he speaks.

另类 lìng lèi

指与众不同的、特殊的、时髦的一种类型。a different, special, completely new or fashionable type or trend

例：他在力求探索一种全新的写作方式，根本不在乎是否别人会将他的作品视为另类。

He is trying a completely new way of writing and doesn't care whether others will consider his work special or not.

琉璃猫 liú li māo

比喻十分吝啬的人。glazed cat/A metaphor for a mean person.

例：大家知道他是琉璃猫，让他出钱实在难。

Everyone knows that he is very mean. It's hard to get any money out of him.

溜 liù

流利；熟练。skilled; fluent

例：她英语讲得挺溜。

She speaks English very fluently.

遛弯儿 liù wānr

散步。take a walk; go for a stroll

例：他带着狗去遛弯儿了。

He took his dog for a walk.

睽 lōu

看。have a look-see

例：1. 让咱睽睽。

Let me peep.

例：2. 我听说你近来买了一块新表，能让咱睽睽吗？

I heard that you have bought a new watch recently. Could I have a look-see?

撸 lū

1. 用手握住条状物向一端滑动。rub one's palm along (sth.)

例：我手上都是泥。你能帮我把袖子撸一下吗？

My hands are dirty. Could you help me push up my sleeves?

2. 撤销（职务）。fire someone; sack someone from his post

例：如果你再不听我的命令我就撸了你。

If you disobey my order next time, I'll fire you.

3. 训斥；斥责。rebuke; dress down; reprimand

例：他考试不及格被他父亲狠狠地撸了一顿。

He failed the examination and was reprimanded severely by his father.

露脸 lù liǎn

1. 指某人出现。show up; appear

例：她几天没露脸了。我想她一定是病了。

She hasn't shown up for days. I think she must be ill.

2. （给某人）增光添彩；争光。do credit to; win honor for

例：他比赛得了冠军，也算给他自己露脸了。

He did credit to himself by winning first prize in the competition.

路子 lù zi

1. 方法；办法；途径。way; method; means

例：他解决问题的路子对头。

He knows the right way to solve the problem.

2. 关系；后门。connections; pull; influence (needed to get sth. done)

例：他有路子买低价钢材。

He has the connections to buy steel at a cheap price.

路子野 lù zi yě

渠道多；关系多；办法多。be well-connected

例：如果你有难处尽管找他帮忙。他认识不少人，路子很野。

If you have any problems you can turn to him for help. He's well-connected and knows a lot of important people.

抡 lūn

1. 抽；打；揍；扔。slap one's face; hit; beat; swing

例1：他狠狠地抡了那家伙一个耳光。

He slapped the guy's face hard.

例2：他差点儿抡我一个跟头。

He nearly knocked me down.

2. 瞎扯；胡说八道。talk rubbish; talk nonsense

例：他们都知道她是个严肃的人，所以很少跟她抡。

They know she is a serious person so they seldom talk rubbish with her.

抡圆了 lūn yuán le

使足劲；甩开手臂。swing one's arms with all one's might; exert all one's strength

例：他抡圆了给那小子一个耳光。

He walloped that guy in the face.

L

裸机 luǒ jī

没有注册登记的手机。unregistered cellular phones

例：这个牌子的裸机在香港买比这儿要便宜的多。

This brand of unregistered cell phone is much cheaper if you buy it in Hong Kong.

落单 luò dān

指失去配偶的人，寡妇或鳏夫。widow / widower

例：孤独寂寞是那些落单老人最大的敌人。

Loneliness is the greatest enemy of widows or widowers.

M

麻利儿地 má lìr di

赶快；立刻。quickly; promptly; at once; immediately

例：他老婆吩咐做什么，他总是麻利儿地去干，而且从无怨言。

He quickly does everything his wife orders and never complains.

马大嫂 mǎ dà sǎo

此为上海话"买"、"洗"、"炒"的谐音，意指干家务活的人。

"Madam Ma"/In Shanghai dialect the three words sound the same as the words for shopping, washing and cooking. It refers to a woman or man who does housework.

例：小李自从结婚后便当上了马大嫂。

Xiao Li became a housewife after she got married.

马屁精 mǎ pì jīng

指爱奉承领导的人。ass-kisser; boot licker; flatterer; brown-noser

例：他看不起办公室那几个马屁精。他觉得他们是世上最没本事的人。

He despises the brown-nosers in his office. He thinks they are the people good for nothing in the world.

马爷 mǎ yé

指警察。cop; policeman

例：别看他现在狂得很，可一见马爷就尿(sóng)。

Although he's very arrogant now, he looks weak and incompetent as soon as he sees a cop.

马仔 mǎ zǎi

指替黑帮头领干活的人或帮凶。gangster; accomplice

例：昨天在一家旅馆里抓到两个马仔,缴获了一些他们随身携带的毒品。

Two gangsters were arrested in a hotel yesterday and some drugs were found on them and seized.

马子 mǎ zi

女朋友;情人。girlfriend; lover

例：今晚他准备带着马子去看电影。

He plans to take his girlfriend to see a movie tonight.

码 mǎ

堆放;摆放。put in order; pile up; stack

例1：把书码在墙角。

Pile up the books in the corner.

例2：她帮我把服装按号的大小码好。

She helped me put the clothes in order according to size.

码长城 mǎ cháng chéng

指打麻将牌。build the Great Wall/A metaphor for playing mahjong.

例：他们天天晚上码长城。

They play mahjong every evening.

埋单 mái dān

结账;付款。"bury the bill"; pay the bill

例1：你们两位别争,我已埋单了。

Don't argue, you two. I've already paid the bill.

例2：伙计,埋单。

Waiter, please bring the bill.

脉门 mài mén

指关键；主要部分。key；heart；the most important part

例：如果你找到事情的脉门，你就能顺利地解决矛盾。

If you get to the heart of the matter, you'll solve the problem easily.

卖青苗 mài qīng miáo

指卖书稿。sell young crops/A metaphor for selling book manuscripts.

例：她非常喜欢写作，以至于她干脆辞去了工作专门在家写作，以卖青苗为生。

She is so fond of writing that she finally gave up her job and stayed at home to write. She makes a living by selling the manuscript of her novels.

卖相 mài xiàng

1.指东西的外观或外包装。exterior；outward appearance；packaging

例：顾客越来越注重商品的卖相。

Customers pay more attention to the packaging of goods than to the goods themselves.

2.指人的长相（多含贬义）。looks；appearance (often used as a derogatory term)

例：你有这么好的卖相，不愁找不到好的工作。

You are so pretty. You needn't worry too much about not finding a good job.

蛮 mán

指很；挺。pretty；quite

例：这人还是蛮能干的。

He is quite a capable man.

满 mǎn

表示程度,有"很"、"挺"的意思。very; rather; fairly

例1:我的身体满好。

I'm pretty well.

例2:这件衣服满漂亮。

This dress is very beautiful.

满地找牙 mǎn dì zhǎo yá

比喻被打得很厉害,鼻青脸肿,牙齿也被打掉了。be badly beaten; be seriously battered (lit., pick one's teeth up from the ground)

例:你听着,下次再来捣乱我就让你满地找牙。

Believe me. I'll have your teeth knocked off next time if you come to trouble me.

满脸车道沟 mǎn liǎn chē dào gōu

比喻人的脸上满是皱纹。a metaphor to describe a face full of wrinkles and furrows

例:你瞧她那张脸,已经是满脸车道沟了。

Look at her face. It is already full of wrinkles and furrows.

满脸旧社会 mǎn liǎn jiù shè huì

形容人的长相很苦,而且布满了皱纹,一副饱经风霜的样子。It refers to someone with a weather-worn face, filled with wrinkles, as if he or she had gone through a very hard life.

例:你长得多喜庆啊,不像我满脸旧社会的,难怪女孩子都爱跟你说话。

You have a joyful look, not like me with my weather-worn face. No doubt girls all like to talk with you.

满脸跑眉毛 mǎn liǎn pǎo méi mao

形容面部表情十分丰富,眉毛上下乱跑。(a person) with dancing eyebrows; with a rich facial expression/An expression used to describe someone who is bright and cheery when talking with others.

例:也许她自己不知道她说话时会满脸跑眉毛。

Perpaps she doesn't know she has such a rich, cheery facial expression when she speaks.

满脸双眼皮 mǎn liǎn shuāng yǎn pí

形容皱纹很多。have a wrinkly face

例:三十年前她是个漂亮的姑娘,可如今是满脸双眼皮。

She was a very pretty girl thirty years ago, but now her face is full of wrinkles.

满世界 mǎn shì jiè

到处;各个地方;处处。everywhere; in all places; all over; the world over

例:她满世界地找她的手表,结果还是没找着。

She looked everywhere and could not find her watch.

忙活 máng huo

指忙碌。be busy; bustle with

例:为了结婚她已经忙活了三天。

She has been busy for three days on account of her wedding.

盲流 máng liú

盲目离家外出寻找工作的人。jobless peasants in search of work

例:每年全国有成千上万的盲流。

There are thousands of peasants seeking work throughout the country every year.

猫 māo

躲藏。hide

例1:你猫在那儿干吗?

Why on earth are you hiding there?

例2:他偷了钱就猫起来了。

He stole some money and went underground.

猫冬 māo dōng

冬天躲在家里不出来干活。to stay at home and work indoors for the whole winter

例:如今的人们都想方设法地挣钱,就连爱猫冬的人也利用冬闲的日子出来找活干了。

Nowadays people are trying everything to make money. Even those who used to stay at home during the winter are going out to look for work in the winter season.

猫儿腻 māor nì

指私下进行的不正常的活动或交易。illegal deal; underhanded activity

例:他们推迟几天宣布获奖名单。谁知道他们要玩什么猫儿腻?

They postponed announcing the winners' names for a few days. Who knows what underhanded activities they're doing?

猫眼(儿)māo yǎn(r)

门镜;窥视镜。peephole, such as those with fisheye lenses found on doors in hotels or households

例：他不开门，只透过猫眼儿就能看清门外的一切。

He can see everything clearly through the peephole on the door without having to open it.

毛 máo

1.指人民币的角。same as *jiao*/A fractional unit of money in China (＝1/10 of a *yuan* or 10 *fen*).

例：从上个月起每份晚报已由四毛涨到了五毛。

Since last month the price of the Beijing Evening Daily has risen from four *mao* (forty *fen*) to five *mao* (fifty *fen*).

2.发火；发怒 get angry; lose one's temple

例：你去见他说话要当心，别把他惹毛了。

Beware of what you say to him when you go to see him. Don't make him angry.

毛毛雨 máo máo yǔ

指某事无关紧要；无所谓；没什么大不了的。drizzle/A metaphor for something not very important or serious.

例：他有的是钱。我们涨这么一点价对他只不过是毛毛雨罢了。

He is well off. It doesn't matter at all if we put the price up a little bit.

毛片 máo piān

指黄色的描写性爱的淫秽录像或电影。pornographic video or movie; porno flick

例：他从境外带回几盘毛片录像带。

He brought home some pornographic video tapes from abroad.

毛票 máo piào

1.指毛泽东纪念邮票。commemorative stamp of Mao Zedong

例:在集邮市场一张毛票能卖到千元。

In the stamp market one commemorative stamp of Mao Ze-dong can be sold at one thousand *yuan* RMB.

2.指一角,两角或五角的纸币。one-*jiao*, two-*jiao* or five-*jiao* note of Chinese currency (One *jiao* equals ten *fen* or ten cents.)

例:我每次都把买东西找回来的毛票给孩子。

Every time I go shopping I give all the small change to my child.

毛腔 máo qiāng

指骂人或发脾气。swear; curse; lose one's temper

例:他总是顺从他老婆,从不发半点儿毛腔。

He's always an obedient husband, and never loses his temper.

冒 mào

指傻,没见过世面。stupid; unexperienced

例:你真够冒的,连车门都不会开。

You're so stupid! You don't even know how to open a car door.

冒泡 mào pào

指开张;有生意;有买卖。have business; have a deal

例:由于下雨,我已三天没冒泡了。

I haven't had a deal for three days because of the rain.

冒傻气 mào shǎ qì

干不明智、不聪明或糊涂的事。do sth. unwise; unclever or stupid

例：别当着客人的面冒傻气。如果你不懂那是什么，就干脆把嘴闭起来。

Don't do anything stupid in front of the guests. If you don't know what you're talking about, don't say anything at all.

冒儿爷 màor yé

指土里土气、傻头傻脑、没见过世面的人。也称"傻冒儿"。clod-hopper; country bumpkin; stupid person; dodo

例：你可真是个冒儿爷，连西装袖口上的商标也不摘就这么穿出去了，不叫人笑话才怪呢。

You're really a bumpkin. How could you wear this suit without removing the label from the sleeves. There is no doubt that people would have laughed at you.

没的说 méi de shuō

1. 没有任何缺点。have no faults or mistakes; be perfect

例：他做的家具没的说。

The furniture he made is perfect.

2. 没有商量或分辩的余地。have no room for discussion; not open to debate

例：没的说，该轮到我用这台电脑了。

There is no room for discussion. It's time for me to use the computer.

3. 指不成问题。have no problem

例：为你办这点儿小事，没的说。

It's no problem for me to do such a little thing for you.

没好气 méi hǎo qì

态度不好；没有礼貌。hostile; impolite; unkind; feel bad; turn a cold eye

例1：我曾被狗咬过，所以每当我看到狗时，我就对它没好气。

I was injured by a dog so whenever I see one, I'll turn a hostile look on it.

例 2：我不喜欢他，所以跟他说话总没好气。

I always speak impolitely to him because I don't like him.

没劲 méi jìn

1. 没意思。uninteresting; boring

例：这电影真没劲，我看了一半就出来了。

This film was so boring that I walked out in the middle.

2. 没出息。(of person) good-for-nothing; not very promising

例：我看那人没劲，压根儿不值得你去为他流泪。

I think he's good-for-nothing. He's no worth crying about at all.

没门儿 méi ménr

1. 没有办法；无出路。have no way out; have no idea

例：别指望我多搞些票，我可没门儿。

Don't depend on me. I have no ideas how to get more tickets.

2. 没有线索；没有成形。get no clues; not take shape

例：我现在不能跟你讲得太多，这计划还没门儿呢。

I can't tell you too much about the plan now. It hasn't taken shape yet.

3. 休想得到；甭想。no way; no go; absolutely impossible

例：没门儿，你别想把女儿从我身边带走。

No way. You can't take my daughter away from me.

没脾气 méi pí qi

指无可奈何；没有办法。have no way out; be at the end of one's rope

例：人家就是不让你进去,你不是也没脾气。

You're at the end of your rope if they refuse to let you in.

没谱 méi pǔ

1.没有影子;没有实现;不着边际。unsure; unrealistic; be irrelevant; unsettled

例1:你还得再多等会儿,这事还没谱。

You have to wait longer because the matter has not been settled yet.

例2:他说话总是没谱。

He always mouths irrelevant talk.

2.不知道。have no idea; not know

例:他何时来我可没谱。

I have no idea when he will come.

没起子 méi qǐ zi

骂人没出息;窝囊。spineless; good-for-nothing; hopelessly stupid

例:他真没起子。

He is good-for-nothing.

没日子 méi rì zi

没有希望;没有盼头。have no hope; expect nothing; not have the day

例:如果老板得到那份材料,你晋升的事就没日子了。

There will be no hope for you to get a promotion if your boss receives the material.

没商量 méi shāng liáng

无商量的余地;主意已定,不容改变。be settled; impossible to change; have no room to reconsider

例:你没必要去找他。无论对错,只要他决定的事就绝对没商量。

You needn't go to see him. No matter what he decides, right or wrong, he won't change his mind.

没完没了 méi wán méi liǎo

无休止的;不停的。ceaseless; endless; restless

例:她喜欢和别人没完没了地说。

She enjoys incessant talk with others.

没戏 méi xì

原指文艺演出不吸引人。现引申为没有希望;没有任何可能。

have no hope; hopeless; impossible/A term that originally referred to a dull and uninteresting performance.

例:想晋升你没戏,你不是他们想要的那种人。

There's no way for you to get promoted. You're not the person they want.

没心没肺 méi xīn méi fèi

指人心胸开阔,不计较。have no heart and lungs/One who is tolerant; broad-minded and doesn't fuss.

例:她这人没心没肺,很快就会忘掉跟你吵架的事,并待你同以前一样好。

She is broad-minded. She'll soon forget the quarrel with you and treat you as well as before.

没着没落 méi zhāo méi lào

1.指不安稳;不踏实。unsteady; unsure; anxious

例:她一接不到儿子的信,心里就没着没落的。

She always gets anxious when she doesn't receive a letter

from her son.

2.指没有决定；没有处理。unsettled；unresolved

例：她调动工作的事还没着没落呢。

Her transfer to a new job is still unresolved.

没辙 méi zhé

没有办法；没有主意。have no other way out；have no solution

例：如果他们不同意放你走，我也没辙。

I have no solution if they don't agree to let you go.

没治 méi zhì

1.没有希望；没有任何办法。hopeless；helpless

例：真没治，他谁的话也不听。

He's completely helpless. He doesn't listen to anyone.

2.特别好。excellent；incredible

例：这节目演得真是没治了。

This is an excellent performance.

没咒念 méi zhòu niàn

没有办法；没有主意。have no other way out；have no solution

例：事已至此，他也没咒念了。

He has no idea what to do when things come to a head.

没主 méi zhǔ

1.没有所属的人。belongs to nobody

例：我捡了一个没主的钱包。

I found a purse which nobody claimed.

2.指女性没有结婚，没有男朋友。unmarried woman；woman who has no boyfriend

例：你能帮她介绍个男朋友吗？她还没主呢。

Would you please introduce a boyfriend to her? She's still single.

没准儿 méi zhǔnr

1. 不一定；可能；或许。perhaps; maybe

例：没准儿他今天不来了。

Perhaps he won't come today.

2. 没有确定的主意、方式、规律等；没有把握。have no definite idea, way or rule; have no certainty

例：能否在一天内完成我可没准儿。

I have no idea whether I can finish it within a day.

眉毛胡子一把抓 méi mao hú zi yī bǎ zhuā

指办事没有条理，不分主次，胡乱处理。try to grasp the eyebrows and the beard all at once/One who tries to handle everything at once.

例：你要学会耐心，一个问题一个问题地去解决，不能眉毛胡子一把抓。

You'd better learn to be patient and to solve the problems one by one. You can't solve them all at once.

美不劲儿的 měi bù jīnr de

指得意、高兴的神情。an expression of delight and joy

例：看他美不劲儿的，一定是有什么好事了。

Look, how delighted he is! Something good must have happened.

美的 měi de

得意；高兴的样子。pleased; complacent; delightful

例：她爸爸同意给她买架钢琴，瞧把她美的。

See how pleased she is when her father agreed to buy her a piano.

美眉 měi méi

漂亮女子。pretty girl

例：你们公司可有不少美眉。什么时候也给我介绍一个行不行？

There are many pretty girls in your company. Would you introduce one to me someday?

美妞 měi niū

指漂亮的女孩。beautiful girl

例：过来，小美妞，让我好好看看你。

Come here, you little pretty girl. Let me have a good look at you.

美食 měi shí

美味食品。delicious food

例：中国被誉为美食国，有丰富的美食文化。

China is known as a country of delicious fare with a rich cuisine.

美食家 měi shí jiā

指爱好吃、懂得吃、会吃的人；对食物品味高的人；食物鉴赏专家。gourmet; good eater

例：我丈夫是个美食家。

My husband is a gastronome.

美子 měi zi

指美元。US dollar; buck

例：她才从美国回来，手头一定有不少美子。

She's just come back from the United States. She must have a lot of US dollars.

闷嘚儿蜜 mēn dēr mì

指背地里独自享受。enjoy sth. privately; do sth. alone behind other's backs

例1：他买了个西瓜，闷嘚儿蜜了。

He bought a watermelon and enjoyed it in delicious solitude.

例2：这笔买卖我应得一半利益，可他什么也没给我，把好处都闷嘚儿蜜了。

I should have received half of the profit from the business, but he took everything as his.

焖骚 mèn sāo

（贬义词）指人在对待个人情感问题上表面装出冷漠、无所谓的样子，而内心却激情似火，喜欢得不得了。有情感上的"假正经"或"伪君子"之意。(derogatory term) refers to one who pretends not care about or be unconcerned about the opposite sex or sexual things, but actually feels the stirrings of love. It means an emotional hypocrite.

例：谭爱琳就是那种焖骚，外人看像个人似的，实际就是贱。

Tan Ailin is an emotional hypocrite. Although she seems like a decent person, actually she is a contemptible wretch.

门槛 mén kǎn

1.指地位高，架子大。threshold/A metaphor for high social status or airs.

例：你们家的门槛高，我们哪敢找你呀？

Your social status is so high that we don't dare to come and visit you.

2.比喻窍门。key to a problem; knack

例：你现在还没摸着门槛呢，所以你总失败。

You haven't found the knack yet, so you failed every time.

3.形容人精明，会算计。a person who is shrewd or good at calculation

例：这家伙是个门槛，不好对付。

This fellow is very shrewd and hard to deal with.

门脸 mén liǎn

1.指人的外表（多指人的面部和头发）。appearance/A term that mostly refers to facial appearance (mainly a beard or moustache) and hair.

例：你该修一修门脸了。

You'd better have a shave and a haircut.

2.商店的外部面貌。the facade of a shop; shop front

例：她在街角开了一家小门脸的商店。

She ran a small shop at a corner of the street.

门前清 mén qián qīng

原指把房屋前的院子或街道打扫干净，后借喻为酒席桌上每个人将自己的酒喝光。clear the ground in front of one's gate or street/A metaphor for one to down their wine or liquor during a meal.

例：他建议大家来个门前清。

He suggested that everyone down their wine.

门子 mén zi

奥妙或秘密。profound mystery or secret

例：魔术可有不少门子，一般人都弄不明白。

Magic is full of profound mysteries, and ordinary people can't understand it.

门儿清 ménr qīng

指了解、明白，一清二楚。know sb. or sth. completely; know like the back of one's hand

例：我们从小青梅竹马，他对我的背景绝对门儿清？

We grew up together, so he knows me like the back of his hand.

闷罐子 mèn guàn zi

1. 比喻令人困惑不解的话或事情。sealed pot/A metaphor for a puzzle.

例：他几句没头没脑的话把我一下子装进了闷罐子。

His ambiguous remarks were really a puzzle to me.

2. 形容不爱说话的人。sealed pot; a clam/A metaphor for someone who doesn't like to talk too much.

例：他是个闷罐子，一天也说不了几句话。

He is like a clam and seldom speaks all day long.

猛料 měng liào

具有很大新闻价值而且是突如其来的消息。unexpected, very important news

例：这家报纸刚上市时登出了很多猛料，一下子吸引了不少的读者。

This newspaper published a lot of big, unexpected news when it hit the market, and attracted many readers.

咪表 mī biǎo

停车自动计时装置。parking meter

例：近来市中心的街道两旁安上了咪表，开始实行咪表收费制度。

Parking meters have recently been installed along some main streets in downtown areas to test an automatic charging system.

眯瞪 mī deng

指小睡；睡一小会儿。have a nap

例：别打搅我。我想眯瞪一会儿。

Don't bother me. I want to have a nap.

秘 mī

藏；贪污；拿走。hide; embezzle; take away

例1：谁把我的新帽子秘起来了？

Who hid my new hat?

例2：他把父亲的手表给秘了。

He took off with his father's watch.

蜜 mì

指女友；情人。girlfriend; lover (female)

例：大款们常带着蜜去郊外兜风。

Rich boys often take their girlfriends for rides in the suburbs.

面 miàn

指人软弱或办事不利索。weak; lax; slow

例：他干事特别面。

He is lax about doing things.

面包会有的 miàn bāo huì yǒu de

指生活会好起来；情况会变好。turn for the better; have a bright future

例：她是个乐天派，她总安慰自己面包会有的。

She is an optimist. She often tells herself that life will get better.

面的 miàn dí

指面包型出租汽车。taxi minivans common in Beijing nick-named "bread boxes" because of their appearance

例：多数人喜欢坐面的，因为它既经济又实惠。

Most people prefer the minivan taxis because they are cheap and practical.

面瓜 miàn guā

1.愚蠢的人。fool; stupid person; idiot

例：你真是个面瓜，我暗示你离开，可你就是不明戏。

You're fool. You couldn't even take a hint that I wanted you to leave.

2.软弱无能的人；没出息的人。weak and incompetent person; good-for-nothing

例：虽然他又高又壮，却是个大面瓜。

Though he's tall and strong, he's really good-for-nothing.

灭 miè

打败；打服。beat; convince sb. by force

例：他总跟我过不去。我找一天非灭了他不可。

He always finds faults with me. Someday I'll beat him and teach him a lesson.

名模 míng mó

著名的服装模特儿。supermodel; famous model

例：她梦想有一天成为一个名模。

She dreams of becoming a supermodel one day.

明戏 míng xì

明白；清楚。understand; be clear about; get (uuderstood)

例：我向他解释了那么多，可他还是不明戏。

I explained it so many times to him, but he still doesn't get it.

命门 mìng mén

指能致人于死地的穴位,比喻关系到生死的重大事物或生死攸关之事。point of weakness; Achilles' heel/A term meaning a matter of vital importance.

例:经济改革是中国未来发展的命门。

The economc reforms are a matter of vital importance in China's future development.

磨合 mó hé

原指汽车在大修后机器零件互相磨擦逐渐互相吻合。现引申为人或事物之间互相适应,逐渐步人正常轨道。break in (fit together perfectly)/A term originally referred to new parts in vehicles that require a period to break in become operating efficiently. During this period, vehicles cannot travel at high speeds. The term now describes someone or something that needs a period of time before working effectively.

例:经济改革需要一个磨合期。

The economic reform needs a period to break in.

磨牙 mó yá

1. 说废话;无休止的争辩。argue endlessly; talk nonsense

例:我没事撑的和你在这儿磨牙。

Have I got nothing to do so I argue with you here?

2. 消磨时间。idle away time; kill time

例:他靠玩儿牌来磨牙。

He kills time by playing cards.

3. 嗑(瓜子等坚硬类食品)。crack sth. between the teeth

(usually nuts, melon seeds, etc.)

例:她就喜欢一边看电视一边嗑瓜子磨牙玩儿。

She likes to crack melon seeds while watching TV.

磨嘴皮子 mó zuǐ pí zi

反复说;说服。(lit.) rub one's lips/A metaphor for talking over and over; persuading sb. to agree with one's ideas.

例:为了得到这份工作,我没少跟领导磨嘴皮子,可是到头来还是一点儿用也没有。

I spent a lot of time rubbing my lips with the head of my unit so that I could keep this work, but it didn't work and I failed completely.

摩的 mó dí

称那些专门用来载客挣钱的两轮或三轮摩托车(包括残疾人专用车)。a motor cycle or motor tricycle (for the handi-capped) used as taxi to carry passengers

例:哪里交通不便,哪里就有摩的的市场。

Where the transportation facilities are poor there is a motor cycle taxi market.

模仿秀 mó fǎng xiù

以模仿他人所进行的演出或表演。imitation show/A show in which people mimic stars (usually singers).

例:北京有线电视台搞的模仿秀节目吸引了全国许多青年人报名参加。

The imitation show program organized by Beijing Cable Television Station has attracted many young participants from all over the country.

磨磨唧唧 mò mo jī jī

比喻言行不直爽；动作迟缓；性子慢；说话吞吞吐吐。

be slow tempered; act slowly; hesitate in speech or in action; talk in a roundabout way; hum and ha

例1：别磨磨唧唧的，如果你真喜欢就买下来。

Don't hesitate. If you really like it, buy it.

例2：快点！别磨磨唧唧的。

Hurry up! Don't dawdle.

木 mù

头脑不灵活；麻木；笨；迟钝。not flexible; insensitive; stupid; slow

例1：她真够木的。我跟她解释了三遍这个东西的用途，她还是不明白。

She is very slow. I explained the usage of the thing to her three times, but she didn't catch on.

例2：他对什么都那么木。

He is quite insensitive to everything.

木头疙瘩 mù tou gē da

1. 木材和木料的统称。wood; lumber; timber

例：你带回这么一块木头疙瘩有什么用？

What's the use of this piece of wood you brought back?

2. 形容愚笨或不灵活的人。wooden-head; slow-wit; slow-poke

例：你真是个木头疙瘩，连这么简单的问题也回答不上来。

You are a wooden-headed boy. You can't even answer this simplest question.

N

N ēn

原本是数学中不定数的符号,后用来形容非常多。originally a mathematical symbol, used to refer to something numerous

例:A:我可以借这张唱片吗?

Can I borrow this CD?

B:拿去吧,这张唱片我已经听过 N 遍了。

Go ahead. I've already listened to it too many times.

拿糖 ná táng

摆架子;装模作样或故意推脱,以抬高自己的身价。put on airs; strike a pose to impress people; give oneself airs

例:他从不拿糖,而且总是有求必应。

He never gives himself airs in front of people and does whatever you ask for.

拿下 ná xià

解决;完成。solve, settle, accomplish

例:他是个数学天才,不管多难的题,他一会儿工夫就拿下。

He is a genius at math. No matter how difficult the problem is, he only needs a little while to solve it.

奶水 nǎi shuǐ

指贿赂他人(行贿后)所得的好处。(lit.) milk/A metaphor for the profit one gets after offering a bribe.

例:这两年他凭着各种关系搞到了不少奶水多的大项目。

In the two years he acquired many profitable projects by relying on his various relations.

奶油小生 nǎi yóu xiǎo shēng

指长相好,皮肤白净,说话举止女性化的男青年。effeminate
young man; good-looking young man with feminine characteristics

例:中国电影里可有不少奶油小生。

There are too many effeminate young men in Chinese movies.

脑体倒挂 nǎo tǐ dào guà

指脑力劳动者(知识分子)和体力劳动者的关系颠倒过来,脑
力劳动者的收入不及体力劳动者高。situation where workers are making more than intellectuals

例:脑体倒挂是一种奇怪的现象。

It's odd to see the phenomenon where intellectuals are earning less than workers.

闹 nào

吵;不安静。noisy

例:这街道白天可真够闹的,我简直无法睡觉。

The street is so noisy in the day time that I can't fall
asleep.

闹心 nào xīn

使人心烦意乱,不得安宁。be terribly upset; be agitated; irritate; be restless

例1:这坏消息真让我闹心。

The bad news made me terribly upset.

例2:把迪斯科音乐关小声点儿,真够闹心的。

Turn down the disco music a little bit. It makes me feel restless.

嫩 nèn

指人没经验,年轻不老练。unexperienced; young

例:处理这件棘手的事,她是嫩了点儿。

She is a bit young to handle such a thorny matter.

能耐 néng nai

指本领;本事;技能。skill; ability

例:别看他人不大,能耐可不小。

He has great ability though he is only a little boy.

腻腻歪歪 nì nì wāi wāi

指人说话吞吞吐吐,办事拖泥带水,没完没了,使人厌烦或厌恶。refers to hemming and hawing in speech, or working sloppily, causing others to feel bored or disgusted

例:让你干点事总是这么腻腻歪歪的,你就不能改改?我真拿你没办法。

You always do things sloppily whenever I ask you to help me with something. Why can't you change a little bit? I simply can't do anything with you.

蔫(儿)不唧唧 niān(r) bu jī jī

1.形容人情绪不高,精神欠佳。(of a person) to be in low spirits

例:她今天怎么了,蔫儿不唧唧的?

What's wrong with her today? She is in low spirits.

2.不声不响;悄悄。quiet

例1:她总是蔫儿不唧唧的,整天不跟人说一句话。

She is always quiet and seldom speaks to others.

例2:我不知道他什么时候蔫不唧唧地走了。

I don't know when he left as he didn't say anything to me.

蔫(儿)坏 niān(r) huài

1.悄悄地干坏事;不声不响地干坏事。privately do bad things

例:他看上去老实,实际上蔫(儿)坏。

He looks very honest, but he does bad things in secret.

2.调皮的;恶作剧的。mischievous

例:这个班上数他最蔫(儿)坏。

He is the most mischievous student in the class.

蔫蔫呼呼 niān niān hū hū

形容人慢性子,说话做事不干净利落。refers to one who is slow by nature, and doesn't speak or act in a straightforward way

例:你这人怎么这么蔫蔫呼呼的,有什么话就赶紧说。

How come you're so slow! Speak up if you have anything to say.

黏糊 nián hu

1.(指东西)黏。sticky; glutinous

例:这种胶特别黏糊。

This kind of glue is very sticky.

2.指人的性子慢,不爽快。slow-tempered; phlegmatic

例:这人特黏糊,我不爱跟他一起办事。

He is so slow-tempered that I don't like to work with him.

3.(指人)行动迟缓,精神不振。delay; betardy

例:这件事你可别再黏糊了,赶快办吧!

You should not delay in this matter. It must be done at once!

撵 niǎn

1.赶走;驱逐。drive out; oust; expel

例：他被撵出了房间。

He was driven out of the room.

2. 赶上；追上。catch up

例：他很快就撵上了他的女友。

He caught up with his girlfriend quickly.

念想 niàn xiǎng

心中惦念的事情，渴望的事情。things hidden in one's mind; hidden longings; desires

例：我这把年纪的人了，你说还能有什么念想，只求你们能平平安安地过日子。

I'm such an old man now. What desires could I possibly have? I only wish that you'll live your lives peacefully.

鸟语 niǎo yǔ

方言，多指粤语（广东话）。dialect, usually the Cantonese dialect

例：他一给女友打电话就说鸟语，生怕我们听到他在说什么。

He speaks Cantonese whenever he calls his girlfriend, so as to keep us from understanding what he says.

捏估 niē gu

1. 欺负。bully; take advantage of

例：很明显地是存心要捏估我。

It's obviously clear that she is taking advantage of me on purpose.

2. 背后说某人坏话；算计、中伤某人。speak ill of sb.; scheme against sb.; malign sb.

例：我讨厌那些背后捏估别人的人。

I hate those who malign others clandestinely.

3. 撮合。act as a go-between

例:如果没有她的捏估,他们俩不会和好。

They wouldn't have made it up if she hadn't acted as a go-between.

拧 nìng

性格倔强;固执。pigheaded; stubborn

例:她很拧。一旦她拿定主意,没人能使她改变。

She is really pigheaded. Once she makes up her mind, nobody can persuade her to change it.

牛 niú

1.形容高傲自大,自命不凡。proud; arrogant; self-important

例:自他兜里的钱多了以后,人也变得牛了。

Since he became rich he's become very arrogant.

2.吹牛;说大话。talk big; boast; brag

例:他喜欢在女孩儿面前牛。

He likes to talk big in front of girls.

牛皮糖 niú pí táng

1.形容难对付的人或缠住某人不放的人。sticky candy/A metaphor for one who is hard to deal with or get rid of.

例:我今天真倒霉,又碰上了一个牛皮糖顾客。

I was unlucky today to meet a customer who was so hard to deal with.

2.指办事拖拉,不利落的人。one who is slow at doing things

例:她是个急性子,最不喜欢牛皮糖。

She is quick tempered and doesn't like those who are slow at their work.

牛气 niú qi

形容得意洋洋,自高自大的骄傲神气。very proud and arrogant; cocky; complacent

例:你既无钱又无房,有什么可牛气的?

What could you be cocky about? You've got neither bags of money nor a beautiful house.

弄 nòng

玩弄;与女性发生关系。dally with(woman);have sexual relations with (women)

例:那家伙把女孩子弄了,并逼迫她嫁给他。

The fellow had a liaison with a girl and forced her to marry him.

弄潮儿 nòng cháo ér

比喻改革者。tide player/A reformer or one who fights against old customs and influences, or a pioneer.

例1:他们被誉为时代的弄潮儿。

They are known as progressives of the age.

例2:自从经济改革以来,涌现出一大批弄潮儿。

Large numbers of groundbreakers have emerged since the economic reform.

努 nǔ

拼全力;使劲;用力。do one's utmost; do all one can

例:他努了半天,只得了第四名。

He did all he could, but only got a fourth prize.

O

呕吔 ōu yè

感叹词，表示高兴、激励、赞同。Oh yeh. / An exclamation expressing happiness, encouragement, or agreement.

例：他刚刚宣布明天去郊游的消息，就听到教室里响起一片呕吔声。

He heard loud cheers of "Oh Yeh" in the classroom as soon as he finished announcing the news of an outing the next day.

P

PK

"player killing"的缩写,指两名选手对垒,淘汰其中一人。

趴车 pā chē

停车。parking

例:这个点开车出来,要想找个趴车的地方特难。

It's very hard to find a place to park the car if you drive at this time of the day.

趴活 pā huó

指出租司机在路边停车等顾客打车。wait for business (usually referring to taxi drivers)

例:昨天的一起交通事故正好被当时在路边一位趴活的出租车司机看见了。他是这起事故的惟一目击证人。

The traffic accident yesterday happened to be seen by a taxi driver who had stopped at the roadside to wait for business. He was the only witness to the accident.

扒拉 pá la

吃(把饭拨到嘴里)。eat; stuff /A term that actually refers to the action of putting food (rice or vegetables from a bowl or dish) into one's mouth.

例:她随便扒拉了两口饭就急急忙忙地走了。

She ate something and left in a hurry.

爬格子 pá gé zi

指从事写作、编辑等文字工作。take up writing or editing

例：她的朋友纷纷下海了，可她依旧喜欢爬格子，为妇女杂志撰写文章。

Most of her friends have gone into business, but she still enjoys writing articles for a woman's magazine.

拍 pāi

1. 拿出或放下（钱）。 take money out; put money down

例：他拍了二千元让店老板把最好的酒拿出来。

He took out 2,000 *yuan* and asked the owner to bring him the best wine in the restaurant.

2. 打败；打人。 defeat; beat

例：她把对手一个个都给拍了。

She beat her opponents one by one.

拍板 pāi bǎn

定夺；决定。 make the final decision; give the final verdict; have the final say

例：这事老板不拍板，谁也不敢承担责任。

Nobody dares to bear the responsibility until the boss gives his final decision on the matter.

拍婆子 pāi pó zi

指寻找，追求女性（含贬义）。 chase a young woman (derogatory)

例：我几天都没见他的影子了。我猜他一定在哪儿拍婆子呢。

I haven't seen him for a few days. I guess he's been chasing a young woman.

拍拖 pāi tuō

谈恋爱。 (lit.) patrol/It refers to courting; being in love;

having a love affair.

例：经过三年的拍拖,他们终于结为夫妻。

After being in love for three years they finally married and became husband and wife.

派 pài

指气派、神气的样子。impressive

例：他穿上这套西装够派的。

He looks quite impressive in his new suit.

派对 pài duì

1.聚会;集会。party

例：今天晚上她要去参加派对,不回来吃晚饭了。

She'll go to a party tonight so she won't be back for dinner.

2.男女通过介绍相互认识产生好感,配成一对,并同意从此开始约会。make pairs; matchmaking

例：这期电视征婚节目下来,有三对派对成功。

Three couples were successfully brought together when this TV dating program was over.

攀高枝 pān gāo zhī

比喻投靠或巴结有权有势的人。climb the social ladder; play up to powerful or influential people

例：他只想当一名普通百姓,不想为了当官而去攀高枝。

He is satisfied with being a common person. He doesn't want to play up to the important people just to get a promotion.

盘儿 pánr

指人的长相、面容。looks; features; appearance

例:他们抱怨说当今社会干什么事都凭一个人的盘儿来决定。

They complained that everything is decided by one's looks in today's society.

盘儿亮 pánr liàng

指人的长相漂亮。good-looking; beautiful

例:你的女友盘儿够亮的。

Your girlfriend is good-looking.

跑光 pǎo guāng

指女人或男人的私密处被人看到。to expose a private part of the body (such as underwear) to others (usually referring to women or man)

例:夏天女孩子穿短裙时一定要注意坐姿,不要翘二郎腿,那样很容易跑光的哟。

Girls wearing short skirts in summer should be aware of how they are sitting. Don't sit cross-legged because you're likely to expose your underwear to others.

跑水 pǎo shuǐ

指水管漏水或管道被堵住而发水。to flood because of a pipe leak or a blocked up pipeline

例:这里怎么有这么多水,一定是哪里跑水了。我们赶快查一下吧。

Why is there so much water here? There must be flooding somewhere nearby. Let's go and check it out right away.

泡妞 pào niū

与女子调情;寻求女性。flirt with girls; spend time with girls; chase girls; womanize

Pop Chinese

A cheng & Tsui
handbook of Comtemporary
Colloquial Expressions.

———————————

例1:他下班后常去酒吧泡妞。

He often flirts with girls in bars after work.

例2:他到哪儿去了？一定又在泡妞。

Where has he gone? He must be flirting with girls some-where.

泡吧 pào bā

指长时间呆在"酒吧"、"网吧"等地。indulge oneself for a long time in bars (wine bars or Internet bars)

例:他一到周末或节假日就去泡吧,这是他特有的休息方式。

He indulges himself in bars every weekend or holiday. This is his special way of relaxing.

泡汤 pào tāng

失败;完蛋;落空。fall flat; fall through (of plans); fail; be done for; be unsuccessful; come to nothing; be fruitless

例1:如果你不抓紧办,你的计划可能要泡汤。

If you don't do it immediately, your plan will come to nothing.

例2:由于今晚下雨,原定的露天晚会泡汤了。

Because of the rain tonight, the open-air party that was planned fell through.

喷粪 pēn fèn

指说脏话或骂人。swear; curse; say dirty words

例:他这个人文化素质太低,一急起来就满嘴喷粪。

He's poorly educated because his mouth is full of dirty words when he gets angry.

坏子 pī zi

指在某方面有天赋、有素质的人。person with a gift or talent for something; gifted person

例：她是一个跳舞的坯子。

She's a person with a gift for dancing.

皮包公司 pí bāo gōng sī

指资产不多，人员不多，主要从事咨询、买空卖空生意的公司或人。由于这种公司或人无其他附属资产和实力，一个皮包足够了，故称为皮包公司。a briefcase company/A company or a person which has few assets, few employees and mainly engages in consulting, buying and reselling. The only thing needed to run this sort of company is a briefcase.

例：跟他打交道你可别全信他。他的公司只不过是个皮包公司。

Don't trust him fully when you do business with him. His company is only a briefcase company.

皮榔头 pí láng tou

指拳头。(lit.) hammer/A metaphor for fist.

例：你要小心，他发火时会给你一只皮榔头。

Be careful! He will punch you if he gets angry.

痞子 pǐ zi

指流里流气，不三不四的人；无赖。rascal; scoundrel; ruffian

例：他在一部电影中扮演一个小痞子。

He played the role of a little rascal in a movie.

屁颠儿 pì diānr

指高兴的样子。happy and gay; pleased; overjoyed

例：他老婆给他买回一瓶酒，瞧把他乐得屁颠儿的。

He was overjoyed when his wife bought him a bottle of wine.

屁驴子 pì lǘ zi

指电动自行车。bicycle that runs on a motor

例:许多人买不起摩托车,便自己动手攒屁驴子。

Many people can't afford to buy a motorcycle, so they assemble bicycles with motors.

片儿警 piànr jǐng

指负责管理某一个地区或居民小区社会治安的警察。

local regional policeman/A policeman in charge of the public order of a local region or a residential area.

例:他是这儿新来的片儿警。

He is a new local regional policeman.

片儿懒 piànr lǎn

指懒汉鞋,一种不用系带,有松紧口的布面平底鞋。

lazy man's shoe/A cloth-covered shoe without shoestrings.

例:在年轻人当中开始流行穿片儿懒。

Lazy man's shoes have become popular with the young.

片儿汤 piànr tāng

一种面食,把和好的面擀成薄片,撕成小块,下锅煮熟后连同汤一起吃。doughflake soup; soup in which flakes of dough are boiled

例:我父亲最爱吃片儿汤。

Doughflake soup is my father's favorite.

片儿汤话 piànr tāng huà

指带有流行语、俚语、俗语等贫嘴逗乐的语言。playful, teasing word (of slang)

例:他这人很有趣,一开口净是些片儿汤话。

He is a very interesting person. His speech is full of playful, teasing words.

漂 piāo

没挣到钱, 完了。to get nothing; come up short; fail to make money

例: 他刚借了点钱做生意, 可偏偏遇上了"非典", 生意全漂了。

He had just borrowed some money to start his business, and then happened to come down with the flu. His business failed entirely.

漂人 piāo rén

到北京寻求发展的艺术人才。artists who come to Beijing seeking career development

例: 许多影视大腕以前都曾是漂人。

Many famous movie or TV actors and actresses of today were once artistic individuals who came to Beijing looking for a future.

飘 piāo

1. 随风摇动或飞扬。float in the air; flutter

例: 我看到天空中有个风筝在飘。

I can see a kite fluttering in the sky.

2. 动作轻快; 技巧娴熟。brisk; elegant; skilful; graceful

例: 这次他翻的跟头又轻又飘。

The somersault he turned this time was light and graceful.

3. 指某人没有正当职业, 在社会上游荡。be unemployed; loaf about; wander

例: 你最好尽快找一份工作, 别总这么飘着。

You'd better find a job as soon as possible. Don't loaf about like this all day long.

漂白 piǎo bái

指黑社会的人或干过坏事的人改变自己的形象,使自己在公众面前更见得人。bleach; whitewash/Refers to sinister gangsters who whitewash their image.

例:一些最大的毒品贩子也想晋身政坛,以政治人物来漂白以前的身份。

Some of the biggest drug dealers want to change their image and go into politics.

票贩子 piào fàn zi

指倒买倒卖车票从中获取利益的人。train ticket scalper

例:春节前警察在北京火车站抓住了一批票贩子。

Police caught some train ticket scalpers in Beijing Railway Station before the Spring Festival.

票提 piào tí

为汽车招揽乘客并从车票中提取报酬的人。a person who asks passengers to take a bus in return for a cut of the fares

例:他曾干过票提,后来又干起了导游。

He used to work as a person who persuades people to take a minibus in return for a cut of the fares, and later he became a tourist guide.

漂亮姐 piào liang jiě

指长相好的女子。beautiful woman; good-looking woman

例:他在那边与一位漂亮姐聊天。

He is talking with a beautiful woman over there.

平蹚 píng tāng

1.形容无法无天地行事。do whatever one likes without interference

例：他在这一带小有名气，而且可以平蹚。

He has a little fame and can do anything he wants in this region without interference.

2.没有阻挡；没有障碍。cannot be blocked（impeded，hindered，stopped）

例：这一带咱哥们儿平蹚，没有谁敢跟我们过不去。

We can do whatever we like here and nobody will dare stop us.

平推 píng tuī

指买进和卖出的价钱相同，没有丝毫盈利。sell without turning a profit

例：现在这种衬衫的样子已过时了，所以摊主决定将余下的衬衫平推出去。

This style of shirt has long since gone out of fashion，so the stall owner decided to sell it without turning a profit.

Q

齐活 qí huó

指活儿全部干完了,也有"完事了"、"行了"、"好了"的意思。

finish; complete; OK; well-done; all right

例:女孩把针放在桌上对我说:"齐活了,穿上看看是否合身。"

The girl put the sewing needle on the table and said to me, "It's finished. Try it on to see whether it fits you."

起腻 qǐ nì

烦扰某人;缠着某人。bother someone; pester; nag

例:爸爸一出门,孩子就跟妈妈起腻,非买那个玩具不可。

The child pestered his mother for buying the toy for him when his father went out.

起子 qǐ zi

1. 出息;胆量。prospects; future; courage; guts

例:瞧你这点儿起子,跟人借书也害怕。

What a coward you are! You even dare not borrow a book.

2. 改锥。screwdriver

例:把起子递给我。

Hand me the screwdriver.

3. 发酵粉。baking powder

例:买些起子回来,我好给你蒸馒头。

Buy some baking powder back so I can make some steamed bread for you.

气不忿儿 qì bù fènr

看不过去;心中不服气。not stand the sight of; be furious;

feel indignant; be unconvinced

例 1:看他那么虐待他亲生父亲,我真气不忿儿。

I can't stand to see him ill-treat his own father like that.

例 2:听到这消息真让我气不忿儿。

I'm furious to hear the news.

气管炎 qì guǎn yán

"妻管炎"的谐音,指怕妻子的男人。tracheitis; hen-pecked husband/Homonym for a husband who is strictly controlled by his wife. A term for man who is afraid of his wife.

例 1:我敢说他在家一定是个气管炎。

I'm sure he's a hen-pecked husband.

例 2:他一结婚就患上了气管炎。

He's suffered as a hen-pecked husband since he got married.

砌墙头 qì qiáng tóu

指打麻将牌。building a wall (with mahjong pieces)/A metaphor for playing mahjong.

例:她每天都到老年活动中心砌墙头去。

She goes to play mahjong at the senior citizens' center everyday.

掐 qiā

1.打架;吵架。fight; scuffle; come to blows; quarrel; kick up a row

例:他们为什么掐起来了?

What did they fight for?

2.指一小把。handful

例:她买了一掐韭菜。

She bought a handful of Chinese chives.

千儿八百 qiānr bā bǎi

指一千元或少一点。(of money) a thousand or slightly less

例：她开了一家小饭馆，每天挣个千儿八百的。

She runs a small restaurant and makes a profit of a thousand or slightly less a day.

前卫 qián wèi

指时髦的；入时的；创新的。fashionable; modern; creative

例：这种发型是当今最前卫的，许多年轻人都喜欢。

This hairstyle is most fashionable at present. Many young people like it.

枪毙 qiāng bì

1. 指用枪打死。be executed by gun

例：那个杀人犯被枪毙了。

The killer was executed by gun.

2. 指否决，没有通过。vote down; veto; shot down; nix

例：他的滑雪计划被老婆枪毙了。

His plan to go skiing was shot down by his wife.

枪手 qiāng shǒu

1. 指专门替代某人考试拿取高分的人。gun shooter/A metaphor for someone who is hired to participate in an examination on behalf of someone else.

例：居然有人公开登报招聘枪手代其考研。

Someone who goes as far as to put a public notice in a newspaper to hire a "gun shooter" to take the entrance examination of a master's degree for him.

2. 指专门为人代笔写东西的人。ghostwriter

例：他是这里出了名的枪手，并以替人写书为生。

He's a famous ghostwriter here and makes a living doing it.

呛水 qiāng shuǐ

指（工作或生活）受挫折或（生意）亏本,吃亏。be choked with water/A metaphor for those who suffer setbacks (in work or life) or suffer losses (in business).

例:他干这份工作以来已呛水好几回了。

He has suffered some setbacks since he got this job.

强努 qiáng nǔ

指硬着头皮,竭尽全力迫使自己去做某事。force oneself to do sth. ; try one's utmost to do sth. beyond one's ability

例:搬不动就别强努,当心闪了腰。

Don't force yourself to carry it if it's too heavy for you. Be careful not to sprain your back.

抢滩 qiǎng tān

指抢先占领市场。seize the shore/A metaphor for to seize a market; fight to be the first on the market.

例:近年来外国有实力的大公司纷纷抢滩中国的电信市场,使这里的竞争更为激烈。

In recent years large and powerful foreign companies have fought each other to seize the telecom market and have made the competition fiercer.

戗行 qiàng háng

在竞争中让人占了上风。snatch away business; take the lead in competition

例1:这本来是我的买卖,可是让他戗行了。他把价格压得很低。

It was my business originally,but he snatched it away from me by selling goods at much lower prices.

例2:他哥的女友让他给戗行了,并同她结了婚。

He stole his brother's girlfriend and married her.

巧劲儿 qiǎo jìnr

1.聪明巧妙的办法。clever way; ingenious method

例:你该学会如何用巧劲儿来对付一件难事。

You should learn how to do hard work in a clever way.

2.碰巧的事。coincidence

例:真是巧劲儿的,我正要给你打电话你就来了。

It's just a coincidence. I was about to call you when you came.

巧嘴八哥 qiǎo zuǐ bā ge

比喻很会说话的;能说会道的人。talking myna bird/Those who have a glib tongue or the gift of the gab.

例:她是个巧嘴八哥,什么场面都能应付。

She's got a glib tongue. She can deal with any situation.

翘辫子 qiào biàn zi

指人死。kick the bucket

例:你要翘辫子呀!过马路干吗不看着点儿车?

Do you want to kick the bucket? Why don't you look around before you cross the road?

切汇 qiē huì

指在买卖外汇当中,买方从卖方应得的款中扣下一部分钱(多数是采用欺骗、弄假的方法少给卖方钱)。swindle someone by secretly withholding some money when changing foreign currency

例:他特别会切汇。

He is good at swindling people by secretly withholding some money when changing their foreign currency.

切入 qiē rù

(突然)插入;加进来;转换进来。cut in (a queue or line)

例 1:电话很忙,所以她请总机帮她切入。

The line was busy, so she asked the operator to help her cut in.

例 2:他不让那个司机从他前面切入。

He didn't let the driver cut in before him.

怯 qiè

1. 不大方,不合时,俗气 in poor taste; vulgar; tawdry

例:你怎么买这个颜色的毛衣,太怯了。

Why did you buy this color sweater? It looks very tawdry.

2. 缺乏知识;浅薄 lacking in knowledge; superficial

例:我不敢当众说话,怕露怯。

I dare not speak in public for fear of making fool of myself.

青春饭 qīng chūn fàn

指有年龄限制(通常指十八岁至三十岁以下)的职业,如运动员、飞机乘务员、舞蹈演员等。a youthful profession, which has a strict age limit usually between 18 to 30 years old, like dancing, air hostessing, athletics, etc.

例:舞蹈是吃青春饭的,所以她父母不同意她当舞蹈演员。

Dancing is a youthful profession, so her parents won't allow her to become a dancer.

青春族 qīng chūn zú

指二十岁左右的年轻人。youth clan; young blood/Refers to people in their teens and early twenties.

例:这种娱乐消费对青春族来说难以承受。

The cost of this kind of entertainment is too audacious for the younger generation to afford.

青瓜头 qīng guā tóu

指涉世不深,经验不足,愣头愣脑(行为莽撞)的年轻人。多用于长辈对晚辈的评说。也称"青不愣"。greenhorn; inexperienced, unsophisticated or crude and impetuous young people/It's mostly used by the elderly to comment on the young.

例:你真是个青瓜头,办事怎么能如此草率。这会给公司招惹来不少麻烦。

You're really a greenhorn. How could you handle things in such a rash way. It could cause many problems for the company.

青一色 qīng yī sè

一个颜色;全是;都是。monotone; entirely; all; whole

例1:我喜欢青一色的红裙子。

I like an all-red skirt.

例2:这个班的学生青一色都是女孩子。

The students in this class are all girls.

清水衙门 qīng shuǐ yá men

指挣钱不多的单位,多指国家机关。water purifier; low salary unit (usually refers to government offices where employees have low salaries)

例:他那个单位是清水衙门,除了挣死工资外什么都没有。

He works in a low salary government unit. He gets nothing besides his fixed salary.

轻子 qīng zi

指小偷行窃他人财物时用的刮胡子刀片。razor blade (which a thief uses to steal things from people's bags)

例：他用轻子划一位女士的皮包时，被一名顾客抓住。

He was caught cutting the woman's leather bag with a ra-
zor blade by a customer.

情儿 qíngr

指情人。(extra marital) lover (man or woman)

例：他整晚跟他的情儿在一起，可却对他妻子说他有一个重
要会议。

He spent the whole evening with his lover, but he told his
wife that he had an important meeting.

穷开心 qióng kāi xīn

自己找快乐的事。amuse oneself at another's expense;
make fun of sb. ; look for fun

例：他们常拿新来乍到的人穷开心。

They often make fun of newcomers.

鞧 qiū

1.（身体）屈卷在一起；缩着；收缩。snuggle up; shrink; curl
up

例1：起来活动一下身体，别整天鞧在床上。

Get up and do some exercises. Don't huddle up in bed all day.

例2：丝绸裙在洗过之后都鞧在一起了。

The silk dress shrank after the wash.

2.呆。stay

例：我不喜欢在这么个小地方鞧着。

I wouldn't like to stay in such a small place.

去你的 qù nǐ de

对某人说的话表示反感。damn you

例：A：别生气，我只不过是逗你玩的。

Don't be angry. I was just kidding.

B：去你的，以后再也不理你了。

Damn you. I won't talk to you any more.

圈 quān

1.把生畜用围栏关在一起。pen in; shut in a pen

例：把小鸡圈起来。

Shut the chickens in a pen.

2.把犯人关押起来。put in jail

例：他被公安局圈起来了。

He was put in jail by the police station.

圈子 quān zi

指由一些兴趣爱好相投的人组成的小团体。也称"圈儿"。

circle/It refers to a small group of people with a common interest getting together.

例：她是那个圈子里的人，所以对这件事的内幕了解得更清楚。

She belongs to the circle so she knows the inside story of the case.

全活儿 quán huór

指什么活儿都干，也指什么坏事都干。do everything（the good and the bad）

例：如我要用你，你可得干全活儿，包括买菜、做饭、打扫卫生、看孩子。当然你会比别人拿的工资要高得多。

If I hire you, you have to do everything in the house including shopping, cooking, cleaning and baby sitting. But you will get paid more than other people.

R

饶 ráo

多给一点儿东西（多用于买东西时）。give sth. extra

例：她让摊主多饶她一个苹果，摊主答应了。

She asked the owner of the stall to give her one more apple，and the owner agreed.

惹火 ré huǒ

1. 引起欲望；刺激。inspire；excite

例：她的歌惹火了全场的观众，气氛也变得越来越热烈。

Her song inspired the audience. The atmosphere became more and more charged.

2. 激怒；使人发脾气。enrage；infuriate；cause one to lose temper

例：小王的话一下子把他惹火了。

He was enraged by Xiao Wang's words.

热昏 rè hūn

指某人头脑发热，一时冲动。have a fever；have heatstroke

例：我想你是热昏了，否则不会做出这种决定。

I think you must have had heatstroke，otherwise you couldn't have made such a stupid decision.

人精 rén jīng

指人非常精明，极善于算计个人的利益得失。devil of a human being/Referring to someone who is clever, smart, or good at calculating their own gains and losses.

例：这些推销员各个都是人精，跟他们打交道可是不容易。

These salesmen are all devils of human beings and are not easy to deal with.

人来风 rén lái fēng

指小孩儿见有客人到家里来就变得异常兴奋,不守规矩,发疯,调皮,不听话。(children) run wild and disobey parents when guests come to the house

例:这孩子就是人来风,你简直拿他没办法。

This child always runs wild and disobeys me when someone come to the house. I just don't know how to control him.

人力的 rén lì dí

指能载客的人力三轮车。pedicab/A three wheeled bike that can take one or two passengers.

例:游客喜欢乘人力的游览市区。

Tourists enjoy taking pedicabs to tour the city.

人脉 rén mài

指人际关系,认识的人多。having many personal relationships; popular; well-connected

例:她这个人特别有人脉,最适合干销售这行。

She knows a lot of people; she's very suitable for sales work.

人模狗样 rén mó gǒu yàng

1.指打扮、穿戴很像样子(含贬义)。dressed up (derogatory)

例:他这是怎么了? 我从未见过他像今天这样人模狗样的。

What's going on with him? I've never seen him as dressed up as he is today.

2.正经的;严肃而认真(含贬义)。serious; grave (derogatory)

例：别装得那么人模狗样的。我知道这根本就不是什么问题。

Don't pretend to be so serious. I know that it's not a problem at all.

人气 rén qì

指某人或某地受欢迎的程度。degree of popularity of sb. or a place

例：由于她在这部电影中的出色表演，她的人气迅速上升，有望摘取今年最佳女主角奖的桂冠。

As a result of her outstanding acting in this movie, her popularity has soared and she is expected to win the best actress award this year.

人蛇 rén shé

指偷渡出境的人。illegal immigrant

例：在香港有一些人蛇从事建筑业来获得一点很微薄的工资。

In Hong Kong many illegal immigrants work in construction for very low wages.

人市 rén shì

非法的劳务市场。black market for labor; illegal labor market

例：她去人市想找个保姆。

She went to an illegal labor market to look for a housekeeper.

人渣 rén zhā

人类中的败类，或指品质十分恶劣、道德败坏的人。

dregs or scum of society, or someone of inferior or evil characteristics or a morally degenerate person

例：老百姓对于那些犯有盗窃、抢劫、强奸罪的人渣真是恨极
了。他们要求政府对他们进行严厉的打击。

The common people have great hatred for those dregs of society
responsible for crimes of robbery, theft, and rape. They want
the government to crack down on them severely.

日子口 rì zi kǒu

指（时刻,时间）时候；日子。time; moment; date; day

例1：这都什么日子口了,天气还这么热。

How come is it still so hot at this time of the year?

例2：她偏偏在我需要她的日子口上病了。

She is sick just at the moment I need her.

柔 róu

指女性妩媚、娇色,也用于动词指做媚态。sweet; lovely;
charming; curry favor; win favor by fawning

例1：她特别柔,每个人都喜欢她。

She is so sweet that everyone likes her.

例2：她最了解如何柔得观众的喜欢。

She knows pretty well how to win favor of the audience by
fawning.

揉巴 róu ba

用于来回搓；团弄。rub; knead; crumple

例1：别总揉巴我的背。

Don't rub my back all the time.

例2：你把我的衬衫揉巴成什么样子了。

You certainly crumpled my shirt.

肉 ròu

1.（食物）不脆；不酥。overcooked

例：这道菜你炒得肉了。

This dish is overcooked.

2.（人）性子慢,动作迟钝。(of a person) slow in getting things done

例：我恨跟他一起干活儿。这人太肉。

I hate to work with him. He's so slow!

3.（人）不爽快；不痛快。not frank; not straightforward

例：他总是肉乎乎的,有事不明说。我得去猜他想对我说什么。

He never is frank with me. I have to guess what he's trying to say.

软 ruǎn

1. 起皱,不平整。rough; wrinkled; soft

例：别把西服那样折起来,那会把西服弄软的。你最好把它们挂在衣橱里。

Don't fold the suits like that—they'll get wrinkled. You'd better hang them in the wardrobe.

2. 软弱,窝囊。cowardly; timid; good-for-nothing; hopeless; weak

例：他真够软的,一点儿也不像个大男人。

He's so cowardly—not a bit like a grown man.

3. 指质量差。poor quality; tacky; inferior

例：这活儿干得不软。

This work is quality.

软档 ruǎn dàng

弱点,缺点。weak point; weakness

例：他深知自己的软档,并在努力改正。

He knows his weakness very well and tries his best to change.

软件 ruǎn jiàn

指电子计算机里装载程序的设备,包括汇编程序、操作系统;编译程序、诊断程序、控制程序、数据管理系统等。比喻人或人才,通常指虚的,如人的素质、人的思想或能力等。

software/A term used to described talented people or a person's qualities.

例:这个公司的软件不错,可是管理太差。

This company has talented people, but poor management.

软拒 ruǎn jù

用有情理的话拒绝别人,最早出现于出租车司机拒绝搭载乘客。

soft excuse; refuse in a reasonable way (first used by taxi drivers in refusing to take passengers)

例:的哥们常用要回家吃饭或收车的手段来软拒乘客。

Taxi drivers often use the excuse of going home for meals or finishing work to refuse to pick up passengers.

软肋 ruǎn lèi

指人或事的薄弱环节或不足之处。someone or something's weak point

例:他一下击中了我的软肋,我不得不按照他的话去做。

He got me right where I'm weakest, so I had to do what he said.

弱智 ruò zhì

智力差;呆傻;不聪明。idiotic; stupid

例:你不能让他为你打这封信。他弱智,根本不会用打字机。

You can't let him type this letter for you. He's stupid and doesn't know how to use a typewriter.

S

仨瓜俩枣 sā guā liǎ zǎo

不贵重的物品。invaluable things

例：他的眼光可高了，你这仨瓜俩枣的，他根本看不上。我劝你还是别费力讨好他了。

His taste is very high. He won't care about your invaluable things. I advise you not to use them to please him.

飒 sà

指潇洒、有风度（多指女性）。(of women) natural and unrestrained; elegant; graceful

例：那个穿晚礼服的妞儿看上去够飒的。

The woman in the evening gown looks natural and unrestrained.

塞车 sāi chē

堵车；交通堵塞。traffic jam; to be held up in traffic

例：你不该往那边走，每天这个时候那边都塞车。

You shouldn't go in that direction. Every day at this time there's a traffic jam there.

塞牙缝 sāi yá fèng

比喻极少的东西。sth. not large enough to fill a tooth gap; sth. very sparse or extremely little

例：这些吃的还不够我塞牙缝的呢。

This food is far from enough for me.

三级跳 sān jí tiào

本指田径运动中的三级跳远,后引申为快速晋升。triple jump/A metaphor to describe someone who gets promoted quickly.

例:他两年内来了个三级跳,一下当上了出版社的副总编辑。

Within two years he made a triple jump, rising to become deputy editor-in-chief of the publishing company.

三青子 sān qīng zi

1. 指鲁莽的人。rough fellow; rude person

例:他是个三青子,干什么都不管不顾。

He is a rough fellow. He doesn't care about anything.

2. 混不讲理的人。a person who is utterly unreasonable, impervious to reason

例:你不必跟他争。他是个三青子。

It's useless to argue with him. He's impervious to reason.

三孙子 sān sūn zi

指受气的人或受到欺负却不敢发火,唯命是从的人;也指地位低下的人,唯唯喏喏的人;应声虫。yes-man; one who is absolutely obedient or always censured

例:他怕老板炒他的鱿鱼,所以像个三孙子似的处处小心谨慎地干活。

He is afraid of being fired by the boss, so he works very carefully and obediently like a yes-man.

三只手 sān zhī shǒu

指小偷。pickpocket

例:他曾是个好孩子。我不知何时他变成了三只手。

He used to be a good boy. I don't know when he became a pickpocket.

扫黄 sǎo huáng

指打击和取缔出版、出售色情读物及音像制品。confiscate pornographic magazines, books, audio and video tapes; ban on the sale of pornographic magazines, books and video tapes

例:政府在全国发起了一场大规模的扫黄运动。

The government launched a nationwide campaign to confiscate all pornographic magazines, books and video tapes on the market.

扫街 sǎo jiē

原指清扫大街或马路,现引用为一种推销手段,即一个店一个店地上门推销产品。同此方法还有"扫楼",即挨家挨户推销产品。to clean streets or roads/A metaphor for selling products door to door along an entire street. Also "clean buildings", meaning to sell to every apartment in a building.

臊着他 sào zhe tā

故意不理某人。put someone aside purposely; ignore someone purposely

例:咱们臊着他,看他怎么办。

Let's ignore him and see what he does.

杀价 shā jià

使买者降低价格。bargain the price down; bargain with a peddler to lower his or her price

例:如果你到自由市场买东西,你得学会如何杀价。

If you go to the free market to buy things, you have to learn how to bargain the price down.

杀青 shā qīng

原泛指著作完稿,现用于电影或电视剧拍摄完成。Originally meaning a completed manuscript, this now refers to a film or television drama which has been shut down or has finished producing.

例：冯小刚的《天下无贼》这部片子刚刚杀青，大概年底公映。
Feng Xiaogang's new film "A World Without Thieves" has just wrapped up. Perhaps it will be shown at the end of the year.

杀熟 shā shóu

专门向熟人索取高价，引申为专门欺负熟人。charge, especially a friend, a high price/It refers only to cheating a friend.

例：公安局抓获了一名专杀熟的盗窃分子。
Policemen caught a thief who made a specialty of cheating his friends.

傻 shǎ

傻眼；没辙；没料到。be dumbfounded; be stunned; be at the end of one's rope

例1：到了银行他们都傻了，所有的钱都被人提走了。
They were stunned when they got to the bank and discovered all their money had been withdrawn by someone else.

例2：他傻了，他原以为她不会一个人回家去。
He was stunned that she would go home by herself.

傻 X shǎ chā

骂人话，多用于书面表达，X 表示那个说不出口的脏字。a swearword often used in written Chinese. X stands for an unspeakably dirty character

傻冒儿 shǎ màor

1.讥讽或戏称人不聪明。stupid person；fool；dodo（scornful or jocular）

例：你是个大傻冒儿。你怎么能让那家伙给骗了？

You're such a fool. How could you let that guy cheat you?

2.傻子。idiot；blockhead

例：我又不是傻冒儿。我知道那里发生的事情。

I'm not an idiot. I know what's going on there.

傻青儿 shǎ qīngr

指涉世不深的年轻人（含讥讽或玩笑意思）。naive young person；unexperienced（scornful or jocular）

例：他才从大学出来，是个傻青儿。

He just graduated from college so he's still a very naive person.

晒 shài

故意把人晾在一边，不管不问不理。ignore someone on purpose

例：顾客几次招呼售货员，可是她把人家晒在那里，依然与另一位售货员聊天。

The customers tried to get the shop assistant's attention, but she deliberately ignored them and kept talking with her co-worker.

晒干儿 shài gānr

指冷落人，把人放在一边不予理睬。be cold to；give the cold shoulder；neglect

例：我们明白他是在有意晒我们的干儿来考验我们的耐心。

We all knew he was purposely giving us the cold shoulder in order to test our patience.

煽 shān

1. 吹嘘；聊天。boast about；lavish praise on；brag about

例：他买了一条狗，只要他见到我就跟我煽他的那条狗。

He bought a pet dog. Every time he meets me he brags about her.

2. 走红；出名。become famous；become popular；make a name for oneself

例：一首好歌就把她煽起来了。

A good song made her popular.

煽火 shān huǒ

煽风点火，比喻鼓动、怂恿别人做某事。fan the flames；stir up trouble

例：这起初是件小事，但他却把它煽火成越来越复杂的问题了。

It was nothing at first, but he stirred up trouble and made it into a big mess.

煽情 shān qíng

1. 鼓动情绪，激发感情。arouse one's enthusiasm，fervor

例：他的报告特能煽情，没有一个学生中途退场。

His lecture so aroused the students' enthusiasm that no one left in the middle.

2. 调情。flirt

例：他一见漂亮的女孩子就去跟人家煽情。

He flirts with every beautiful girl he meets.

闪 shǎn

1. 躲闪，闪开 to dodge，get out of the way

例：你这个人真差劲，一碰上难题你就闪。

You're such a disappointment. You dodge difficulties

whenever you meet them.

2. 甩下，丢下。 to leave someone or something behind

例：你们真不够朋友，出了事你们都跑了，把我闪那儿了。

Some friends you are! When things went wrong, you all ran away and left me behind.

闪客 shǎn kè

电脑动画制造者 a flash-animation cartoonist

例：珍妮迷恋于漫画，她立志长大后要当一名闪客。

Jenny is mad about cartoons and determined to be a flash animator when she grows up.

上班族 shàng bān zú

指不从事体力劳动阶层的人（机关职员、教师等）。 class of people who do white-collar jobs (white-collar workers; office workers)

例：这套衣服是专为上班族设计的。

This suit of clothes is designed specially for white-collar workers.

上帝 shàng dì

原指基督教所崇奉的神，现引申为顾客或消费者。 god/A term used for a customer or consumer.

例：买东西时我们就是上帝，我们应该得到一流的服务。

When we buy things we should be treated like a god. We should receive the best service.

上赶着 shàng gǎn zhe

单方主动的；积极的。 enthusiastically

例：尽管他上赶着为老板玩儿命干，可是老板却并不给他加薪。

Although he works enthusiastically, his boss won't give him a pay rise.

上脸 shàng liǎn

1. 指喝酒后脸上泛出红色。become flushed after drinking

例：每次喝酒他都上脸。

Every time he drinks, he becomes flushed.

2. 得寸进尺。give him an inch and he'll take a mile

例：我不想同他吵，但他认为我怕他，反而上脸了。

I didn't want to quarrel with him, but he thought I was scared of him and he took a mile after I gave him an inch.

上路 shàng lù

明白；领悟；熟悉。understand; comprehend; get to know

例：没有人教他，可他就是脑子好使，上路快，如今生意经念得比谁都好。

Nobody has ever taught him, but he's got a good brain and is quick on the uptake. Now he does business better than anyone.

上面 shàng mian

1. 指上级领导单位。(leader of) unit at the higher level

例：上面让我们尽快组织学习"政府公报"。

The unit at the higher level has asked us to organize people to study the "Government Report" as soon as possible.

2. 指中央政府。the central government

例：上面三令五申不用公款请客吃饭。

The central government has made repeated injunctions that no unit is allowed to use public money to treat guests or hold banquets.

上眼药 shàng yǎn yào

指到领导处说某人的坏话。rub one's eyes with eyedrops/
An expression for those who go to the boss and tell tales or
speak ill of others.

例：我知道她妒忌我，所以到头儿那儿给我上眼药。

I know that she's jealous of me, so she went to the boss to
tell tales of me.

烧 shāo

1. 指购买东西。go shopping; buy sth.

例：我今天出去烧了一个真皮皮包。

I went out today and bought a new leather bag.

2. 指某人非常想做某事（常指花钱）。want to do sth. (normally related to spending money)

例1：近来他挣了不少钱，这便烧得他三天两头下馆子。

He's earned a lot of money recently, so he eats out almost
every day.

例2：瞧这点儿奖金把她烧得，想买很多很多新衣服。

Because of her bonus she wanted to buy lots of new
clothes.

烧包 shāo bāo

指爱购买东西的人或爱花钱的人。shopping fanatic

例：她是个烧包，每天下班就去烧。

She is a shopping fanatic. She goes shopping everyday after
work.

烧机 shāo jī

指利用窃取的"大哥大"密码，炮制同样号码的大哥大进网无
偿使用。to produce a copy of cellular phone with the same
code number by stealing the code number of the real cellu-

lar phone so that one can use it without paying, but the one
with the real cellular phone will suffer and pay a lot

例:他十分聪明,烧机技术也很高超。别人将窃取的大哥大
密码送来,他只花二三分种就能复制一只。每烧一只收取一
千元。

He is very clever and very skilled at making false cellular
phones. When one gives him a code number, he only
spends two or three minutes making a copy and gets 1,000
yuan for it.

烧钱 shāo qián

形容快速地耗费钱财。to burn money, used to describe
someone who spends money very quickly

例:卓越网向众人宣布将为中国音像业打造一项全新大奖。
为此卓越网开出 1000 万的赏金征集畅销影视音乐精品。这
是卓越网在融资 5000 万之后推出的最大的一次"烧钱"活
动。

Joyo announced to the public that it would launch a brand
new award for the Chinese audio and video industries. It
gave a 10 million *yuan* prize for the best collection of music
from movies or television dramas. This is its largest "money burning" activity since it was financed with 50 million
yuan.

捎带脚儿 shāo dài jiǎor

顺便。in passing; incidentally

例:不麻烦,这件事等我回家的时候捎带脚儿就能给办了。
It's no trouble at all. I can do this on my way home.

哨 shào

1. 说;聊。chat; gossip; talk

例：她又和朋友哨上了。

She gossiped with her friend again.

2.吹牛。boast; talk big; brag

例：他跟我哨他在股票交易所七分钟就赚了二千元。

He bragged to me that he made 2,000 *yuan* in seven minutes on the stock market.

折 shé

失败，没有成功。fail; not succeed

例：这次期末数学考试我们班折了五个。

Five students in our class failed the final examination in mathematics this semester.

蛇头 shé tóu

指专门从事把人偷渡出境的人或组织。a person or gang that ferries people illegally across the border

例：他是东南亚最大的蛇头。

He is the biggest human trafficker in Southeast Asia.

神经搭错线了 shén jīng dā cuò xiàn le

指某人神经不正常；举止言行反常。have one's nerves crossed (to act strangely or behave differently from normal)

例：别理他，他今天神经搭错线了。

Don't talk to him. He's acting very strangely today.

神聊 shén liáo

指漫无目的长时间兴致勃勃地聊天。a long rambling talk; a long, animated discussion on many topics

例：他们俩一见面就神聊上了，也不知哪有那么多话可说。

They started a long discussion as soon as they met. Who knows how they found that much to talk about.

神哨 shén shào

1. 特别能说、能聊。very talkative

例：她特能神哨，从不觉得累。

She is very talkative and never feels tired.

2. 胡说八道，乱吹一通。talk trash; talk big; talk nonsense

例：当他不做生意时，他就喜欢跟哥们儿神哨。

He likes to talk nonsense with his friends when he doesn't have any business to do.

生 shēng

指对男士的称呼，意同"先生"。sir; mister (Mr.)

例：请告诉王生大厅里有人正在等他。

Please tell Mr. Wang that someone is waiting for him at the lobby now.

省油的灯 shěng yóu de dēng

容易对付的人；勤俭的人。an oil-saving lamp; someone industrious and thrifty/A metaphor for someone who is easy to deal with.

例：她可不是省油的灯。她花的钱比她挣的还多，而且与人合作十分不友好。

She's not an oil-saving lamp. She spends more than she earns and is not very cooperative.

狮子大张口 shī zi dà zhāng kǒu

向人提出要求时，索要的数目很大，也指非常贪心。

be too greedy; ask for (demand) a huge sum of money

例：我同意借钱给他，但我没想到他狮子大张口，要我一个月的工资。

I agree to lend him some money. But I didn't expect him to ask for the equivalent of my monthly salary.

十三点 shí sān diǎn

形容有些傻气,办事鲁莽或言行不合情理的人。A metaphor for simple-minded person; stupid person; rash person.

例:我之所以没雇他是因为与他谈话时我觉得他是个十三点。

I didn't employ him because when I talked with him I felt he was a bit simple-minded.

十有八九 shí yǒu bā jiǔ

指绝大数。mostly; in eight or nine cases out of ten

例:由于下雨,他十有八九不会来了。

Most likely he won't come because of the rain.

十一路 shí yī lù

指步行,走路。walk

例:办公室离我家不远,所以我每天乘十一路去上班。

The office is not far from my home, so I go to work on foot everyday.

时下菜 shí xià cài

指大量上市的适合季节的蔬菜（多指价钱便宜的）。vegetables in season (seasonal vegetable in abundant market supply and cheap)

例:她很省钱,常买时下菜。

She usually buys vegetables in season to save money.

屎 shǐ

指水平低;很差;愚笨。poorly; of low quality; like shit

例:这球踢得真够屎的。

The soccer team played like shit.

屎盆子 shǐ pén zi

比喻过错、坏事、罪过。crap pot，meaning fault；mistake；
bad thing；sin

例：这完全是他们的过错，可是他们却把屎盆子扣在我头上。
It's their fault completely. But they made me take the responsibility for it.

事儿 shìr

1.爱管闲事；啰唆。meddlesome；troublesome

例：我们最好别让她看见我们在这儿。她特事儿。万一她看
见我她会告诉我妈的。

We'd better not let her see us here. She is too meddle-
some. She would tell my mother if she sees me.

2.谨小慎微；多虑。overly concerned

例：你真够事儿的。我又不是小孩子了，我知道如何照顾自
己。

You're overly concerned. I'm not a child any more. I
know how to take care of myself.

事儿妈 shìr mā

1.形容爱管闲事，爱挑剔的，言语啰唆的人。meddler；wordy
speaker；picky person

例：她是个事儿妈。她很少对她丈夫买给她的东西表示满意。

She's a very picky person. She is seldom satisfied with the
things her husband buys for her.

2.形容多虑，谨小慎微的人。worrywart；overanxious person

例：她可是个事儿妈。一件事她能反复考虑半天。

She is a worrywart. She thinks over one matter over
and over again.

事儿事儿的 shìr shìr de

指人老于世故；会来事儿。sophisticated；worldly-wise

例：他可是非常事儿事儿的人，对我的工作常挑剔，而且还指手划脚地告诉我该做什么不该做什么。

He's very sophisticated. He always analyzes my work and advises me what I should do or should not do.

收线 shōu xiàn

挂断电话。hang up the receiver

例：我想我该收线了，否则又要耽误你的工作了。

I think I should hang up now otherwise I'll interfere with your work.

收心 shōu xīn

控制心情，让心从激动、兴奋状态恢复平静（通常指节假日后将心情调整到日常工作状态）。

to return one's mood to normal after play or excitement；to readjust to work after holidays or vacations

例：明天就开学了，你也该收收心了。今天就别出去了，在家里复习一下功课。

School will start tomorrow. You should get your mind off play. Don't go out today—stay at home and review your homework.

手榴弹 shǒu liú dàn

指走后门用的，作为礼品送人的酒。grenade/A term for a bottle of wine that people give as a gift in order to cotton up to someone.

例：他昨天才从美国回来就给头儿送去两枚外国造的手榴弹。

He came back from the United States yesterday and gave two foreign-made "grenades" to his boss.

手艺潮 shǒu yì cháo

手艺不高；技术不好。(of skill) inadequate；unskilful；not proficient

例：她的手艺潮，我可不让她给我做外套。

I won't ask her to make my coat because her skill is not up to scratch.

手壮 shǒu zhuàng

指手气特别好。luck at gambling, cards, etc.

例：今天她手壮，盘盘都是她赢。

She got a lucky hand today. Every time we played, she won.

书商 shū shāng

指以盈利为目的，并用个人的资金投资策划、组织出版并发行图书的商人。book trader who plans, organizes and invests in the publication and distribution of books to make a profit

例：在当了几年编辑之后，他便辞职做起书商来了。

After several years' work as an editor, he gave up his job and started to work as a book trader.

数落 shǔ luo

1. 责备。scold；rebuke；blame

例：由于回来晚了，妈妈就数落我一通。

My mother rebuked me for coming home late.

2. 一件事接着一件事不停地说。talk on and on；say sth. again and again

例：她爱没完没了地数落她们家的事。

She likes to go on and on about her family.

刷卡 shuā kǎ

指使用信用卡记账、付款。pay by credit card

例：她喜欢刷卡，不愿付现金。

She prefers using her credit card to paying in cash.

刷课 shuā kè

逃学；旷课。cut class; play truant; play hooky; skip school

例：他跟我说他曾是个淘气鬼，三天两头刷课。

He told me he used to be a naughty boy and skipped school every other day.

刷夜 shuā yè

指与不三不四的人鬼混，在外过夜。stay away from home all night; spend the night outside with shady characters

例：他昨晚又刷夜去了。

He fooled around with shady characters again last night.

耍 shuǎ

1. 玩。play; have fun

例：我们到海边耍了几天。

We enjoyed a few days on the beach.

2. 折腾整弄某人；骗。make fun of sb.; fool sb.; play tricks on sb.

例：我没耍你。我是认真的。

I'm not fooling you. I'm serious.

耍单儿 shuǎ dānr

不顾天冷，仍穿单薄的衣服。wear less on purpose; be thinly clad/Someone who refuses to put on more clothes just for beauty's sake or to flaunt good health in cold weather.

例:由于她在特别冷的那天要单儿,结果患了感冒。

She caught a cold by wearing too few clothes on a freezingly cold day.

耍大牌 shuǎ dà pái

摆出明星的架子。to put on airs; to affect a movie-star pose

例:他由于有事没能参加那台晚会,结果被人说是他在耍大牌。

He didn't attend the party because he had something else to do, and everyone said he was playing the movie star.

耍钱 shuǎ qián

1. 赌博。gambling

例:我对他真是没辙了。他总去耍钱,谁说他都不听。

I want nothing to do with him. He's always going gambling and won't listen to anyone.

2. 炫耀自己的富有。to show off one's wealth

例:听说他的婚礼就花了十几万,这不是明明在耍钱玩吗。

People are saying that he spent over ten thousand on his wedding. Obviously he took the opportunity to show off his wealth, didn't he?

帅呆 shuài dāi

指某人或某事物极为漂亮,或某行为非常出众。the appearance of sb. (usually male)or sth. that is very beautiful or handsome; sb. demeanor or bearing that is outstanding or extraordinarily unusual

例:你儿子的长相真是帅呆了,完全可以去当模特。

Your son is extremely good looking. He has the right qualifications to be a model.

帅哥 shuài gē

指英俊、潇洒、帅气的男子。handsome young chap；smart man

例：小男孩穿着一身牛仔装去问妈妈自己像不像个小帅哥。

The little boy asked his mother whether he looked smart wearing jeans.

涮 shuàn

耍弄；骗。make fun of；make a fool of；deceive；be stood up

例1：如果你真爱他，就别再涮他了。

If you really love him you shouldn't make fun of him any more.

例2：她答应昨晚请他吃饭，所以他在饭店前等了两个小时，但她没来。最后他明白他被涮了。

She promised to treat him to dinner last night，so he waited two hours outside of a restaurant for her to show up. He finally realized that he was being stood up.

爽 shuǎng

1.指人的性格开朗、直率，说话爽快，办事干净、利落、痛快。（nature of sb.）straightforward；frank；forthright；efficient；do sth. quickly；to the point

例：她这人特爽。我喜欢跟她一起共事。

She is very frank. I like working with her.

2.指使人感到身心畅快。to feel well；comfortable

例1：干完活后，冲个热水澡那才爽呢！

It feels great to take a hot shower after working.

例2：你知道什么能让我爽到家吗？那就是大热天里喝上一瓶冰镇啤酒。

Do you know what makes me feel best? Having a bottle of

ice-cold beer in a hot summer day.

水 shuǐ

1.指质量差。poor quality；shoddy

例：那个公司生产的香肠越来越水了。

The quality of the company's sausages became worse and worse.

2.赔本。lose money；be in the hole；run a business at a loss

例：这趟广州之行我可是水了，没有人买我的产品。

Not one client bought my product. I lost money during my business trip to Guangzhou.

水分 shuǐ fèn

本指物体内所含的水，引申为一件事情中所含虚假、不可信的成分或数量。moisture content/A term used to describe something that has been exaggerated or falsified.

例：这笔款可有不少水分。

The sum of money has been exaggerated.

水货 shuǐ huò

1.指质量差的商品。low-quality goods；shoddy goods

例：市场上的水货太多。

There are too many shoddy goods on the market.

2.指走私来的货物。smuggled goods

例：这台摄像机一定是水货，否则不会卖得这么便宜。

This video camera recorder must be a smuggled good, otherwise it wouldn't be so cheap.

水穴 shuǐ xuè

指赔钱或盈利极少的走穴演出。privately organized show

that makes little profit

例:走穴通常分火穴和水穴两种。一般没有名气的歌手都先从走水穴开始。

There are mainly two kinds of privately organized shows in China: those that are profitable and those that are not. Usually new pop singers have to work their way up starting with shows that do not make much profit.

顺 shùn

1. 随手拿走;偷。walk off with sth.; pick up sth. on the sly; shoplift; steal

例:在回家的路上他顺了一棵白菜。

He walked off with a cabbage on the way home.

2. 将某物直着抬或扔。move sth. in a vertical way

例:我帮他把竹杆顺出窗外。

I helped him push the pole out off the window.

3. 方便;顺利。handy; convenient and easy to use; smoothly; without difficulty

例:这钢笔特别好,所以用起来特顺。

This pen is very handy because it's got a good point.

顺出去 shùn chū qù

1. 指把某物竖着抬出去。carry sth. out vertically

例:请帮忙把这个桌子顺出去。

Please help me to put this big desk on its side and move it out of the room.

2. 把某人打倒或痛打一顿后再抬出去。carry sb. out after knocking him down or giving him a good thrashing

例:你怎么还不走,是不是想让我的手下把你顺出去?

How come you haven't left yet. Do you want my men to carry you out vertically after giving you a good thrashing?

顺溜 shùn liu

1. 有次序；不乱。in good order

例：把鞋都摆顺溜了。

Put the shoes in good order.

2. 顺当；流畅；无阻拦。smoothly

例：这首歌她唱得挺顺溜的。

She rendered the song smoothly.

3. 顺从听话。obedient

例：相对面言，女孩子比男孩子顺溜多了。

Girls are more obedient than boys.

4. 长相不难看；使人看得舒服。look comfortable; good looking; nice

例：这女孩长得顺溜。

This girl is good looking.

顺毛驴 shùn máo lú

指只听顺耳的话、表扬的话的人，或让别人顺从他的意志办事的人。one who only listens to pleasing words and makes others fall in with his wishes

例：他是个顺毛驴。你若求他办事就得顺着他。

He likes to listen to compliments. If you ask him to do you a favor, you'd better fall in with his wishes and make him happy.

顺走 shùn zǒu

指顺手拿走；偷走。steal; sneak away with sth.

例：我的手袋放在这个椅子上，不知让谁给顺走了。

I put my handbag on the chair here and don't know who stole it.

说摞了 shuō luò le

说出事情真相；全部抖搂出来；招供。confess; tell the truth

例：他在晚饭上一口白兰地酒也没喝，因为他怕喝醉了把那

最新中国俚语

New Slang of China

S

件事给说摞了。

He didn't take a sip of brandy during the dinner because he was afraid to get drunk and tell the truth of the matter.

说胖就喘 shuō pàng jiù chuǎn

形容经不住别人的夸奖。to puff and blow when others say you are fat/A metaphor for one who cannot stand praise from others.

例:瞧你这个人说胖就喘,昨天刚夸你身体好,你今天就病了。

Look at you. I just praised your good health yesterday and you are sick today.

说脱落了 shuō tuō luò le (口语中念"shuō tū lu le")

说走嘴。make a slip of tongue; let an inadvertent remark slip; spill the beans

例:她没把住自己的嘴,把这事说脱落了。

She didn't hold her tongue and ended up spilling the beans.

私了 sī liǎo

指私下解决,不诉讼,不打官司。settle a dispute privately (without lawsuit)

例:他们在拿到司机给的一大笔钱之后,就撤消诉讼并把这个案子私了了。

They dropped the lawsuit and settled the case privately after they received a large sum of money from the driver.

死碴 sǐ chá

指拼命地打架,以决输赢。fight fiercely

例:他们是冤家对头,一见面就死碴。

They are enemies. They will fight fiercely when they meet.

死扛 sǐ káng

1.拼命支撑或承担责任。go all out to support or shoulder responsibilities

例：你无需有任何顾忌,我会为你死扛的。

You needn't worry about anything. I will go all out to support you.

2.顶住压力死也不说或招供。refuse to confess or reveal information

例：他们折磨他,但他一直死扛着。

They tortured him but he refused to reveal any information.

死磕 sǐ kē

玩儿命;拼命。risk one's life

例：你没必要为这点儿事跟那家伙死磕下去。

It's not necessary for you to risk your life to fight him over such a trivial matter.

死性 sǐ xing

固执;死心眼;不灵活。stubborn; obstinate; having a one-track mind; inflexible; stiff

例：他这人特别死性,一但他决定了的事情,没有人能改变他。

He's as stubborn as a mule. Once he makes up his mind, no one can make him change.

死轴子 sǐ zhóu zi

形容人固执。a metaphor for one who is stubborn

例：这件事这么做行不通,你不会换种方式做吗? 你呀,真是个死轴子!

It won't work in this way. Why don't you change to another way? What a stubborn person you are!

夙 sóng

讥讽人软弱无能。weak and incompetent

例：他特别夙，一遇到困难就往后退。

He is weak and incompetent. He always backs away from difficulty.

耸 sǒng

指太夸张，过分。overdo sth.；go too far；excessive；exaggerated

例：送太大包的鲜花反而被人认为是耸。

It would be considered too excessive if you send a super large bundle of flowers.

送死 sòng sǐ

自寻死路；找死。court death

例：他可不想白白地送死。

He didn't want to court death for nothing.

馊主意 sōu zhǔ yi

不高明的办法。rotten idea；lousy thought

例：这一定是你出的馊主意。

It must be your rotten idea.

碎催 suì cuī

伺侯，听从他人支使，干杂事或跑路的人。errand-boy

例：我辞了那份工作，因为我厌倦做公司老板的碎催。

I resigned the job because I hate to be the boss' errand-boy.

碎嘴子 suì zuǐ zi

1. 说话啰唆，没完没了。talk on and on；chatter away

例：只要你跟她说一句话，她就跟你来碎嘴子。

She talks on and on with you as long as you have a word with her.

2.指说话没完没了的人。windbag；garrulous person

例：什么时候你变成碎嘴子老太婆了。

When did you become a prattling old woman?

损 sǔn

1.残忍；阴险；狠毒。vicious；wicked；cruel

例：他这手可真够损的。

That was really a mean idea of his.

2.挖苦；嘲讽。caustic；sarcastic

例：她这人说话特别损。

She is good at making savage remarks.

缩头乌龟 suō tóu wū guī

比喻胆小怕事的人。turtle with its head in its shell/A metaphor for a cowardly person.

例：那小子是个缩头乌龟，没有一点儿男子汉气。

He's not a man, he's a coward.

T

他妈的 tā mā de

　　骂人话。fuck

塔儿哄 tǎr hòng

　　起哄；捣乱；添乱。create a big disturbance; make trouble

　　例：他成心跟我们在这儿塔儿哄。我们决定往东,他却偏要往西。

　　He made trouble for us on purpose. We decided to do it this way, but he insisted on doing it the opposite way.

抬 tái

　　1.揭发；供出来。expose; confess; reveal one's accomplices

　　例：在审讯中他把同伙抬了出来。

　　He revealed the name of his partner in the interrogation.

　　2.请出；说出(有势有名望的人来压别人)。drop name (of a famous or powerful person) in order to achieve one's aims; ask for help

　　例：不管你抬出谁来,就是总统也帮不了你。

　　It doesn't matter who you ask for help, even the president won't be able to help you.

抬杠 tái gàng

　　争论。argue; wrangle

　　例：他们俩到一起准抬杠。

　　The two wrangle whenever they meet.

抬轿子 tái jiào zi

比喻吹捧、奉承、拍马屁。(originally) to carry sb. in a sedan chair；(metaphor) to flatter；sing the praises of；lick sb. 's boots

例：他这个人最喜欢别人为他抬轿子。

Most of all he likes to be flattered.

抬轿子的 tái jiào zi de

比喻好吹捧、奉承他人的人或拍马屁者。sedan chair carrier；flatterer (someone who flatters or sings the praise of others)；booster；boot polisher；sycophant

例：这里的大部分人都不喜欢他，只有几个抬轿子的整天围着他转。

Most of the people here don't like him. Only a few sycophants stay with him.

抬人 tái rén

使人显得更美。make sth. look better；beautify；doll up

例：这身新衣服真抬人。

This new suit makes you look wonderful.

太空人 tài kōng rén

指常乘飞机来往于两地的人（常指工作单位在一处，而家住他乡，两地相距甚远，需乘飞机来住的人）。(lit.) spaceman；commuter, normally by airplane/A term referring someone who works in one place, but whose family lives in another place, so he or she has to fly back and forth between the two places frequently.

例：为了得到香港这份高薪工作，他宁愿去做太空人。

He'd be willing to commute in order to do this highly paid job in Hong Kong.

太平公主 tài píng gōng zhǔ

戏称胸部平坦的女子。(jocular term) girl with flat breasts

例1:不少太平公主都热衷于通过各种方式改变自我形象,她们无疑成了商家推销各种隆胸产品的对象。

Many young girls are keen on changing their self-image by various means. They have no doubt become the targets of merchants who sell various products to make breasts bigger.

例2:这种产品最适合于那些太平公主们使用。

This product is most suitable for girls with flat breasts.

弹 tán

变软,比喻身体筋疲力尽,动弹不了;瘫软。unable to move; turn soft/Someone who is exhausted or whose arms or legs have become weak and limp.

例1:他把行李抬上楼后就弹了。

He was tired out after he carried the suitcase upstairs.

例2:坏消息立刻使她弹了。

The bad news immediately made her weak and limp.

探班 tàn bān

到影视剧拍摄现场看望或采访演职人员。to visit or interview actors and actresses at the filming location

例:前不久,我们节目组到《天下无贼》影片的拍摄现场探班,打探到不少最新拍摄动态。

Not long ago, our program team went to visit actors and actresses at the filming location of the film "A World Without Thieves" and got a lot of the latest news of the film.

探底 tàn dǐ

探察底细或背景。to find out the ins and outs; to dig up

the exact details or background

例：为了增加影片对观众的神秘感，这部电影在拍摄之中不许任何人前来探底。

In order to make the film more mysterious to the audience, no one is allowed to find out about the shooting process.

蹚道 tāng dào

先找门路；了解情况；先试一试。get information in advance

例1：他很快就毕业了，他让他父亲为他的工作蹚道。

He will graduate from school soon. He has asked his father to help him find a job.

例2：如果你不先蹚道，你就不知如何办合资公司。

If you don't get information in advance, you won't know how to set up a joint venture.

蹚混水 tāng hún shuǐ

一起干；参加；凑趣儿。do sth. together; participate; join in

例：他们准备编本字典。你想跟他们蹚这个混水吗？

They're going to compile a dictionary. Would you like to join in and work with them?

趟雷 tāng léi

扫除障碍。to clear off/remove obstacles

例：你就大胆去干吧。别担心，有我给你趟雷呢！

Just go and do it bravely. Don't worry. You have me to clear the way for you.

掏心窝 tāo xīn wō

说心里话，说真实的话。tell the truth; pour out one's innermost thoughts and feelings; talk frankly

例：他跟我掏心窝地聊了两个多小时，最后我被他的真诚所打动,与他和解了。

He talked with me and poured out his innermost thoughts and feelings for more than two hours. At last I was moved by his sincerity and placated him.

淘 táo

1. 寻找;找到。to look for; find

例:我总爱在周末上街淘我喜欢的东西。

On weekends I love to go shopping and look for my favorite things.

2. 买。buy

例:你这双靴子是从哪儿淘来的?

Where did you buy this pair of boots?

逃票 táo piào

指乘公共汽车不买车票。take a bus without paying the fare; evade bus fare

例:他总在汽车拥挤的下班高峰时逃票。

He always evades bus fares when the bus is crowded at the rush hours.

讨个说法 tǎo ge shuō fǎ

要一个公正的答复或解释。want to have a fair judgment, answer or explanation

例:他就此事提出上诉的真正目的是为了讨个说法,其他的一切都是次要的。

The ture reason why he lodged an appeal on this matter is that he wants to get an explanation.

套瓷 tào cí

指与不太熟悉的人拉关系;表现出亲近的样子。cotton up

to；try to establish a relationship with someone；act as if one has a close relationship with someone else

例：他只见过我一面,但他使劲儿与我套瓷仿佛就像是我的老朋友一样。

He only met me once, but he acted as if we were old friends.

套近乎 tào jìn hu

指极力与某人拉关系。try to get in with sb.；try to create a close relationship with sb.

例：他有求于我,所以他才来跟我套近乎。

He wanted me to do him a favor, so he tried to get in with me.

套儿 tàor

指圈套;陷阱;罗网。snare；trap

例：你千万别去,说不定那是人家给下的大套儿。

You should never go there. It might be a big trap they laid for you.

提气 tí qì

1.使情绪振奋。excite；inspire；raise one's morale

例：这台晚会真提气。

The performance inspired the audience.

2.使人显得精神,有气派。make one look better

例：好衣服就是能给人提气。

Good clothes can really make a person look better.

T tì

指钱。money

例：他经不住 T 的诱惑走上斜路。

He couldn't resist the temptation of money and took to evilways.

T 恤 tì xù

指短袖圆领汗衫。T-shirt

例：她买了十件不同颜色的 T 恤。

She bought ten T-shirts in different colors.

添堵 tiān dǔ

增加烦恼；使人不愉快。trouble; disturb; annoy; displease

例：他今天本来就不开心。你就别为这点儿小事给他添堵了。

Don't trouble him with such a small thing. He is already in low spirits today.

添乱 tiān luàn

增加麻烦。trouble; disturb

例：你不该在他忙得团团转的时候去添乱。

You shouldn't disturb him when he's up to his ears in work.

甜 tián

1. 指获利很大，收入很多。profitable; well-paying

例：这笔买卖挺甜的。

This business is really profitable.

2. 指人长得漂亮，可爱。(of women) sweet; pretty; nice; lovely

例：她长得很甜，很受大家的喜欢。

She is very sweet and everyone likes her.

甜姐 tián jiě

指容貌漂亮、温柔善良、可爱的女子。sweet girl; cutie-pie

例：她虽已年过三十岁，但她在银幕上仍然保持着甜姐的形象。

She's over thirty but she's managed to maintain her cutie-pie image in the movies.

挑刺儿 tiāo cìr

挑毛病；指责他人的缺点或短处。find fault with sb.；pick holes in

例：她总盯着我的工作，并总想给我挑刺儿。

She always keeps her eyes on my work and always tries to find fault with me.

挑工 tiāo gōng

辞职；辞工；罢手不干。quit；resign；leave a job

例：他不喜欢这活儿，所以挑工走了。

He didn't like the work, so he quitted.

条儿 tiáor

指身材。figure；shape

例：她的条儿够棒的。

She's got a beautiful figure.

调侃 tiáo kǎn

1. 开玩笑。joke；tease；make fun of

例：我常跟他调侃说他是面条师傅，因为他只会做面条。

I often tease him about being a noodle chef because he only knows how to make noodles.

2. 耍贫嘴；闲聊。empty talk；chitchat

例：这部电视剧充满了调侃的味道。

The soap opera is full of empty talk.

跳槽 tiào cáo

1. 指调换工作。change johs；job-hopping

例：他一直不断地跳槽，直到找到满意的工作为止。

He kept changing jobs until he found one he was satisfied with.

2.离婚与别人结婚。divorce in order to marry someone else

例：她比他丈夫小得多,看上去也不太可靠。我担心有一天她会跳槽另寻一个年轻的男人。

She is much younger than her husband and seems very un-reliable. I'm afraid she'll divorce her husband one day to marry a younger man.

跳水价 tiào shuǐ jià

最低的价钱。the lowest price

例：A：这件衣服还能再便宜点吗？

Could you lower the price of this jacket a little?

B：不行,这已经是跳水价了。

No. That's already the lowest price.

贴 tiē

指判处死刑。sentence to death; to be burned

例：他知道他从银行贪污了那么大数额的巨款,怎么也得贴了。

He knew he would be sentenced to death for embezzling such a large sum of money from the bank.

铁 tiě

指关系紧密、牢固。(of a relationship) intimate; close; firm; stable

例：我们的关系很铁,他不会出卖我。

Our relationship is very stable. He won't betray me.

铁磁 tiě cí

1.指关系特别紧密的朋友。intimate friend; close friend; soul mate

例：我们是铁磁,所以你的困难就是我的困难。

We are close friends, so your difficulties are my difficulties.

2. 指关系极好、忠实可靠。（of relationship）very good；faithful；reliable

例：他的哥们儿都跟他铁磁。在需要帮助时，他们都会拉他一把。

All his friends are very good to him. They give him hands when he needs them.

铁哥们儿 tiě gē ménr

指关系极好、亲密无间的男性朋友。intimate male friend；close male friend

例：他叫了几个铁哥们儿帮他盖房子。

He asked some of his close friends to help him build the house.

铁公鸡 tiě gōng jī

比喻吝啬、小气，一分钱也不出的人。iron rooster；a miser/A mean person who is extremely stingy and unwilling to lend money to others.

例：你别指望她可怜你，她可是个十足的铁公鸡。

You can't count on her showing you any mercy. She is a miser indeed.

铁姐们儿 tiě jiě ménr

指关系极好，亲密无间的女性朋友。intimate female friend；close female friend

例：这是我的铁姐们儿，刚从美国回来。

This is my close friend. She's just come back from the United States.

铁嘴 tiě zuǐ

比喻能说会道、能言善辩的人。iron mouth/A term for a

good talker; a talkative person; a chatter box

例:他天生一张铁嘴,一说起来就没完,从不觉得累。

He was born with an iron mouth. He talks on and on and never gets tired.

挺 tǐng

1. 坚持;支撑;承受。stand; endure

例:这点儿疼痛还挺得住。

I can stand the pain.

2. 对付。deal with; handle

例:这件事你自己挺一下就成。

You can deal with it yourself.

挺尸 tǐng shī

指平躺;睡觉。lie; take a cat nap; snooze

例:他在凉快的地方挺尸呢。

He's snoozing in the shade.

通吃 tōng chī

无论什么全能对付;什么都吃。sweep the deck; be able to deal with everything; eat everything; defeat everyone

例:他这个人厉害,黑道白道通吃。(黑道指黑社会,白道指警察或法制社会。)

He is really terrific. He can sweep the deck no matter if it's legal or illegal.

同道儿 tóng dàor

指同是从事干坏事的人。partners in crime; people involved in the same illegal trade

例:他们是同道儿,所以经常相互包庇。

They are involved in the same illegal trade so they often

help each other.

同志 tóng zhì

同性恋者之间的相互称呼。comrade (a form of address between homosexuals)

例：七八十年代人们之间常称呼"同志"，如今都改用"先生"
和"小姐"了，你知道为什么吗？因为怕引起别人误会。

People usually addressed each other as "Comrade" in the
1970s and 1980s. But now they use "Mr." or "Miss" instead. Do you know why? Because they're afraid that others will misunderstand.

筒子楼 tǒng zi lóu

指一种长走廊，两边有门，形状似长筒子的楼房。tube-
shaped building with lining on both sides of a long corridor/
In China, this type of building is mainly used for offices or
classrooms but can also be used for residential quarters.

例：他终于从破旧的筒子楼搬进了新的高层建筑。

He finally moved out of the shabby tube-shaped building into a new apartment highrise.

头彩 tóu cǎi

第一名，大奖。first prize in a lottery

例：上次摸奖他中了头彩，一辆汽车外加 50 万元奖金。

Last time he won the first prize, a car plus a 500,000 *yuan*
bonus, in the lottery.

头大 tóu dà

指头痛，比喻感到为难或发愁。be puzzled; have a head-
ache; be in a stew

例 1：看见这封信他的头立刻大了，他不知怎样答复才妥当。

This letter puzzled him. He didn't know how to answer it properly.

例 2：一提找一个照顾孩子的人,她的头就大。

She is in a stew over finding a baby-sitter.

头儿 tóur

指单位领导或团体、帮派中掌权的人。leader；head of a unit, group or a gang；boss

例：这件事头儿不同意,我没法干。

I can't do it unless the head of the unit agrees.

头头脑脑 tóu tóu nǎo nǎo

指大小领导。all the deparment heads and leaders of a unit, company，organization

例：今天上午单位里的头头脑脑们都去开会了。

All the heads of the unit had a meeting this morning.

透心凉 tòu xīn liáng

1. 很冷。extremely cold；freezing；heartfelt cold

例 1：他在回家的路上让雨给浇了个透心凉。

On his way home he got wet all over in the rain.

例 2：冬天西北风一刮,吹得人是透心凉。

The winter northwest wind freezes people to the marrow.

2. 灰心；寒心。be bitterly disappointed；be discouraged

例：她的一句话说得我透心凉。

Her words made me bitterly disappointed.

透着 tòu zhe

显得。look；seem；appear

例 1：夏天白色的衣服本身就透着一种凉爽的感觉。

White clothes look cool in summer.

例2：她的表情透着一丝恐惧。

She seems a little frightened.

秃瓢儿 tū piáor

1. 没有头发的人；秃子。baldhead

例：他不敢当众脱帽，因为他是个秃瓢儿。

He doesn't dare take off his hat in front of people because he is a baldhead.

2. 指男孩子。boy; baby boy; son

例：她想要个女孩，却生了个秃瓢儿。

She wanted to have a girl, but she gave birth to a boy.

土 tǔ

1. 见识少；没见过世面。unsophisticated; not well-informed; ignorant; unexperienced/A term used to describe someone who hasn't seen very much of the world.

例：你真土，连西餐都没吃过。

You're really unsophisticated. You haven't even had Western-style dishes yet.

2. 土里土气。uncouth; rustic

例：这裙子的颜色对我来说太土了一点儿。

The color of the dress is too rustic for my taste.

土鳖 tǔ biē

1. 地鳖的通称。beetle

例：我小时候常抓土鳖到药店去卖。

I used to catch beetles and sell them in a drugstore when I was young.

2. 比喻懂得很少，土里土气的人。ignorant person; clodhopper; a country bumpkin

例：你真是个土鳖，连这个也没见过。

You're really a clod-hopper. You haven't seen such a thing like this.

土得掉渣儿 tǔ de diào zhār

形容人十分土气,无知;见识极少。very ignorant; rustic; unrefined

例:她刚进城时土得掉渣儿。

She looked very unrefined when she first came to the city.

土老冒儿 tǔ lǎo màor

讥指农村人或见识少的人。a country bumpkin; clod-hopper; ignoramus; hillbilly (scornful)

例:他根本不懂什么是艺术。他是个土老冒儿!

He doesn't understand art. What a bumpkin!

吐血 tù xiě

指拿出一笔钱。"spit blood"; to foot the bill; pay for sth.

例:你不能总吃白食。今天轮到你吐血了。

You can't have free meals all the time. It's your turn to foot the bill today.

吐腥 tù xīng

暴露自己生意上的手法。to reveal one's secrets or methods of doing business

例:他为人非常谨慎,从不轻易吐腥。

He is very cautious and never reveals his business secrets to anyone.

腿着 tuǐ zhe

指步行。to walk; to go on foot

例:我的自行车坏了,只好腿着去了,反正又不远。

My bicycle's broken so I'll have to walk there. It's not very far though.

托儿 tuōr

1.指雇来冒充顾客购物以吸引他人、帮助雇主促销的人。
someone hired by a store owner to pretend to be a customer in order to attract customers

例：她是我哥哥雇来的托儿。

She was hired by my brother to be an "enthusiastic customer".

2.指为办成事暗地里所托咐的人。someone entrusted to perform a task

例：她找了两个托儿跟踪她丈夫，看他下班后干什么。

She found two people to follow her husband to see what he does after work.

托儿姐 tuōr jiě

指当"托儿"的女青年。a young woman hired by a store owner to pretend to be a customer in order to attract customers

例：最近生意不好，你能帮我找两个托儿姐吗？

My business is not going well. Would you find two young women to be "enthusiastic customers" for me?

脱口秀 tuō kǒu xiù

演讲，用谈话的方式表演。talk show

例：每年在各大学都要举行脱口秀比赛，获奖者有机会步入电视主持人的行列。

All the colleges and universities will hold a talk show competition each year and the winners might have an opportunity of stepping into a career as a television host.

脱星 tuō xīng

专门从事拍摄裸露性的照片或电影的明星。a star who has been photographed nude, or who is well known for roles in sexy scenes particularly those involving nudity

例:玛丽莲·梦露被人们视为是一颗永不坠落的脱星,至今人们还会记得她。

Marylin Munro is regarded as a star that never sets and is still remembered by people.

W

哇塞 wā sài

表示惊讶，惊叹。Wo si! /A term to express surprise, an exclamation，etc.

例：哇塞，这地方简直是太美了！

Wo si，what a beautiful place!

歪才 wāi cái

指与众不同的才华；小聪明。unique artistic talent；cleverness in a certain field

例：我真没料到他干这事还有点儿歪才。

I had no idea he was so talented in this area.

歪瓜裂枣 wāi guā liè zǎo

指长得不正的瓜和裂开口的枣，但这种瓜和枣却十分甜。比喻人或物虽长得不好看，却很实惠，心地善良。crooked melon and split open date/A metaphor for someone who is not good looking but honest，sincere and kindhearted.

例：别看他长得跟歪瓜裂枣似的，可还有不少女孩子喜欢他。

He looks like a crooked melon and split open date，but many girls like him.

崴泥 wǎi ní

陷进泥水里，比喻遇上麻烦事；事情不好办；糟糕。get stuck in the mud/get into trouble；make things worse；go wrong.

例：这次她崴泥了，到了海边才发现忘记带游泳衣了。

She got into trouble this time. When she arrived at the beach，

最新中国俚语 New Slang of China

she found she had forgotten to bring her swimming suit.

外活 wài huó

指本职工作以外的活或工作；额外的工作。extra work

例：她在完成本职工作以后常干些外活。

She often does some extra work after she finishes her own job.

外快 wài kuài

指额外的临时性的收入。additional income; temporary income; extra money

例：她靠晚上辅导学生挣些外快。

She makes some extra money by tutoring in the evening.

外来妹 wài lái mèi

从外地来到城市里打工的女孩子。a young woman from elsewhere who finds temporary work in a city

例：北京的外来妹越来越多。

There are more and more young women from other parts of the country who find temporary work in Beijing.

玩儿蛋去 wánr dàn qù

滚蛋；让人一边呆着去（斥责或骂人话）。(swearword) fuck off; go away; beat it; scram

例：我不听任何人的话，无论是谁统统给我玩儿蛋去。

I don't listen to anyone no matter who they are. I simply tell them to beat it.

玩儿得转 wánr de zhuàn

（对某人、某事）运用自如；掌握得住；会使用。handle (sb. or sth.) easily; use (a tool) with skill; master with ease; able to use or operate

例1：这匹马除了我没人能玩儿得转。

No one can easily handle the horse except me.

例2：他太淘气，没人能玩儿得转他。

He is naughty that nobody can keep him under control.

玩儿活儿 wánr huór

指干活儿；干事情；干工作。do sth.；work

例：这些天我们没玩儿活儿，因为机器全都坏了。

We haven't worked these past few days because all the machines have broken down.

玩儿闹 wánr nào

1. 指淘气鬼；调皮捣蛋的人；流里流气的人。mischievous person；naughty guy；ruffian；rascal；troublemaker

例：这个班有许多小玩儿闹。

There are many troublemakers in this class.

2. 指吃喝玩乐，胡打胡闹。idle away one's time in seeking pleasure；fool around；run wild

例：他什么也不会只知道玩儿闹。

He knows nothing but how to fool around.

玩儿飘 wánr piāo

故意显示自己的技巧，水平。show off one's skill or talent on purpose

例：那两个男孩在马路上骑车玩儿飘。

The two boys are showing off their bike riding skills on the street.

玩儿去 wánr qù

走开；一边呆着去；滚开。（斥责或骂人话）（swearword or a

curse of anger) fuck off; beat it; go away; scram

例：你们统统给我玩儿去，我现在不想见任何人。

You should all beat it. I don't want to see anyone right now.

玩儿深沉 wánr shēn chén

指故作含蓄、老练或说话慢且带有思考状。pretend to be sophisticated; speak in a way so as to deliberately mystify others

例：你不必在我面前玩儿深沉。

You needn't pretend to be sophisticated in front of me.

玩儿完 wánr wán

垮台；失败；死亡。be over; collapse; be finished; be dead and done for

例：一旦计划败露，我们就得玩儿完。

Once the plan is revealed, we'll be dead and done for.

玩儿稀的 wánr xī de

指干别人没干过的事情；干不寻常的事或稀奇古怪的事。do sth. unique

例：他喜欢玩儿稀的，以显示他与众不同。

He likes to do unique things to differentiate himself from others.

玩儿潇洒 wánr xiāo sǎ

指无拘无束、自由自在的样子。act and behave in a natural, carefree and unrestrained manner; be happy-go-lucky

例：年轻人喜欢玩潇洒。他们从不管明天该怎么过。

Young people like to act in a carefree way. They don't care what tomorrow will bring.

玩儿一把 wánr yī bǎ

干一回;玩一次。play (do) sth. once

例:这棋很有意思。你不想跟我玩儿一把吗?

This is a very interesting game. Don't you want to play it with me once?

玩儿阴的 wánr yīn de

指背后使坏,算计他人。play dirty tricks on sb.; secretly scheme against sb.; employ underhand means

例:他当着我的面装出一副笑脸,可背后却给我玩儿阴的。

He puts on a false smile in front of me, but plays evil tricks on me behind the scene.

玩主 wán zhǔ

指好生事、捣乱、能打能闹的人。fop; dandy; trouble-maker

例:他过去曾是个玩主。

He used to be a troublemaker.

王八犊子 wáng bā dú zi

坏孩子;混蛋小子(长者骂年轻人或孩子时说的话)。犊子是指小牛。有时也可以用羔子替代。羔子是指小羊。bastard; son of a bitch, bad boy (a curse used by the elderly to the young)

例:好你个王八犊子,竟敢背着我把家里的电脑给卖了。

You bastard, how dare you sell my computer behind my back.

网吧 wǎng bā

指以收费方式提供客人使用其电脑上网的场所。Internet bar

例:大学里都有网吧。学生在课后泡网吧已成为一种时尚。

There are Internet bars in all colleges and universities. Indulging in Internet bars after classes has become a fashion for students.

网虫 wǎng chóng

热衷于上网，对网络入迷，并且具有一定的网络知识和技能的人。web worm/A metaphor for web fanatics who have a certain knowledge and skills on the Internet.

例：他是一个不折不扣的网虫，每天一回到家就上网，而且一呆就是数小时。

He's a real web worm. He connects to Internet as soon as he comes home and stays on the web for hours.

网恋 wǎng liàn

在网上谈恋爱。web dating；fall in love on web

例：他们经过一年的网恋终于喜结良缘。

They finally got married after web dating for a year.

网友 wǎng yǒu

在网络上结交的朋友。web friend

例：小李上网不到半年，已交了不少网友，还经常参加网友组织的聚会。

Xiao Li has made many web friends in the six months since he was connecting to the Internet. He often goes to parties organized by web friends.

腕儿 wànr

指大人物，名家，权威。celebrity；famous person；expert

例：别小看他，他正经也是个腕儿。

Don't look down on him. He's a famous celebrity.

危 wēi

指情况不好，危险，要出事。far from settled；dangerous；

not too encouraging

例：她担心这事有点儿危。

She is afraid this matter is far from settled.

微面 wēi miàn

微型面包车。minivan

例：我知道哪儿有修微面的地方。

I know a place where minivans can be repaired.

尾巴长 wěi ba cháng

1.指进出门后不随手关门。long tail/A term used for someone who never closes the door when he or she walks in or out.

例：他的尾巴特别长。

He has a long tail (he never closes the door behind him).

2.指人身后拖着很长的东西。long tail/A term used for someone who is carrying something long behind his or her back.

例：他在腰上系了一条绳子，这样他就可以安全地攀岩了。别人看见他身后拖着那条绳子都笑他尾巴长。

He tied a rope around his waist so that he could go rock climbing safely. Some other people saw the rope hanging behind him and made fun of his long tail.

3.比喻事情干得不彻底，不干净。long tail/A term used for something that is done incompletely or not thoroughly.

例：她办什么事尾巴都长。

Nothing she does is done thoroughly.

温 wēn

指温和，老实，胆小。mild；gentle；well-behaved

例：这小男孩特温，从不与其他孩子打架。

The boy is very well-behaved. He never fights with other boys.

温吞水 wēn tūn shuǐ

指慢性子的人。lukewarm water; slow coach or slowpoke

例：她是典型的温吞水，所以你跟她干事要有耐心。

She is a typical slow coach, so you must be extremely patient when you work with her.

文化打工族 wén huà dǎ gōng zú

指除本职工作外兼为他人做临时性文化工作并领取报酬的文人或知识分子。intellectuals who get extra money from second jobs

例：京城近来出现了一批文化打工族。

Lately a group of Beijing intellectuals have started to do second jobs for extra money.

搵钱 wèn qián

赚钱。make money

例：大多数人都搞投机搵钱，可他却要投资办厂当实业家。

Most people engage in speculation to make money quickly, but he wants to invest in a factory and become an industrialist.

窝脖 wō bó

1.（意见、说话等）被别人驳回；被人拒绝；哑口无言。
turn down; overrule; reject; be rendered speechless

例：他不知道他会弄个大窝脖。

He didn't know his idea would be turned down.

2.吃亏；上当。be fooled; be taken in; be duped

例：她被朋友弄了个大窝脖，损失了不少钱。

She was fooled by her friend and lost a lot of money.

3.憋气;不顺心。feel oppressed; be depressed; chafed

例:这些天感到特别窝脖,什么事似乎都干不成。

I feel depressed these days. Everything seems to go wrong.

窝里反 wō lǐ fǎn

指内部的人互相争斗,或在内部闹事、造反;内哄。uproar; internal rebellion; internal dissension; domestic conflict

例:敌人还没打进来,他们自己却先窝里反了。

There was internal dissension among them before the enemy's invasion.

窝里横 wō lǐ hèng

指在自己家中厉害,发脾气。be harsh and unreasonable at home/A term that refers to those who only act in a rude and unreasonable manner at home.

例:他从不在外面发脾气,只会窝里横。

He never loses his temper outside, but at home he is harsh and unreasonable.

卧底 wò dǐ

潜伏在对方的内部。hide (lie low) in middle of opponents

例:这家伙是准备派往敌方卧底的人。

This fellow will be sent to lie low in the heart of the enemy.

无厘头 wú lí tóu

指没有由头,没有任何意思,格调不高的事情。something meaningless, unmotivated, vulgar and unreasonable

例:谁也没想到这么好的原作却被一名香港导演演绎成了无厘头风格的幽默搞笑片。

No one thought that such a good manuscript would be made into such a pointless, vulgar comedy by a Hong Kong director.

五指山红 wǔ zhǐ shān hóng

即"五指煽红"的谐音,指抽嘴巴并留下五个手指印。a slap in the face so hard it leaves five finger marks remaining

例:他给她来了一个五指山红。

He gave her a huge slap in the face.

五毒俱全 wǔ dú jù quàn

指吃、喝、嫖、赌、抽。be totally addicted to the five vices (gluttony, drunkenness, lechery, gambling and drug abuse)

例:我这人五毒俱全,没有救了。

I'm totally depraved. I have all five vices.

雾里看花 wù lǐ kàn huā

对某事看不清楚,朦胧的样子。unable to see things clearly; to see things blearily

例:对于房价到底有多大水分,消费者只能是雾里看花。只有房地产开发商心知肚明。

Consumers can hardly see it through the extras in a houseing price. Only the real estate developers themselves know.

X

吸引眼球 xī yǐn yǎn qiú

引人注目。eye-catching；attractive

例：前几年电视台最吸引眼球的节目是模特大赛。如今搞的太多了，收视率下降了。

The most eye-catching program on TV was a model contest a few years ago. Now the viewer ratings have gone downhill because there are too many contests like that.

洗钱 xǐ qián

把不是从正道上赚来的钱（通常指出售军火、毒品）存入银行，并通过正当的渠道把钱取出，这一过程叫洗钱。

laundering money/A term that describes putting money made through illegal means (such as drug or weapons smuggling) into a bank and then withdrawing it in a proper way.

例：他可是个洗钱的老手。他在贩毒道上已混了三十多年了。

He is an expert at laundering money. He has been in the gang smuggling drugs for over thirty years.

细发 xì fa

细致；精细；不粗糙。exquisite；delicate；careful；fine

例1：她的皮肤真够细发的。

She's got fine skin.

例2：以前我还没见过工艺做得这么细发的手表。

I haven't seen such delicate workmanship in a watch before.

瞎 xiā

指不知如何办；毫无办法；抓瞎。not know what to do；have

no idea; be at a loss

例：他今天可是瞎了，不知怎样才能进到办公室里去，因为他把钥匙锁在里面了。

He had no idea how to get into the office today for he had locked the key inside.

瞎掰 xiā bāi

1. 没有道理或没有根据乱说，乱干；胡闹。act senselessly; talk nonsense

例：别信他的话。他就会瞎掰。

Don't believe him. He's only talking nonsense.

2. 没有用；没有意义。be worthless; be useless

例：喝酒止渴纯粹是瞎掰。

It's completely useless trying to quench your thirst with wine.

瞎菜 xiā cài

指不好办；没辙；完蛋。have no way out; be finished; be at the end of one's hope

例：如果你告我卖假货，我就瞎菜了。

If you sue me for selling fake goods, I'll be finished.

瞎咧咧 xiā liē liē

胡乱说；乱讲。make irresponsible remarks; speak groundlessly; talk nonsense

例：在没弄清真相以前别瞎咧咧。

Don't make irresponsible remarks before the truth of the matter is clarified.

瞎迷 xiā mí

1. 傻眼；抓瞎。be dumbfounded; be stunned; find oneself at

a loss

例：他们说得好听，但真正干起来就瞎迷了。

They talked a big game, but they were at a loss as to what they should actually do.

2. 指白费劲；白干。make an effort in vain; make a wasted effort

例：你最好先跟他商量一下，否则他不同意你不就瞎迷了。

You'd better consult with him beforehand. Otherwise you'll be making a wasted effort if he doesn't agree.

下海 xià hǎi

原指某人加入帮会组织或良家女子沦为妓女，现指某人辞职经商或从事商业活动；做生意。

go to sea/Originally this term referred to someone who joined a gang or a woman from a good family who became a prostitute. Now it refers to someone who has given up a stable job to engage in business.

例：许多人辞职下海去了。

Many people gave up their regular jobs and started to do business.

下课 xià kè

被解雇（多用于指教练）。to be fired; to be dismissed (usually referring to sports coaches)

例：一年来由于这个队没能打进四强，王强作为这个队的教练最终还是逃脱不了下课的命运。

One year had passed, and the team hadn't gotten into the top four list yet. Wang Qiang, the coach of the team, finally couldn't avoid getting fired.

下面 xià mian

1.指下级单位。unit at the basic level

例:不管政策如何定,下面就是不执行。

No matter what policies are made, the unit at the basic level refuses to carry them out.

2.指群众;老百姓。masses; common people

例:你得多听听下面的意见。

You'd better listen more carefully to the views of the masses.

下片儿 xià piànr

指(警察)深入所管辖的地区或居民小区了解情况。

(policeman) go to get informaton in locat beat

例:今天所有警察都下片儿了。

All the local police have gone to their beats today.

先生 xiān sheng

指丈夫。husband

例:她先生是位教师。

Her husband is a teacher.

闲磕牙 xián kē yá

闲谈;闲聊天。chat

例:他们不是聚在一起闲磕牙就是下象棋。

They get together either to chat or play chess.

显摆 xiǎn bai

炫耀;显示。show off; flaunt

例:她把礼物带到幼儿园向小朋友显摆去了。

She took her gift to the kindergarten to show it off to her friends.

现 xiàn

现眼；出丑。lose face；make a fool of oneself；bring shame on oneself

例：他算是现了，刚讲了一半就说不出话了。

He felt shamed by losing his voice in the middle of the speech.

现炒现卖 xiàn chǎo xiàn mài

1. 比喻人没有功底，现学现卖弄。sell while cooking/Someone who teaches，uses or shows off what he or she has just learned.

例：对于电脑我懂得不多，只是现炒现卖罢了。

I know a little about computers. I'm simply teaching you what I have just learned.

2. 指做无本买卖；做转手买卖。do business without capital；engage in buying and reselling

例：多数人经商都是从现炒现卖开始的。

Buying and reselling goods is a popular way to start up in business.

线人 xiàn rén

为公安机关提供情报的人。informer；spy

例：据线人报告，今晚他们将有一批毒品走私进关。

According to the informer's report，a group of drugs will be smuggled in through the border tonight.

香饽饽 xiāng bō bo

原指好吃的糕点或馒头，现比喻受欢迎、受人喜爱、被人重视的人。delicious pastry or cake/A popular，welcome or valuable person.

例：我不是老板的香饽饽，如果我离开这儿，他不会在乎。

I'm not a favorite of the boss. He won't care if I leave here.

向毛主席保证 xiàng máo zhǔ xí bǎo zhèng

一种发誓用语,用于二十世纪七十年代,表示绝对真实,没有说谎。In Chairman Mao's name/A term to indicate that what one says is absolutely true, mostly used in the 1970s of the 20th century.

例:我敢向毛主席保证,我没拿你那本书。

I swear in Chairman Mao's name that I didn't take your book.

消防队员 xiāo fáng duì yuán

指解决或平息矛盾、纠纷或争端的调解人。fire fighter/A metaphor for a mediator.

例:这里的邻居们都知道他是个好消防队员。他总是热心地帮助邻居们处理纠纷。

Everyone in this neighborhood knows that he is a good mediator and he is always willing to help them settle their quarrels.

小巴 xiǎo bā

小型公共汽车;小型出租汽车。minibus; small bus

例:为了缓解320路大巴的拥挤现象,汽车公司又开辟了320路小巴业务。

To ease up the overcrowding on bus No. 320, the bus company is running minibuses along that route in addition to the normal bus service.

小菜 xiǎo cài

指小碟的冷食蔬菜、鱼肉等。比喻非常容易的事情。common

or cold dish（meat，fish，vegetable）/Referring to an easy task or a child's play；a piece of cake；no sweat.

例：唱英文歌对她来说简直是小菜。

It's a pushover for her to sing an English song.

小炒 xiǎo chǎo

1.指用小菜锅，为顾客单独炒菜。an individual quick-fried dish

例：今天我请你吃小炒。

I'll treat you to small dishes today.

2.指投资不多，从事小生意的买卖。engage in small business；buy and resell by using small amounts of money

例：我没有你那样雄厚的资本，我只能从小炒开始。

I don't have abundant funds like you. I can only start with some small business.

小打小闹 xiǎo dǎ xiǎo nào

指小范围、小规模地做事。do sth. on a small scale

例：他现在是小打小闹挣些小钱，等有一些经验后再玩大的。

He is doing some small-scale business to make a little money. He'll join the big leagues when he has more experience.

小儿科 xiǎo ér kē

1.原指医疗机构中治疗儿童疾病的一科，现多比喻微不足道或不被人重视甚至被人瞧不起的事物。pediatrics/A term used to describe something trivial and insignificant or something that is neglected or looked down upon by others.

例：他干的那些事太小儿科了，不值得一提。

His work is so trivial that it isn't worth mentioning.

2.比喻人的幼稚。pediatrics/A term used to describe someone simple, naive or childish.

例：如果连这个也不懂我就太小儿科了。

I would be very naive if I didn't know this.

小皇帝 xiǎo huáng dì

形容独生子女或被宠爱坏了的孩子。little emperor/A term referring to children from one-child families or spoilt children.

例：如今中国的小皇帝越来越多，这将成为中国未来的一个社会问题。

There are more and more little emperors now in China. It will become a social problem in the future.

小晃 xiǎo huàng

指小流氓；小痞子。little rascal; little ruffian

例：这些小晃常到歌舞厅来捣乱。群众恨透了他们。

These little hooligans often come to make trouble in this karaoke bar. The customers really don't like them.

小金库 xiǎo jīn kù

个人私下存的钱；私房钱。private hoard

例：我丈夫用他小金库的钱买烟抽。

My husband uses his private hoard to buy his cigarettes.

小蜜 xiǎo mì

1. 称陪伴有钱人的女子。cutie-pie; little sweetie; little honey/A term describing a young woman who accompanies rich men.

例：那个姑娘一定是老板的小蜜。她总跟老板一起外出。

The girl must be the boss' little sweetie. She often goes out with him.

2. 女友；女伴。girlfriend

例：最近我听说张三交了个漂亮的小蜜。

I've heard recently that Zhang San has got a beautiful girl-friend.

小时工 xiǎo shí gōng

1. 指按小时为单位支付报酬的工作。hourly job

例：我想找个小时工干一干。

I'm looking for an hourly job.

2. 指按小时为单位工作并领取报酬的人。hourly worker

例：我雇了一个小时工，每星期来帮我打扫一次厨房。

I've hired an hourly worker to help me clean my kitchen once a week.

小样 xiǎo yàng

模样。appearance；look

例：你也不看看你那小样，是当总经理的料吗？

Look at yourself. Are you suitable for the position of general manager?

笑星 xiào xīng

指有名气的相声和小品演员。comedy celebrity；comedy star/Usually refers to "cross talkers" (TV celebrities who perform short monologues) or comedians.

例：全国各地的笑星们纷纷云集到北京，参加中央电视台1999年春节联欢晚会。

Comedy stars from all over the country have gathered in Beijing to attend the CCTV 1999 Evening Show held on the eve of the lunar new year.

歇菜 xiē cài

指歇着，让人停止做某事；不行；算了；靠边站。stop doing

sth. ; have a rest; stand aside; get out of the way

例：你还是歇菜吧。这活儿技术性太强，你干不来。

You'd better stand aside. You can't do it. It's too technical for you.

邪 xié

1. 不正当；非法的。not right; illegal; unconventional

例：我真担心他，他无论干什么总爱玩邪的。

I'm worried about him. No matter what he does, he likes doing it in unconventional ways.

2. 不正常；不对劲。strange; odd

例：今天真是邪了，所有倒霉的事都让我赶上了。

It was very strange today. I ran into a series of problems.

邪门儿 xié ménr

1. 奇怪；不正常。strange; odd; out of the ordinary

例：真邪门儿，今天办公室一个人也没有。

That's very strange. Nobody is in the office today.

2. 指不正常；反常。strange; odd; abnormal

例：真邪门儿！今天我怎么也找不着我的眼镜了。我通常都把它放在桌子上。

That's strange! I can't find my glasses today. I usually put them on the table.

邪乎 xié hu

1. 指不正常；不可信。out of the ordinary; incredible

例：这个季节西瓜的价格高得都邪乎了。

At this time of the year the price of watermelons is incredibly high.

2. 夸张；过火。exaggerated; overstated

例：这消息越传越邪乎。

As the news got passed by word of mouth it kept getting exaggerated.

3. 严重;厉害。severe

例:这事有那么邪乎,到了今天非解决不可的地步?

Is this matter so severe that we have to solve it today?

邪行 xié xing

特别;不同寻常;不正常。peculiar; extraordinary; strange

例:这天真邪行。四月初的天气不该像夏天那样热呀。

What extraordinary weather! It shouldn't be as hot as summer in early April.

心里美 xīn lǐ měi

1. 水萝卜的俗称,形容人的思想品质、道德情操高尚。turnip (which is light green on the outside and red on the inside)/ Someone who has a good heart, noble mind and solid virtues.

例:她长得不漂亮,但却心里美。

Though she's not pretty, she's got a good heart.

2. 指人的内心十分高兴。happy; pleased

例:听到这好消息他心里美着呢。

He was very pleased to hear the good news.

星 xīng

指明星。star; celebrity

例:她梦想成为一个星,拥有一大批追随者。

She dreams of becoming a star and having a lot of fans.

星哥 xīng gē

对男明星的昵称。intimate term for a male star

例:你最喜欢哪个星哥?

Which male star do you like the best?

星姐 xīng jiě

对女明星的昵称。intimate term for a female star

例：她女儿的房间里贴满了星姐星哥的照片。

Her daughter's room is full of pictures of male and female stars on the walls.

行头 xíng tou

原指唱戏穿的戏装，现指衣着穿戴。apparel; dress; clothes; outfit/A term that originates from the word for a theatrical costume.

例：为接受电视台的采访他特意换了一身行头。

He changed his outfit for the interview with the television station.

醒 xǐng

明白；发觉；醒悟。realize; understand; wake up to reality

例1：我给他反复解释，但他还没有醒过来。

I explained it to him again and again, but he still didn't get it.

例2：她突然醒了，觉得这事有点儿不对头。

She suddenly realized that something was wrong.

熊 xióng

申斥；批评。scold; rebuke; criticize

例：他把新自行车丢了，为此他让父亲熊了一顿。

He was scolded by his father for losing his new bike.

雄起 xióng qǐ

1.原意为"崛起"，后常用于体育比赛中，意为"加油"。Originally means "spring up; grow up" / A term often used in sport games, meaning "go!", to cheer on.

例：在足球比赛中，热心的球迷向他们喜欢的球队大喊："雄起！"

During a football match the enthusiastic football fans shouted, "Go! Go! Go!" to their favorite teams.

2. 指某人做得最好，最棒。refers to one who does the best

例：我相信她是受欢迎的，用我们的四川话来说，就是：李宇春，雄起！

I believe that she is the most popular. In our Sichuan dialect, we'd say that Li Yuchun is the best!

修长城 xiū cháng chéng

指玩麻将牌。play mahjong

例：老年人靠修长城来消磨时间。

The old people like to kill their time by playing mahjong.

修理 xiū lǐ

指整治；收拾；教训。teach someone a lesson; make someone suffer

例：他们准备好好修理一下那个坏蛋。

They decided to teach the scoundred a lesson.

修地球 xiū dì qiú

耕田；种地；从事农业劳动。farm; till land

例：他父亲修了一辈子地球，从没离开过这块土地。

His father farmed his entire life and never left the land.

嗅 xiù

指追求（女性）。to be after (a woman); chase; court; pursue a woman

例：单位里刚分配来一个女大学生，他马上就嗅上了。

He was after the new graduate as soon as she started working in the unit.

嗅蜜 xiù mì

追求女性；寻觅女友。chase a woman；look for a girlfriend

例：他到这儿不是为了锻炼身体，而是嗅蜜寻欢来了。

He didn't come here to exercise，but to chase women and have fun.

秀 xiù

演出，表演。show

例：如今各种秀特别多，有模仿秀、脱口秀、现场秀、电视秀、内衣秀等等，真是五花八门。

Now there are so many kinds of shows including talk shows，live shows，TV shows，and lingerie shows，etc. It is indeed a rich variety.

绣花枕头 xiù huā zhěn tou

比喻表面好看，却没有大用途的人或物。embroidered pillow/A person or a thing which looks beautiful，but is not useful or practical.

例：她漂亮极了，但她从不喜欢别人把她看成是绣花枕头。

She is extremely beautiful，but she hates others to look on her as an embroidered pillow.

悬 xuán

危险。dangerous

例1：真悬呀！差一点儿打着我的眼睛。

How dangerous! It nearly hit my eyes.

例2：你想说服他，我看有点儿悬。

I think you have little hope of persuading him.

悬的乎 xuán de hū

危险。dangerous

例：离电线远点儿，我觉得你站在那儿有些悬的乎。

Keep away from the wire. I think it's dangerous to stand there.

穴头 xuè tóu

指组织演员"走穴"，主持演出的经纪人或代理人。agent or middleman who organizes performances and runs the show

例：他是个大穴头，这两年搞走穴挣了不少钱。

He is a big agent. He's made a lot of money from organizing performances these past two years.

寻开心 xún kāi xīn

逗乐；开玩笑。look for fun; amuse; make fun of

例：别跟人恶作剧寻开心。

Don't amuse yourselves by playing tricks on others.

寻模 xún mo

1. 寻找；看来看去。hunt for; look around

例：我正寻模我的钥匙呢，我忘了把它放在哪儿了。

I'm hunting for my key. I forgot where I put it.

2. 打算；考虑。plan; intend; consider

例：我寻模着是否该添辆新车。

I'm considering whether I should buy a new car.

Y

丫头片子 yā tou piàn zi

指女孩子。girl；baby girl

例：这小丫头片子的嘴还挺厉害。

This little girl have got a sharp tongue.

压根儿 yà gēnr

1. 根本。at all；simply

例：他压根儿就不同意。

He didn't agree at all.

2. 本来。at first；originally

例：我压根儿没觉得这个主意好，过后想一下认为它似乎还不错。

At first I didn't think of that than it seemed like a good idea.

亚市民 yǎ shì mín

指居住在都市边缘村镇里的年轻人；指无城市户口，但生活着装已城市化的人。second-class citizen/Refers to those who live in city suburbs with no urban residence card but lead a lifestyle like that of regular residents.

例：别小看人家亚市民，他们的生活比你的还强呢！

Don't look down upon second-class citizens. They lead a better life than you do.

轧马路 yà mǎ lù

指在街上散步；溜达。saunter；take a walk；stroll

例：小两口总是在晚饭后轧马路。

The couple always take a walk after supper.

眼力见儿 yǎn lì jiànr

指人机灵懂事,看得见该干的或该帮忙干的活儿。sensible; intelligent; smart; referring to someone who has initiative, and can figure out what should be done

例:你这人一点眼力见儿都没有。没看见我两手都拿着东西吗? 还不赶紧帮我开一下门?

You're totally senseless. Can't you see my hands are full? Why don't you help me open the door?

阳光 yáng guāng

形容人朝气蓬勃,年轻靓丽。sunny; young and pretty/handsome; full of youthful spirit

例1:他给人一种非常阳光的感觉,不仅在电影中,而且在生活中也一样。

He gives people a spirited, youthful feeling, not only in his movies, but also in real life.

例2:他是大家喜爱的阳光男孩。

He has a sunny disposition, and is loved by people.

洋插队 yáng chā duì

指到国外读书、打工、生活。study, work or live in a foreign country

例:这几年在青年中流行一种洋插队热。

In recent years it has been a growing trend for young people to study or work abroad.

洋倒儿 yáng dǎor

指倒买倒卖的外国人,也称"洋倒儿爷"。foreign profiteer

例:他结识了一位洋倒儿。那位洋倒儿每月都从莫斯科来一趟北京。

He met a foreign profiteer who travels between Moscow and

Beijing once a month.

洋妞 yáng niū

指外国女青年。foreign girl; young woman from the West

例:这位男士想娶个洋妞作为跳板出国。

This man wanted to marry a foreign girl so he could go abroad.

养小 yǎng xiǎo

指有小老婆。have concubine

例:这么点儿钱我怎么能养小呢?

How can I afford a concubine with such little money?

养眼 yǎng yǎn

形容某人或某物看了令人愉悦。pleasant-looking, pleasing to the eye

例1:人们不得不承认如今电视剧里众多的俊男靓女的确能使观众养眼。

People can't help but admit that all the handsome boys and pretty girls in today's TV dramas are really pleasing to the eyes.

例2:这幅油画可真够养眼的。

This oil painting is very pleasing.

幺蛾子 yāo é zi

指鬼点子;坏主意;坏事。a crafty plot; a wicked idea or thing; a trick

例:你怎么不说话,又想什么幺蛾子呢?

Why don't you speak? What wicked ideas are you thinking?

摇羽毛扇的 yáo yǔ máo shàn de

指出谋划策的人。counsellor; advisor

例:他是给老板摇羽毛扇的。

He is an advisor to the boss.

咬耳朵 yǎo ěr duo

指小声低语。whisper; murmur sth. in sb.'s ear

例：上课时不能咬耳朵。

Don't whisper to each other in class.

野鸡 yě jī

1. 指无营业执照而非法经营的人或集团。illegal trader or corporation without any business licenses or certificates

例：野鸡一旦被抓着是要受重罚的。

Once an illegal trader is caught, he will be fined heavily.

2. 指妓女；暗娟。prostitute; whore

例：那家饭店有不少野鸡。

There are many prostitutes in that hotel.

野模 yě mó

非专业团体的、非正式的服装模特。amateur model/someone hired to be a model with no previous experience.

例：商店雇了一些野模，向顾客展示店里所售的新服装。

The shop hired some amateur models to present the shop's new clothing to customers.

夜猫子 yè māo zi

指睡得很晚，擅长熬夜的人。night owl; a person who stays up late at night

例：他是典型的夜猫子。他很少能在晚上十二点以前睡觉。

He is a typical night owl. He seldom goes to sleep before midnight.

夜陪 yè péi

指夜间陪出租车司机拉客的帮手。person who accompanies a taxi driver at night; taxi driver's night assistant

例:如果我有他作夜陪,她就可以放心了。

If I had him as a night assistant she would be relieved.

页子 yè zi

指钱(专指纸票)。paper money; note

例:对我来说整天在银行点页子真枯燥。

It would be boring for me to count money all day in a bank.

页子活 yè zi huó

指有钱;能挣钱。make big money; be rich

例:他想找个页子活的工作。

He wants to find a job where he can make big money.

一个数 yī ge shù

指一百元人民币。one hundred *yuan*

例:她给了我一个数,便把那条裙子拿走了。

She took the dress away and gave me a hundred *yuan*.

一根筋 yī gēn jīn

指死心眼;不灵活。stubborn; having a one-track mind; inflexible

例:他干任何事都是一根筋。

He has one-track mind when he comes to doing anything.

一号 yī hào

指厕所。lavatory; toilet; bathroom; John

例:几分钟前他们去一号了。

They went to the bathroom just a few minutes ago.

一脸旧社会 yī liǎn jiù shè huì

指面相苦；脸上无表情，没有笑容。expressionless face; painful looking face; solemn face; sad; unhappy; solemn; doleful

例：姑娘们笑一笑。别那么一脸旧社会。

Girls, please cheer up. Don't look so sad.

一水儿 yī shuǐr

指一种颜色或性别。single color or sex only; completely; totally

例：他教的那个舞蹈班一水儿的女生，没有一个男生参加。

The students of the dancing class he teaches are all girls, not one boy participated.

一通 yī tòng

表示动作或时间的连续性。a spell; a fit

例：她在床上折腾了一通，最后终于睡着了。

She tossed about in bed for a while before she fell asleep at last.

一头雾水 yī tóu wù shuǐ

对某事不清楚，弄不明白。to make one puzzled or confused; to cast a mist before someone's eyes

例：这个案子对他简直就是一头雾水，根本不知从何入手。

This case completely puzzled him. He had no idea how to handle it at all.

衣服架子 yī fu jià zi

比喻（某人）身材好，穿什么都很好看，合适。clothes hanger; clothes-horse; clothes holder/Someone with a beautiful figure and fit to all kinds of clothes.

例：你真是个衣服架子，穿什么都那么好看。

You've got a clothes-horse figure. You would look good in anything.

医托 yī tuō

指受雇在医院门口以帮助病人为由,拉病人去他雇主的医院或科室看病。someone hired by a hospital or a certain department of a hospital to pretend to help those patients coming to a hospital, in order to convince them to go to the hospital or certain department of the hospital.

例:近期,在医院门前活动猖獗的"号贩子"、"医托"行为引起媒体的关注,也引起相关部门的重视。

Recently, the conduct of registration — ticket scalpers and "enthusiastic hospital customers" who are working unchecked in front of hospitals has aroused the attention of the media, and the relevant units of the government.

意思 yì si

指通过送礼或其他方式,向对方作出感谢或诚意的表示。presenting gifts as a token of affection, appreciation or gratitude

例:请人家帮忙总得意思意思。

We have to send something to him as a token of appreciation for his help.

瘾君子 yǐn jūn zǐ

指吸毒者。drug addict

例:他给人的印象挺好的,谁也不知道他会是一个瘾君子。

He gave good impression to people, so nobody knew that he could have been a drug addict.

硬派小生 yìng pài xiǎo shēng

指坚强不屈,有胆有识,具有男子汉气派的男青年。stud;

role model; a strong-minded, brave and unyielding young man

例:他是影视界里为数不多的硬派小生之一。

He is one of the few role models in film and television circles.

勇 yǒng

指勇敢,胆大。brave; bold; daring

例:尽管你都四十七岁了,但还是像年轻人那样勇。

Although you are 47, you're still as bold as a young man.

悠着点儿 yōu zhe diǎnr

掌握尺度,不要过度。be careful; keep oneself under control; take it easy

例1:悠着点儿,别玩儿命地干。

Take it easy. Don't overstrain yourself at work.

例2:她让她丈夫悠着点儿,别喝太多的酒。

She told her husband to keep himself under control and not drink too much.

油 yóu

狡猾;老于世故;滑头。foxy; cunning; sly; crafty

例:他很油。他干一件事你很少能抓住他什么把柄。

He is very crafty. He seldom lets you know what he's doing.

油倒儿 yóu dǎor

1. 指倒买倒卖汽油或汽油票的人。a person who resells gasoline or gasoline tickets for a profit/In China all vehicles are rationed a certain amount of gasoline tickets. A driver uses the tickets to get gasoline for his or her vehicle at a gas station.

例:他刚从加油站附近一个油倒儿手上买了十公斤油票。

He's just bought ten-kiloliter worth of gasoline tickets from someone reselling them near the gas station.

2.指倒买倒卖食用油的人。a person who buys and resells edible oil

例:现在市场上食用油短缺,油倒儿乘机高价出售他们的油。

There is currently a shortage of edible oil. The oil profiteer took advantage of the situation to sell oil at a higher price.

油耗子 yóu hào zi

指专门偷汽油的人。gas mouse/Someone who steals gas from other vehicles.

例:他昨天上午给汽车加的油,昨天夜里就让油耗子偷走了。

The gas he filled his car with yesterday morning was stolen by a gas mouse last night.

油葫芦 yóu hú lu

一种形体像蟋蟀,黑褐色,有油光的昆虫,用以比喻人的身体和头发很脏。a kind of dark brown and shiny field cricket; a grungy person/A term to describe someone who is extremely dirty and hasn't taken a shower in such a long time that his or her body and hair is oily.

例:我必须好好洗个澡。我觉得我活像个油葫芦。

I must take a shower. I feel like a shiny field cricket.

有板有眼 yǒu bǎn yǒu yǎn

指人办事说话有条理,有次序。(of speech and action)orderly; methodical; rhythmical

例1:虽然他还是个孩子,但办每件事情都有板有眼。

Although a boy, he does everything methodically.

例2:她是位有板有眼的人。

She is an orderly person.

有碍市容 yǒu ài shì róng

指长相不好或穿着太破旧。be an eyesore; be repugnant to the eye; be a monstrosity/Something or someone who is ugly; poorly dressed or looks shabby and poor.

例：别那样看着我，我想我这身打扮不会有碍市容。

Don't look at me like that. I don't think my dress is that much of an eyesore.

有把豆 yǒu bǎ dòu

有办法，有能耐。have skill, capability or ability

例：你真有把豆，别人管不了的事，到你这儿一下子就解决了。

You are really capable. You can solve problems which others can't.

有鼻子有眼 yǒu bí zi yǒu yǎn

指叙述或描述得详尽透彻，活灵活现。vivid description; description full of details

例：我想他不会骗我，因为他说得有鼻子有眼。

I don't think he lied to me because he described the whole thing in vivid detail.

有病 yǒu bìng

（口头禅）表示对某人不满，讽刺或讥笑别人行为古怪，不正常。nuts; neurotic; sick; (behavior) strange; unusual, out of the ordinary; odd / A phrase to express one's dissatisfaction or opinion that someone's conduct is strange mentally

例1：这人砍完价了，又不买了，有病。

After this guy bargained the price down, he didn't even buy it. Nuts!

例 2：你有病呀！你怎么能这样跟你父亲说话。

Aren't you mentally sick? How can you speak to your father like that.

例 3：她这人真有病，非要还我两分钱不可。

She is very strange. She insists on returning the two cents to me.

例 4：他今天有病呀？怎么在办公室见谁就跟谁嚷嚷。

Isn't he acting a bit strange today? He shouted at everyone he saw in the office.

有根儿 yǒu gēnr

指有后台；有关系；有基础。have connections; have support

例：这事对他不难，这方面他有根儿。

It's not hard for him to do this because he's got connections in this field.

有两把刷子 yǒu liǎng bǎ shuā zi

有办法，有能耐。意同"有把豆"。have skill, capability or ability

例：如果你没有两把刷子，这活还真做不了。

If you don't have the ability, you can't do it.

有头有脸 yǒu tóu yǒu liǎn

指有名气；有地位；有身份。have fame (social status, dignity); leader; head; famed person; VIP

例：坐在主席台上的那些人都是学校有头有脸的人物。

Those who sit on the rostrum are somebodies of the school.

有戏 yǒu xì

原指文艺演出吸引人，现引申为有希望，有可能。hopeful; possible/A term that originally described a show that appealed to a wide audience.

例 1：他拿冠军绝对有戏。

There's a good possibility he'll win first prize.

例 2：我想这件事十之八九有戏。

I think there's a good chance that this will work.

有一搭,无一搭 yǒu yī dā, wú yī dā

1. 不重视；冷漠。not take sth. seriously; pay little attention

例：他对别人的忠告总是有一搭,无一搭的。

He doesn't take other's suggestions seriously.

2. 指办事没有准备；不可靠。do sth. without certainty; be unreliable

例：他这人有一搭,无一搭的,我可不让他干这项工作。

I won't let him do the work. He is very unreliable.

有一号 yǒu yī hào

指有些名气；算得上一个人物。have some fame; be considered one of the tops in one's field

例：在这幢大楼里他算是有一号的象棋高手了。

He enjoys the reputation of being the best chess player in this building.

淤 yū

指多余,富余。extra; surplus; spare

例：如果买衬衫的钱淤了,你还打算买些什么？

What else do you plan to buy if you have money left after buying that shirt?

郁闷 yù mèn

(年轻人口头禅)表示心情不好,烦躁。bored; depressed/A phrase used by the young to express a fretful bad mood.

例：我朋友这次期中考试没考好,现在正郁闷着呢。

My friend didn't get good marks in the mid-term examination, so he is depressed now.

原装 yuán zhuāng

1. 指原生产厂家生产组装的产品。(genuine) product

例：这台录音机是日本原装的。

This tape recorder is a Japanese product.

2. 指天生的。inborn; innate

例：他的高鼻梁是原装的，不是整形出来的。

He was born with a high-bridged nose. It's not plastic surgery.

3. 原配的。attached; included

例：他们买了一套新房，房内的家具全是原装的。

They bought a new house with a set of furniture.

冤大头 yuān dà tóu

枉费钱财的人；干事不讨好的人；大傻瓜。fool; a person who spends time or money but gets no return; a person who is fooled or cheated

例 1：他承认这次他犯了一个错误，当了一次冤大头。

He admitted that he made a mistake and looked like a fool this time.

例 2：他后悔没听我的话，结果如今成了个冤大头。

He regrets not listening to me. Now he looks like a fool.

月嫂 yuè sǎo

指帮助照顾产妇、护理新生儿平安度过生产后第一个月的妇女。a maid who cares for a woman in the month after she's given birth to a child

例：我老婆很快就要生了，你能帮我找个月嫂吗？

My wife is going to give birth. Would you help me find a maid to care for her?

越活越抽抽 yuè huó yuè chōu chou

1.指个子越来越矮。shrink；become shorter

例:我记得我比你高,现在我们一样高。我怀疑我越活越抽抽了。

I remember I was taller than you，but now we're the same height. I doubt I've shrunk.

2.指人胆子越来越小;没有勇气和魄力;没有精神。become more timid, more meek; feel low in spirit; have less interest in something

例:随着年龄的增长,你是越活越抽抽了,一个人竟不敢过马路。

You're becoming more timid as you've gotten older. You even dare not cross a street alone.

晕菜 yūn cài

指晕了;糊涂;晕头转向。feel dizzy; get confused; be muddleheaded

例1:你一次别教她那么多新字,否则她会晕菜的。

Don't teach her too many new words at one time or she'll get confused.

例2:他忙得晕菜了。

He's so busy he feels a bit dizzy.

云山雾罩 yùn shān wù zhào

比喻事情很神秘,难辨真伪。covering the mountain with mist and clouds/An expression for something that is described or told in a vague and mysterious fashion.

例:他故意把事情说得云山雾罩以吸引我们的注意力。

He deliberately told us the story in a mysterious way in order to draw our attention.

Y

最新中国俚语

New Slang of China

Z

砸 zá

指(某事)失败;搞糟;不成功。fail; fall through; be bungled

例:所有的好事都让你给弄砸了。

All good things were bungled by you.

栽 zāi

指栽跟头;丢面子;失败;输了。suffer a setback; feel embar-rassed; be defeated

例1:这次运动会我算是栽了,什么奖也没得着。

I was embarrassed that I didn't get any rewards at the sports event.

例2:他不知他竟会栽在一个女人的手里。

He didn't know that a woman could beat him.

宰 zǎi

指生意人故意多要顾客的钱。overcharge; rip off

例1:这么一个小玩意儿你宰我宰得也太多了。

You overcharged me for this small thing.

例2:他知道今天被人宰了。

He knows he was ripped off today.

在行 zài háng

指内行;懂行;了解。be expert at sth.; know sth. well

例1:她在电脑方面很在行。

She is an expert with computers.

例2:在汽车方面他比我在行。

He knows more about cars than I do.

在乎 zài hu

指计较;认真;重视。care; mind; take to heart

例1:多干一天他不在乎。

He doesn't mind to work one more day.

例2:她对你谈论她的每一句话都很在乎。

She takes every single word you say about her to heart.

糟践 zāo jian

1. 伤害;损坏。harm; hurt; ruin; spoil

例:别抽那么多烟糟践自己的身体。

Don't harm your health by heavy smoking.

2. 玩弄;污辱。insult; humiliate; vilify; sully

例1:一个好姑娘让这个畜牲糟践了。

A good girl was insulted by this beast.

例2:他们画这幅画来糟践我。

They dragged me through the mud by painting this picture.

造 zào

1. 指胡折腾。run wild; mess things up

例:你可以带朋友到家来,但不能在家里造。

You may bring your friends to our home, but don't mess things up.

2. 指大吃大喝;大肆挥霍。spend without restraint

例:她和她的男友一顿饭就造了一千多元。

She spent more than a thousand *yuan* on a dinner with her boyfriend.

造势 zào shì

即制造声势、影响力。make a noise; promote

例:这部电影还未公演,各家媒体便开始造势。

Before this movie was screened, all the media began to promote it.

贼肉 zéi ròu

（贬义）指人身体胖。（derogatory term for someone）extremely fat; overweight

例：自结婚后他便长了一身贼肉，因为他老婆特别会做饭。

He got fat after getting married because his wife is very good at cooking.

扎 zhā

1. 即"扎啤"。draught beer

例：他喝扎喝上了瘾，顿顿饭都离不了扎。

He's got into the habit of drinking draught beer. He can't have his meals without it.

2. 指装扎啤的杯子。mug for draught beer

例：我要一扎，你要几扎？

I would like a mug of draught beer. How many do you want?

3. 钻。plunge into; dive into; swerve into

例：小汽车突然扎到人群里，撞倒许多人。

The car suddenly swerved into the crowd and hit a lot of people.

4. 骗。cheat; defraud

例：那个司机扎了我一百元。

The driver cheated me out of a hundred *yuan*.

5. 欠款。owe a debt

例：这个月我手头紧，房钱先扎着，下月给行吗？

I'm running short of money this month. Could I owe you a debt and pay the rent next month?

扎堆儿 zhā duīr

指众人聚集在一起（聊天、议论等）。get together to chat

例：他们一上班就扎堆儿聊世界杯赛。

They got together to talk about the World Cup as soon as they arrived at the office.

扎款 zhā kuǎn

指搞钱；赚钱。get money; make money

例：他想扎款买辆汽车。

He wants to make money to buy a car first.

扎蜜 zhā mì

指追求女性；寻觅女友。chase a woman; look for a girl-friend

例：自他有了钱以后，他便开始扎蜜、赌博。

Since he became rich he's started to chase women and gamble.

扎啤 zhā pí

指散装鲜啤酒(借自粤语)。draught beer

例：他渴极了，一下喝了两杯扎啤。

He was so thirsty that he drank two mugs of draught beer.

扎势 zhā shì

指派头；架子。style; manner; airs

例：看他那扎势，想必他一定很有钱。

From the looks of the airs he puts on he must have a lot of money.

扎账 zhā zhàng

欠账，拖欠账款。owe a debt

例：现在的生意都不好做，所以许多公司都扎账。

Now it's hard to do business, so many companies are in debt to other companies.

扎针(儿) zhā zhēn(r)

指到领导处说某人的坏话或告状。give or receive acupuncture treatment/A term to describe when someone speaks ill of a co-worker or lodges a complaint against him or her with the boss.

例：我知道昨天他又去老板那儿给我扎针儿了。

I know he spoke ill of me again with the boss yesterday.

咋呼 zhā hu

1. 吆喝；大声说话。shout; bluster; yell

例：别咋呼了，快干活吧！

Stop shouting, get to work right now!

2. 炫耀。make widely known; show off

例1：什么事她都爱咋呼。

She always makes petty things widely known.

例2：他从不在人前咋呼。

He never shows off in front of others.

渣儿 zhār

指缺点；不好的东西；阴暗面。weakness; shortcoming; defect

例：这部电影描写的多是社会的渣儿，没有意思。

This film is not interesting. All it describes are the problems of society.

乍刺儿 zhà cìr

指不顺从；不听话；顶牛；对抗。disobey; disagree

例：他不管你是谁，都敢跟你乍刺儿。

No matter who you are he'll have the audacity to disagree with you.

炸 zhà

1. 发怒；吵；发脾气。quarrel；fly into a rage；lose one's temper；get angry；explode with anger

例：她是个急脾气，遇事就爱炸。

She is hot tempered and easily gets angry.

2. 大声喊叫。roar；cry out；shout

例：到外面炸去。

Go and shout outside the room.

3. 一轰而散；受惊而四处奔逃；乱起来。break up into a hub-bub；fall into disorder；become chaotic；scamper，flee in terror

例1：老师刚离开不大一会儿工夫，教室就炸了起来。

The class fell into disorder not soon after the teacher left.

例2：地震发生时，人们都炸了窝地往外跑。

When the earthquake came, people all fled in terror from their houses.

炸篷 zhà péng

生意没做好或表演不成功，而遭到人们反对或责难。to raise the roof；raise a ruckus；raise hell / A metaphor for a bad scene or unsuccessful performance which aroused anger and protest from people.

例：小贩的表演出了漏子，结果炸了篷不说，还让市容管理人员给带走了。

The vendor's performance went badly. As a result it raised a ruckus, and the vendor himself was taken away by the market administration staff.

炸药包 zhà yào bāo

指作为礼品送人的盒装点心或整条烟,是走后门、拉关系的一种"武器"。explosive package/A gift (usually pastries or cigarettes) used to go through the back door and "buy" someone off or establish a relationship with someone. Giving such a gift is regarded as an important way to build up one's connections and gain back-door access.

例:你不是有实权的人,谁会给你送炸药包。

No one sends you explosive packages because you don't have any important connections.

奓 zhà

指衣服、头发等向外翘着或张开。(of clothes or hair) stand up on end; stick up; turn upwards; bristle

例1:当猫受到惊吓时,它身上的毛会奓起来。

When a cat is frightened its fur bristles.

例2:瞧你的衣服都奓起来了。

Look at your clothes. They are sticking up.

择 zhái

1.分解开;从中分离出来;挑选出。select; choose; pick

例:这本书是他从书架上择出来的最好的一本。

The book he selected is the best on the bookshelf.

2.摆脱;抽身;排除。get away from; distance oneself from; extricate oneself from

例:遇上麻烦事,他先把自己择出来,并称他是清白的。

He extricated himself from the trouble and declared he was innocent.

粘客 zhān kè

向路人兜售非法盗版软件光盘的人。pirated software or

CD-ROM seller

例:春节刚过,粘客们就又出现在街头巷尾或地铁站里,向路人兜售各种光盘。

As soon as the Spring Festival was over, pirated software and CD-ROM sellers appeared again in streets and lanes or at the subway stations.

斩客 zhǎn kè

指向顾客索要高价。slay customers with exorbitant prices

例:他靠斩客赚钱。

He makes a killing by charging customers high prices.

张 zhāng

1. 指十元人民币。ten-*yuan* note

例:我花了三张买这本字典。

I spent thirty *yuan* for this dictionary.

2. 指数字"十",多指岁数。unit of ten (usually refers to age)

例:我已经是快奔四张的人了。

I'm going to be forty years old soon.

长份儿 zhǎng fènr

指提高地位,威信。raise one's social status and prestige

例:三年不见,她长份儿了,也当上了车间主任。

She has raised her social status and become the director of the workshop since I last saw her three years ago.

长行市 zhǎng háng shi

指身价提高或各方面的要求提高。a rise in one's social status, prestige, etc.

例:他突然长行市了,从一名工人变成市长了。

He experienced a sudden rise in his social status when he

went from being a worker to a city mayor.

掌柜的 zhǎng guì de

1. 商店老板;负责人。shopkeeper; manager; boss

例:掌柜的不同意,她就拿不到钱。

She can't get the money without the permission of the boss.

2. 家庭中主事的人。head of the household, the one who wears the pants in the house

例:这事我得问我们家掌柜的。

On this matter I have to ask the head of the house.

招事(儿) zhāo shì(r)

招惹是非;引人注意。call down trouble; stir up trouble; bring trouble upon oneself

例1:她儿子时常在学校招事。

Her son often stirs up trouble in school.

例2:漂亮姑娘易招事。

It's easy for a beautiful girl to bring trouble upon herself.

着 zháo

指入睡。fall asleep; go to sleep

例:她一躺下就着了。

She fell asleep soon after she lay on the bed.

着实 zháo shí

确实;的确。really; indeed

例1:这景象着实壮丽。

The sight is really magnificent.

例2:这着实是个好主意。

This is a good idea indeed.

找不着北 zhǎo bù zháo běi

形容忙得晕头转向;打晕。unable to find where north is; to get confused; knock out; beat up

例1:她忙得都找不着北了。

She was so busy she became muddled.

例2:他一拳就把我打得找不着北了。

He knocked me out with one punch.

找辙 zhǎo zhé

想办法;找出路。think of a way (idea, solution); look for a way out; seek a way (solution) out

例:我正找辙,怎么能尽快赶到那儿。

I'm thinking of a way to get there as soon as possible.

照 zhào

1.指用眼睛盯着上下看,带有挑衅的意思。give someone a cold stare; give someone the evil eye

例:这孩子也学会照人了。我真不知道谁教他的。

This child has learned how to give someone the evil eye. I really don't know who taught him.

2.指营业执照、驾驶执照等。license; permit

例1:我昨天拿到了驾照。

I got my driver's license yesterday.

例2:你该把饭馆的照挂在正面的墙上。

You should hang the business permit on the front wall of the restaurant.

照镜子 zhào jìng zi

指检查自己;反省。look at oneself in the mirror/An expression for assessing oneself.

例:我们应该常照镜子,以求自己更加完善。

We should frequently assess ourselves in order to improve ourselves.

折进去 zhē jìn qù

1.受连累。be involved in; get into trouble

例：我不知他怎么把我也都折进去了。

I don't know how he got me into trouble.

2.赔本。lose (money) in a business or through gambling

例：为了赌博他把老本都折进去了。

He lost his penny by gambling.

3.因犯罪而被公安局关起来。put in jail; lock up in prison; be taken to prison

例：他因走私毒品而折进去了。

He was put into jail for smuggling drugs.

褶子了 zhě zi le

失败；不行；不成功；完了。fail; not work; be finished; be done for; be over

例：他没来电话。我担心这事八成褶子了。

He didn't phone me. I'm afraid that matter is most likely done for.

真格的 zhēn gé de

正经地（的）；真正地（的）；认真地（的）。really; truly; seriously; real; true; serious

例 1：我骗他说我病了不能上班。他却动真格的来看我了。

I lied to him saying I was sick and could not go to work. He took me seriously and came to see me.

例 2：说真格的，你到底爱不爱他？

Tell me truthfully. Do you love him or not?

例 3：这次他可是真格的，不是玩笑。

He is serious this time, not joking.

枕边风 zhěn biān fēng

指利用妻子给当官的丈夫施加影响,说好话。advice on public matters given to a public official by his wife while they are in bed

例:没有她给你吹枕边风,你不可能那么快拿到营业执照。

You wouldn't have gotten the business license so quickly if it weren't for the persuasive words of the official's wife.

震 zhèn

1.指引起轰动;震动。cause a sensation; create a stir

例:她打破女子马拉松世界纪录的消息把整个世界给震了。

The news that she broke the world record in woman's marathon caused a sensation.

2.胜过。surpass

例:女儿的英语把我震了。

My daughter's English has surpassed mine.

蒸馏水衙门 zhēng liú shuǐ yá men

指没有多少奖金,挣钱又很少的单位(比清水衙门还要低一等)。distilled water unit/A term for government offices that give the lowest salaries and no bonuses.

例:现在没有人愿意在蒸馏水衙门做事。

Now no one wants to work in a "distilled water unit".

整个 zhěng gè

指完完全全,的的确确。completely; entirely; absolutely

例1:这东西整个不能用。

This can't be used at all.

例2:你整个错了。

You're completely wrong.

正炒 zhèng chǎo

指通过传播媒界从正面予以吹捧。flatter (lavish praise on) sb. or sth. through the mass media

例：大多数流行歌手都是正炒出名的。

Most pop singers are made known to the public by overpromotion through the mass media.

正根(儿) zhèng gēn(r)

真正的根源，也指正牌的、纯粹的、正经八百的。real reason; true motive; pure; true; serious

例1：为了多挣钱，这才是农民离家进城打工的正根儿。

The real reason farmers are leaving their homes to work in cities is to make more money.

例2：全是瞎掰，好好学习才是正根儿。

It's useless to listen to what others promise do to for you. It's true for you to study hard and get good marks.

支招 zhī zhāo

出主意；想办法。give counsel; think of a way

例1：她输了这盘棋，因为她丈夫没给她支招。

She lost the game because her husband didn't give her any advice.

例2：你们给我支个招，怎么才能让她不生气。

Would you please help me think of a way to cheer her up?

直肠子 zhí cháng zi

性格直爽，直来直去的人。straight intestines/A metaphor for a straightforward (open, frank) person.

例：他是个直肠子，说话从不拐弯抹角。

He's a straightforward person, never beats about the bush.

直来直去 zhí lái zhí qù

比喻言行直爽。(of speech or action) get to the point; do sth. straight out; be blunt

例 1:咱们直来直去的谈这个问题。

Let's get to the point.

例 2:她喜欢说话办事直来直去。

She likes to do and say things in a straightforward manner.

中 zhōng

成;行;好。all right; OK

例:中,咱们就这么办。

All right, let's do it this way.

中巴 zhōng bā

中型客车。medium-sized bus/Privately run buses in cities that run the same routes as public buses. They usually run more frequently and are more comfortable than public buses, but cost five times as much.

例:中巴虽然比大巴贵,可比面的还是便宜多了。

Although the medium-sized buses are more expensive than public ones, they are much cheaper than taxis.

钟点工 zhōng diǎn gōng

按小时计算并支付劳动报酬的工作。hourly worker

例:小张下岗后干起了钟点工。

Xiao Zhang worked as an hourly worker after being laid off.

轴 zhóu

1.指人动作不灵活,僵硬。(of one's action) inflexible; stiff;

awkward

例：你的动作太轴,放松一些。

Your movements are rather stiff. Relax a little.

2.指人性格直爽,做事直来直去。straightforward；forth-right

例：他父亲告诉他待人接物不要太轴。

His father told him not to be too straightforward in dealing with people.

怂 zhòu

指人固执。obstinate；stubborn

例：这家伙特别怂,不爱接受别人的建议。

This fellow is very pigheaded and never takes other people's advice.

主儿 zhǔr

指人。person

例：歌词创作是一门学问,绝非是个主儿就能玩儿的玩意儿。

Writing the words of a song is a branch of learning. Not every person can do it.

煮饺子 zhǔ jiǎo zi

形容人多拥挤的样子。boil dumplings in a pot/A metaphor for a place that is full of people or overcrowded.

例：我不想这时去庙会,现在那儿正是煮饺子的时候。我想晚一点儿去。

I don't want to go to the fair at this time of the day. It is overcrowded now. I would rather go later.

抓瞎 zhuā xiā

指忙乱中无法应付。find oneself at a loss；be in a rush and

muddle

例：他对考试有充分的准备，所以不管考试多难从不抓瞎。

He is well prepared for examinations, so he never finds himself at a loss no matter how hard a test is.

转磨 zhuàn mò

指来回转悠。turn; walk about

例1：这是他的习惯，一遇到问题就在屋里转磨开了。

It's his habit to pace up and down a room when he meets with problems.

例2：他转磨了半天，也没能想出一个更好的主意。

He walked to and fro for a long time, but couldn't think of a better idea.

转腰子 zhuàn yāo zi

指由于不认识路而绕了许多弯子或由于不懂某事而一直找不到正确的解决办法。walk around; wander; take a long time to find a right way to solve sth.

例：你们家可真难找。我一直在这片儿转腰子，最后才找到。

It's so difficult for me to find your home. I kept walking around and around in this area for long time but found it at last.

装嫩 zhuāng nèn

指人在言行和装扮上故意做出一副天真、可爱、年少的样子。pretending to be childish, lovely or young / refers to one who speaks, dresses, or acts like a young girl or boy

例：瞧那些港台明星多会装嫩，三十好几了，还一口一个女生、男生的称自己。

Look, those pop and movie stars from Hong Kong and Taiwan are really good at pretending to be young. They are over 30 years old, but they always address each other as girls or boys.

装尿 zhuāng sóng

指故意装成无能、胆小的样子。pretend to be incompetent and chicken-hearted

例：只要见到对手又高又大，他准装尿。

He always pretends to be incompetent and chicken-hearted when he sees an opponent who is taller and stronger than he is.

装洋蒜 zhuāng yáng suàn

装糊涂，装腔作势。pretend; fake; play dumb

例：别装洋蒜了，我知道你的腿根本没毛病，你只不过不想跟我们一起去罢了。

Don't pretend. I know there's nothing wrong with your leg.

You simply don't want to go with us.

撞大运 zhuàng dà yùn

试一下；碰运气。try one's luck; hit the jackpot; have a try

例1：他到赌场撞大运去了。

He went to try his luck in a gambling house.

例2：他希望自己能撞上大运，考上大学。

He hopes he will hit the jackpot and pass the entrance exam of a college.

撞枪口上 zhuàng qiāng kǒu shang

1. 指自寻死路；自找麻烦。look for trouble; bring about one's own downfall

例：他偷便衣警察的钱，正撞枪口上。

He brought about his own downfall by picking the pocket of a plainclothes cop.

2.正巧赶上；碰上。run into；meet；bump into；be in time for

例：她想悄悄离开，但没想到在大门口却撞在老板的枪口上。

She wanted to get away quietly, but she didn't expect she would bump into her boss at the gate.

追捧 zhuī pěng

指人纷纷争先恐后地推崇，大加赞扬某人或某事。vying to praise someone or something highly

例：这个方案一出台，就得到众多商家的追捧，因为他们看到了更多的利益。

As soon as the project was announced, many business people vied with each other in praising it highly, because they knew there was profit in it.

追尾 zhuī wěi

汽车在行驶中，后面的汽车紧跟在前面汽车的尾部追赶。tailgate

例：很多交通事故都是由汽车追尾造成的。

A lot of traffic accidents are tailgating caused by people.

追星 zhuī xīng

疯狂地追逐明星、崇拜明星。go crazy pursuing or worshipping a movie star or pop singer

例：大多数年轻人都爱追星。他们从街上买来他们喜欢的歌星的照片，贴在家里的墙上。

Most young people go crazy following pop stars. They buy posters of their idols and put them up on the walls of their rooms.

追星族 zhuī xīng zú

指疯狂追逐、崇拜明星的人。groupie; class of people who go crazy pursuing or worshipping a movie star or pop singer

例:她女儿才十五岁,就已成为追星族的一员了。

Her fifteen-year-old daughter has become a groupie.

滋 zī

即滋润,指舒服。comfortable

例:这么大的办公室就你一个人用够滋的。

It must be really comfortable working alone in such a big office.

滋扭 zī niu

闹别扭;胡闹;生事端;不服气。be at odds; make trouble; refuse to obey

例:所有人都听他的指挥,没人敢跟他滋扭。

Everyone does what he orders and no one dares disobey him.

滋润 zī rùn

指舒服;自在。comfortable; at ease; free; in heaven

例:饭后一支烟,他感到十分滋润。

He really feels in heaven having a smoke after a meal.

子弹 zǐ dàn

钱。money

例:你有子弹吗? 借我点儿。我想买一本字典。

Do you have any money? Please lend me some. I want to buy a dictionary.

子儿 zǐr

钱。原指铜子儿,旧时的钱。money / Referred to copper coins in the old days.

例:他挣的不多,每月下来就没剩几个子儿了。

He doesn't earn a lot. There is not much money left at the

end of each month.

自炒 zì chǎo

指自我宣传；毛遂自荐；自吹自擂。boast; introduce oneself to public; crack oneself up; blow one's own trumpet

例：她是第一个自炒歌手。

She is the first singer who inflates her own image to the public in China.

自儿 zìr

指自在、舒服。at ease; comfortable

例：她住在新房里可真够自儿的。

She feels very comfortable in her new house.

自找 zì zhǎo

自找麻烦；自作自受。ask for it; suffer from one's own actions

例：你不听我的忠告执意要那么做，这些后果都是你自找的。

You didn't listen to my suggestions and insisted on going ahead. Now you got what you deserve.

走板 zǒu bǎn

本指唱戏不合韵律节拍，现引申为走样，不对劲，有问题，不对路子。be out of form; be different from what is expected; go wrong/Originally referred to when an opera singer slipped or sang out of tune.

例：这事你不能指望他。他一插手，这事准走板。

You can't depend on him to handle the matter. He'll certainly make things go wrong.

走背字 zǒu bèi zì

比喻不走运,办任何事情都不顺利。be unlucky; do sth. not well or unsuccessfully

例:他最近老走背字。上星期手机被人偷了,这星期车又被撞了。

He has been unlucky recently. Last week his cellular phone was stolen and this week his car was run into and damaged.

走道 zǒu dào

走路。walk

例:他连走道的力气都没有了。

He was too tired to walk.

走合 zǒu hé

指在买卖两方之间搭桥,利用价格差牟取利益。make a profit by buying and reselling goods; make money by working as a middleman

例:这两年他靠走合挣了不少钱。

He has made a lot of money by working as a middleman in the past two years.

走红 zǒu hóng

指(人或事物)发展顺利并不断获得成功;受众人的喜爱或欢迎。become popular or welcomed by public;(someone or something) develop smoothly and make unceasing progress and success

例:她由于演唱一首电视剧的主题歌而走红。

She became popular by singing a theme song from a TV show.

走火入魔 zǒu huǒ rù mó

1. 比喻干某事过了头。overdo; go too far; go to extremes

例：小男孩看功夫片走火入魔了。他也学着从树上往下跳，结果摔断了双腿。

The boy overdid it with *kung-fu* films. He thought he could jump from a tree and ending up breaking his legs.

2. 形容不顾一切地干某事。be absorbed in; utterly devoted to

例：她写小说都写得走火入魔了，经常废寝忘食。

She's so absorbed in writing her novel she often forgets to eat and sleep.

走你 zǒu nǐ

指把东西扔出去或交给某人。Here you are; here you go

例：A：书包好了吗？

　　Have you wrapped the book up?

　　B：马上就好，走你。

　　Right away. Here you go.

走人 zǒu rén

走开；离开。go; leave

例：你再呆在这儿也没有什么用了，还不赶快走人。

It's no use for you to stay here any more. You'd better scram immediately.

走穴 zǒu xuè

旧时指走江湖卖艺。现指参加临时组织起来的商业性演出。take part in a short-term commercial performance/In old times referred to being a traveling performer who put on street performances for a living.

例：她一年大部分时间都在全国走穴，很少能和家人团聚。

She spends most of her time each year taking part in short-term commercial performances around the country and therefore seldom gets together with her family members.

走眼 zǒu yǎn

看错或判断错误。to see something mistakenly; to misjudge something; mistake sb. or sth.

例：A：昨天在电影院我看见你和一个女孩子在一起。

I saw you with a girl in a cinema yesterday.

B：你一定是看走眼了。我昨天哪儿也没去，一直待在家里。

You must have mistaken someone else for me. I didn't go anywhere yesterday. I was at home all day.

走嘴 zǒu zuǐ

说错话；泄密。say things wrong; let the cat out

例1：我这个人，说话多了的时候，就容易走嘴。

It's easy for me to say things wrong when I say too much.

例2：这事要绝对保密，说话时千万不能走嘴。

This thing must be kept under hat, and don't ever let the cat out in talks.

钻石王老五 zuàn shí wāng lǎo wǔ

指非常有钱的单身男人。a very wealthy bachelor

例：35岁的丹麦王储腓烈特是丹麦第一王位继承人，曾是欧洲最炙手可热的"钻石王老五"。

Philiet, the thirty-five-year old crown prince of Denmark, is the first heir to the kingship of Denmark. He was once the most celebrated wealthy bachelor in Europe.

嘴臭 zuǐ chòu

形容某人说话粗鲁，不干净，没礼貌。have a sinking mouth/ A metaphor for someone who is rude of impolite, can be used to describe people who swear.

例:他这家伙就是嘴臭,其实心眼儿还是挺不错的。

He swears a lot, but actually he is not bad-natured.

作 zuò

胡闹;胡搞。run wild; mess things up

例:在她外出时,她儿子常带一帮哥们儿到家作。

Her son often invites his friends over to run wild at her home when she goes on a trip.

作脸 zuò liǎn

争光;争气。win the honor for; bring credit to

例:我女儿真给我作脸,考入世界名牌大学。

My daughter brouglt credit to me by entering a world-famous university.

作死 zuò sǐ

指找死。look for trouble; court death

例:你作死呢? 喝那么多酒。

Are you looking for trouble by drinking too much wine?

凿实 zuò shi

指物品结实,牢固。hard; solid; durable

例:这块木头可够凿实的。

This piece of wood is pretty hard.

坐二等 zuò èr děng

坐在自行车后座架子上。perch on the back of a bicycle

例:他是坐二等来上班的。

He came to the office perching on the back of a bicycle.

坐蜡 zuò là

陷入困境;遇到难办的事情。land in a predicament; be put in a tight spot; fall into a plight

例:他感到这事让他很坐蜡。

He found himself in a very difficult situation over the matter.

坐冷板凳 zuò lěng bǎn dèng

不受重用。sit on a cold stool/A metaphor for someone who is passed over or has suffered a cold shoulder.

例:他在公司工作干得十分出色,可是由于性格倔强不招老板喜欢,所以总坐冷板凳。

He works excellently for his company. But because of his hard nature he cannot win favor with his boss, so he is always passed over.

坐台小姐 zuò tái xiǎo jiě

指在酒吧、夜总会、歌舞厅里前台服务的小姐或领班。front desk girls; waitresses or head waitresses at the front desk of bars, night clubs or karaoke (entertainment) clubs

例:最近公安局抓到了一名罪犯,他专门在深夜以坐台小姐为对象进行抢劫。

Recently a police station caught a criminal who targeted for robbery at midnight only those girls who worked as waitresses or head of waitresses.

做 zuò

指做手脚整治人。play tricks to punish someone

例:他们下一步不知又要做谁了?

We don't know who they'll play tricks on next time.

做瘪子 zuò biě zi

1. (心情)不舒畅。feel unhappy; worry; be in low spirits

例：这消息准会让他做瘪子。

This news will surely make him unhappy.

2. 没有办法。have no way out; have no other option

例：如果他不同意我们的计划，我们可就做瘪子了。

We'll have no options if he doesn't agree to our plan.

3. 失败。fail

例：这次考试我做瘪子了。

I failed the examination this time.

做东 zuò dōng

当主人；做主人招待或款待。play host; act as host

例：今天的晚宴我来做东。

I'll act as host at tonight's dinner party.

做辣 zuò là

使人难堪；使人难以处理；出难题。put someone in a difficult situation; make someone feel embarrassed; put someone in a bind

例：你提出的要求真让我做辣。

Your request put me in a very difficult situation.

做秀 zuò xiù

演出，表演。show

例：电视台邀请他去做秀，他婉言谢绝了，生怕在众人面前出丑，毁了自己的好名声。

He was invited to give a show at the TV station, but he politely refused as he was afraid that he would make an exhibition of himself and ruin his good reputation.

图书在版编目(CIP)数据

最新中国俚语(修订版):汉英对照/李淑娟,颜力钢编.—北京:新世界出版社,2000.8

ISBN 7 - 80005 - 564 - 7

Ⅰ.最…　Ⅱ.①李…②颜…　Ⅲ.汉语－俚语－汉、英　Ⅳ.H136.4

中国版本图书馆 CIP 数据中心核字(2000)第 40700 号

最新中国俚语(修订版)

编　　著:李淑娟　颜力钢　　　翻译:李淑娟

责任编辑:钟振奋　刘丽刚

装帧设计:兆友书装

责任印制:李一鸣　黄厚清

出版发行:新世界出版社

社址:北京市西城区百万庄路 24 号(100037)

总编室电话:＋86 10 6899 5424　　　6832 6679(传真)

发行部电话:＋86 10 6899 5968　　　6899 8705(传真)

本社中文网址:hhtp://www.nwp.cn

本社英文网址:hhtp://www.newworld-press.com

本社电子信箱:nwpcn@public.bta.net.cn

版权部电子信箱:frank@nwp.com.cn

版权部电话:＋86 10 6899 6306

印刷:北京中印联印务有限公司

经销:新华书店

开本:880×1230　　　1/32

字数:280 千字　　　印张:12.5

印数:3001—6000

版次:2006 年 1 月第 3 版　2006 年 9 月北京第 2 次印刷

书号:ISBN 7 - 80005 - 564 - 7/H·022

定价:28.00 元